THE BIG BOOK OF

TAROT

How to Interpret the Cards
and Work with Tarot Spreads
for Personal Growth

JOAN BUNNING

WEISER
BOOKS

This edition first published in 2019 by Weiser Books, an imprint of
Red Wheel/Weiser, LLC
With offices at:
65 Parker Street, Suite 7
Newburyport, MA 01950
www.redwheelweiser.com

ISBN: 978-1-57863-668-6

Library of Congress Cataloging-in-Publication Data available upon request.

Cover and text design by Kathryn Sky-Peck

Printed in the United States of America

10 9 8 7 6 5 4 3

CONTENTS

PART ONE: TAROT BASICS

PART TWO: ENERGY AND CARD ORIENTATION

PART THREE: CARD DESCRIPTIONS

PART FOUR: TAROT SPREADS

PART FIVE: REFERENCE

APPENDIXES

PREFACE

I discovered the tarot at a time in my life when I was seeking and exploring. I was open to whatever might help me understand my inner experiences. It was in that spirit, when by chance I sat next to a psychic at a conference. We got to talking, and he eventually gave me an intuitive reading. The first words he said to me were "You should study the tarot." I had heard about the cards, but knew very little about them. My inner guidance suggested I heed his advice, so I did.

I bought some books, a deck of tarot cards, and began to practice and take notes. I immersed myself as I tend to do. One day, a rough, but fully-formed chapter about the court cards appeared in my mind. "What is this?" I thought. I was puzzled, but intrigued, so I wrote down what I was receiving. One thing led to another, more chapters followed, and eventually I had written a book. I tried to get it published, but with no success, so I put the manuscript away.

Some years later, I developed a course and created a website for it, *www.learntarot.com*. My goal was simply to share what I had written while pursuing what seemed like a fun project. I began receiving feedback the very next day.

And so began many years of correspondence with people from all over the world. Some had been using the tarot for years, others were curious seekers such as myself. Many told me they had always wanted to study the cards, but didn't know how to begin until they found my site. I was deeply grateful for this chance to learn more about how the cards enhanced others' lives and experience.

From the beginning, my inner guidance has been rather clear that my contribution to the tarot is as a writer and teacher. Now I'm able to look back and follow the train of synchronicities that has guided me along this deeply rewarding path. It led me to write and publish three —and now—four books. I can appreciate the purpose the tarot has offered me and, I hope, the benefit to other people drawn to it.

The Big Book of Tarot brings together all the key information and techniques from my earlier books in a unified, comprehensive format. The material is organized so that the content flows naturally from the basics to more advanced concepts, and I've refined and supplemented it with what I've learned in the intervening years. I walk you through learning the tarot step-by-step. I also include exercises to help you practice and teach you how to develop a relationship with your Inner Guide, that wise intuitive voice that is essential to any meaningful tarot practice.

This book is divided into five parts:

PART ONE covers the basics—what you need to know to get started with the cards.

PART TWO covers the reading process itself—how to carry out a tarot reading with techniques for interpreting the cards.

PART THREE is the core of the book. It offers a detailed description of the meaning of each card, including reversals. This section is designed to be a continuing source of reference and inspiration.

PART FOUR covers tarot spreads and teaches you how to use the Celtic Cross Spread and my own Flex Spread, a basic framework that you can customize to fit any reading.

PART FIVE includes a number of helpful references such as shuffling methods and step-by-step reading procedures.

My main purpose in all my writings is to show you how to use the tarot for yourself. The tarot can help you better understand yourself and teach you how to tap your inner resources more confidently. You do not have to have psychic powers to use the tarot successfully. All you need is a willingness to honor and develop your natural intuitive abilities.

The tarot remains an amazing tool for self-discovery. It just may be the tool you've been looking for to develop your own unrealized potential. May the cards always bring you many insights!

Joan Bunning
Vienna, Virginia
December 26, 2018

INTRODUCTION

Years ago, when I told my brother I was studying the tarot, his first comment was, "How can a deck of cards possibly tell you anything about anything?" I laughed because I thought his reply summed up pretty well the common-sense view of the cards. I, too, had my doubts about the tarot, but I found out the cards can make a real difference in the way you perceive and deal with the challenges in your life. In this introduction, I'll try to explain why.

The origin of the tarot is a mystery. We do know for sure that the cards were used in Italy in the fifteenth century as a popular card game. Wealthy patrons commissioned beautiful decks, some of which have survived. The Visconti-Sforza, created in 1450 or shortly thereafter, is one of the earliest and most complete.[i]

Later in the eighteenth and nineteenth centuries, the cards were discovered by a number of influential scholars of the occult. These explorers were fascinated by the tarot and recognized that the images on the cards were more powerful than a simple game would suggest. They revealed (or created!) the "true" history of the tarot by connecting the cards to Egyptian mysteries, Hermetic philosophy, the Kabbalah, alchemy, and other mystical systems.

These pursuits continued into the early part of the twentieth century when the tarot was incorporated into the practices of several secret societies, including the Order of the Golden Dawn.[ii] One of these practitioners was Arthur Edward Waite who collaborated with illustrator Pamela Colman Smith to create the Rider-Waite deck in England in 1910. This deck was originally published by Rider and Company. It is still in print and is arguably the most popular tarot deck in use today. The illustrations in this book are adapted from the Rider-Waite deck.

Although the roots of the tarot are in the occult tradition, interest in the cards has expanded in the last few decades to include many perspectives. New decks have been created that reflect these interests. There are Native American, herbal, mythological, and Japanese decks, among many others.[iii]

The tarot is most commonly viewed as a tool for divination. A traditional tarot reading involves a seeker—someone who is looking for answers to personal questions—and a reader—someone who knows how to interpret the cards. After the seeker has shuffled and cut the deck, the reader lays out the chosen cards in a pattern called a spread. Each position in the spread has a meaning, and each card has a meaning as well. The reader combines these two meanings to shed light on the seeker's question.

A simple process, but rarely presented in a simple way. In films, we always see the tarot being used in a seedy parlor or back room. An old woman, seated in shadows, reads the cards for a nervous, young girl. The crone lifts her wrinkled finger and drops it ominously on the Death card. The girl draws back, frightened by this sign of her impending doom.

This aura of darkness clings to the tarot cards even now. Some religions shun the cards, and the scientific establishment condemns them as symbols of unreason, a holdover from an unenlightened past. Let us set aside these shadowy images for now and consider the tarot for what it is—a deck of picture cards. The question becomes, what can we do with them?

The answer lies with the unconscious—that deep level of memory and awareness that resides within each of us, but outside our everyday experience. Even though we ignore the action of the unconscious most of the time, it profoundly affects everything we do. In his writings, Sigmund Freud stressed the irrational, primitive aspect of the unconscious. He thought that it was the home of our most unacceptable desires and urges. His contemporary Carl Jung emphasized the positive, creative aspect of the unconscious. He tried to show that it has a collective component that touches universal qualities.

We may never know the full range and power of the unconscious, but there are ways to explore its landscape. Many techniques have been developed for this purpose—psychotherapy, dream interpretation, visualization, and meditation. The tarot is another such tool.

Consider for a moment a typical card in the tarot deck, the Five of Swords. This card shows a man holding three swords and looking at two figures in the distance. Two other swords lie on the ground. As I look at this card, I begin to create a story around the image. I see a man who seems satisfied with some battle he has won. He looks rather smug and pleased that he has all the swords. The others look downcast and defeated.

What I have done is take an open-ended image and project a story onto it. To me, my view is the obvious one—the only possible interpretation of this scene. In fact, someone else could have imagined a totally different story. Maybe the man is trying to pick up the swords. He's calling to the others to help him, but they refuse. Or, maybe the other two were fighting, and he convinced them to lay down their arms. The point is that of all possible stories, I chose a certain one. Why?

Because it is human nature to project unconscious material onto objects in the environment. We always see reality through a lens made up of our own inner state. Therapists have long noted this tendency and have created tools to assist in the process. The famous Rorschach inkblot test is based on such projection.[iv]

Projection is one reason why the tarot cards are valuable. Their intriguing pictures and patterns are effective in tapping the unconscious. This is the personal aspect of the tarot, but the cards also have a collective component. As humans, we all have certain common needs and experiences. The images on the tarot cards capture these universal moments and draw them out consistently. People tend to react to the cards in similar ways because they represent archetypes. Over many centuries, the tarot has evolved into a collection of the most basic patterns of human thought and emotion.

Consider the Empress. She stands for the Mother Principle—life in all its abundance. Notice how her image conjures up feelings of luxuriance. She is seated on soft, lush pillows, and her robe flows in folds around her. In the Empress, we sense the bounty and sensual richness of nature.

THE EMPRESS.

The power of the tarot comes from this combination of the personal and the universal. You can see each card in your own way, but, at the same time, you are supported by understandings that others have found meaningful. The tarot is a mirror that reflects back to you the hidden aspects of your own unique awareness.

When we do a tarot reading, we select certain cards by shuffling, cutting, and dealing the deck. Although this process seems random, we still assume the cards we pick are special. This is the point of a tarot reading after all—to choose the cards we are meant to see. Now, common sense tells us that cards chosen by chance can't hold any special meaning—or can they?

To answer this question, let's look at randomness more closely. Usually we say that an event is random when it appears to be the result of the chance interaction of mechanical forces. From a set of possible outcomes—all equally likely—one occurs, but for no particular reason.

This definition includes two key assumptions about random events: they are the result of mechanical forces, and they have no meaning. First, no tarot reading is solely the product of mechanical forces. It is the result of a long series of conscious actions. We decide to study the tarot. We buy a deck and learn how to use it. We shuffle and cut the cards in a certain way at a certain point. Finally, we use our perceptions to interpret the cards.

At every step, we are actively involved. Why then are we tempted to say a reading is "the chance interaction of mechanical forces"? Because we can't explain just how our consciousness is involved. We know our card choices aren't deliberate, so we call them random. In fact, could there be a deeper mechanism at work, one connected to the power of our unconscious? Could our inner states be tied to outer events in a way that we don't yet fully understand? I hold this possibility out to you.

The other feature of a random event is that it has no inherent meaning. I roll a die and get a six, but there is no purpose to this particular result. I could just as easily roll a one, and the meaning would be the same—or would it? Do we really know these two outcomes are equal? Perhaps there is meaning and purpose in every event, great or small, but we don't always recognize it.

At a party many years ago, I had the sudden urge to pick up a die sitting on the floor. I knew with great conviction that I would be able to roll this die six times without repeating any number. As I began, the laughter and noise of the party faded away. I felt a growing excitement as a different number appeared with each roll. It was only with the last successful roll that my everyday awareness returned, and I sat back, wondering what had happened.

At one level, these six rolls were unrelated, random events, but at another level, they were very meaningful. My inner experience told me this was so, even though an outside observer might not agree. What was the meaning? At the time, it was a lesson in the strange interaction between mind and matter. Today, I know it had another purpose—to be available to me now, years later, as an illustration for this very lesson!

Meaning is a mysterious quality that arises at the juncture of inner and outer realities. There is a message in everything—trees, songs, even trash—but only when we are open to perceiving it. The tarot cards convey many messages because of the richness of their images and connections. More importantly, tarot readings communicate meaning because we bring to them our sincere desire to discover deeper truths about our lives. By seeking meaning in this way, we honor its reality and give it a chance to be revealed.

If there is meaning in a reading, where does it come from? I believe it comes from that part of ourselves that is aware of the divine source of meaning. This is an aspect of the unconscious, yet it is much more. It acts as a wise advisor who knows us well. It understands what we need and leads us in the direction we need to go. Some people call this advisor the soul, the superconscious, or the Higher Self. I call it the Inner Guide because that is the role it plays in connection with the tarot.

Each of us has an Inner Guide that serves as a fountain of meaning for us. Your Inner Guide is always with you because it is part of you. You can't destroy this connection, but you can ignore it. When you reach for your tarot deck, you signal to your Inner Guide that you are open to its wisdom. This simple act of faith allows you to become aware of the guidance that was always there for you.

We are meant by nature to rely on the wisdom of our Inner Guide, but somehow, most of us have forgotten how to access it. We trust our conscious minds instead and forget to look deeper. Our conscious minds are clever, but unfortunately, they just don't have the full awareness we need to make appropriate choices day by day.

When we are operating from our conscious minds, we often feel as if events are forced upon us by chance. Life seems to have little purpose, and we suffer because we do not really understand who we are and what we want. When we know how to access our Inner Guide, we experience life differently. We have the certainty and peace that come from aligning our conscious will with our inner purpose. Our path becomes more joyous, and we see more clearly how we bring together the scattered elements of our lives to fulfill our destinies.

I use the tarot because it is one of the best tools I have found to make the whispers of my Inner Guide more available consciously. The ideas, images, and feelings that emerge as I work through a reading are a message from my Inner Guide. How do I know there is a message, and it's not just my imagination? I don't, really. I can only trust my experience and see what happens.

You do not really need the tarot to access your Inner Guide. The cards serve the same function as Dumbo's magic feather. In the Disney movie, Dumbo the Elephant really could fly on his own, but he didn't believe it. He placed all his faith on the special feather he held in his trunk. He thought this feather gave him the power to fly, but he found out differently when it blew away, and he was forced to fall back on his own resources.

The tarot cards may help you fly until you can reach your Inner Guide on your own. Don't worry for now about how this might happen. Just read through the text, play with the cards, and see if you don't experience a few surprises.

Part One

TAROT BASICS

Chapter One

ELEMENTS OF THE TAROT

The Major Arcana

The standard tarot deck consists of seventy-eight cards divided into two sections: the major and minor arcanas. The word *arcana* is the plural of *arcanum,* which means "profound secret." To the alchemists of the Middle Ages, the arcanum was the secret of nature. The tarot cards are therefore a collection of the "secrets" that underlie and explain our universe.

The twenty-two cards of the major arcana are the heart of the deck. Each of these cards symbolizes some universal aspect of human experience. They represent the archetypes—consistent, directing patterns of influence that are an inherent part of human nature.

Each card in the major arcana has a name and number. Some names convey a card's meaning directly, such as Strength, Justice, and Temperance. Other cards are individuals who personify a particular approach to life, such as the Magician or the Hermit. There are also cards with astronomical names, such as the Star, Sun, and Moon. They represent the elusive forces associated with these heavenly bodies.

The major arcana cards are special because they draw out deep and complex reactions. The images on the Rider-Waite deck are evocative because they combine esoteric symbolism with recognizable figures and situations. The symbolism is subtle, but effective.

A major arcana card is always given extra weight in a reading. When one of these cards appears, you know the issues at stake are not mundane or temporary. They represent your most basic concerns—your major feelings and motivations.

The major arcana is often considered as a unit. Different schemes have been developed to show how the cards form patterns that cast light on the human condition. Numerology, astrology, and other esoteric sciences often play a role in these schemes.

Many interpreters view the major arcana as showing the different stages on an individual's journey of inner growth—what some call the Fool's Journey (see Appendix A, p. 337). In these systems, each card stands for some quality or experience that we must incorporate before we can realize our wholeness.

We all travel this road to self-actualization, though our trips more often involve detours, backups, and restarts than smooth progression! Our specific paths are unique, but our milestones are universal. The twenty-two major arcana cards are markers on the path of inner development leading from earliest awareness (card 0) to integration and fulfillment (card 21).

The Fool's Journey seems to move smoothly from one order of experience to the next, but our learning adventures are usually not so tidy. We make mistakes, skip lessons, and fail to realize our potential. Sometimes we lack the courage and insight to discover our deepest levels. Some never feel the call of the Hermit to look inward or never experience the crisis of the Tower that might free them from their ego defenses.

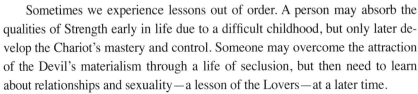

Often, we try to overcome our difficulties, but fail repeatedly. The lesson of the Hanged Man—to let go and surrender to experience—is one that is particularly hard and may need to be faced over and over before it is fully incorporated.

Sometimes we experience lessons out of order. A person may absorb the qualities of Strength early in life due to a difficult childhood, but only later develop the Chariot's mastery and control. Someone may overcome the attraction of the Devil's materialism through a life of seclusion, but then need to learn about relationships and sexuality—a lesson of the Lovers—at a later time.

The major arcana contains many levels and models of experience. These cards hold all the patterns of growth, whether they occur within one segment of a life or a whole life span. We could even say that an entire lifetime is really just one growth episode within the larger saga of our soul's development.

No matter what our pattern of self-discovery, the major arcana shows us that wholeness and fulfillment are our destiny. If we keep this promise as our polestar, we will eventually realize our true nature and gain the World.

STUDYING THE MAJOR ARCANA CARDS

Choose any major arcana card to explore from the Card Descriptions section (page 57). Become familiar with keywords and actions. Notice how keywords reinforce each other to create a certain kind of energy or focus. Note also how the actions flesh out the keywords. Read the description, but just glance at the other information for now. Repeat this exercise for as many major arcana cards as you like. Don't worry about memorizing anything. The goal is simply to get comfortable with the card descriptions.

The Minor Arcana

While the major arcana expresses universal themes, the minor arcana brings those themes down into the practical arena to show how they operate in daily events. The minor arcana cards represent the concerns, activities, and emotions that make up the dramas of our everyday lives.

The Suits

There are fifty-six cards in the minor arcana divided into four suits: Wands, Cups, Swords, and Pentacles. Each of these suits stands for a particular approach to life. Our everyday experiences are a blend of these four approaches. Your tarot readings will show you how the different suit energies are impacting your life at any given moment.

THE BIG BOOK OF TAROT

Wands

The Wands are the suit of creativity, action, and movement. They are associated with such qualities as enthusiasm, adventure, risk-taking, and confidence. This suit corresponds to the yang, or masculine principle, in Chinese philosophy and is associated with the element Fire. A flickering flame is the perfect symbol of the Wands' force. This energy flows outward and generates passionate involvement.

Cups

The Cups are the suit of emotions and spiritual experience. They describe inner states, feelings, and relationship patterns. The energy of this suit flows inward. Cups correspond to the yin, or feminine principle, in Chinese philosophy and are associated with the element Water. The ability of water to flow and fill up spaces, to sustain and to reflect changing moods makes it the ideal symbol of the Cups suit.

Swords

The Swords are the suit of intellect, thought, and reason. They are concerned with justice, truth, and ethical principles. Swords are associated with the element Air. A cloudless sky, open and light-filled, is a symbol of the mental clarity that is the Swords' ideal. This suit is also associated with states that lead to disharmony and unhappiness. Our intellect is a valuable asset, but as an agent of ego, it can lead us astray if it is not infused with the wisdom of our Inner Guide.

Pentacles

The Pentacles are the suit of practicality, security, and material concerns. They are associated with the element Earth and the concrete requirements of working with matter. In Pentacles, we celebrate the beauty of nature, our interactions with plants and animals, and our physical experiences in the body. Pentacles also represent prosperity and wealth of all kinds. Sometimes this suit is called the Coins, an obvious symbol of the exchange of goods and services in the physical world.

The Ranks

Each suit is structured much as our everyday playing cards with ten numbered cards (Ace–Ten) and four court cards (King, Queen, Knight, and Page). Each card has a role to play in showing how the energy of its suit is expressed in the world.

Aces

An Ace announces the themes of a suit. The Ace of Cups stands for love, emotions, intuition, and intimacy—ideas that are explored in the other cards of the Cups suit. An Ace always represents positive forces. It is the standard-bearer for the best its suit has to offer.

Middle Cards

Each of the middle, numbered cards present a different aspect of a suit. The Wands explore such themes as personal power (card 2), leadership (card 3), excitement (card 4), and competition (card 5). A card may approach an idea from several angles. The Five of Pentacles shows the many faces of want—hard times (material want), ill health (physical want), and rejection (emotional want).

Tens

A Ten takes the themes introduced by an Ace to their logical conclusion. If you take the love, intimacy, and emotions of the Ace of Cups to their ultimate, you have the joy, peace, and family love of the Ten of Cups.

Court Cards

The court cards are people with personalities that reflect the qualities of their suit and rank. The court cards show us certain ways of being in the world so that we can use (or avoid!) those styles when appropriate.

King

A King is mature and masculine. He is a doer whose focus is outward on the events of life. He demonstrates authority, control, and mastery in some area associated with his suit. A King's style is strong, assertive, and direct. He is concerned with results and practical, how-to matters.

Queen

A Queen is mature and feminine. She embodies the qualities of her suit, rather than acting them out. Her focus is inward, and her style, relaxed and natural. A Queen is less concerned with results than with the enjoyment of just being in the world. She is associated with feelings, relationships, and self-expression.

Knight

A Knight is an immature teenager. He cannot express himself with balance. He swings wildly from one extreme to another as he tries to relate successfully to his world. A Knight is prone to excess, but he is also eager and sincere, and these qualities redeem him in our eyes. We can admire his spirit and energy.

Page

A Page is a playful child. He acts out the qualities of his suit with pleasure and abandon. His approach may not be deep, but it is easy, loose, and spontaneous. He is a symbol of adventure and possibility.

You now have a basic idea of the role of each card in the tarot deck. You have a feel for how they all fit together and what each one contributes to the whole. In the following sections, you will learn more about these cards and how to interpret them in your readings.

EXPLORING SUIT QUALITIES

Review the lists of suit qualities in Part Five, page 333. Don't try to memorize these lists, just read them over quickly. These word collections are designed to give you a feel for the energy of each suit in all its many manifestations.

SUIT QUALITIES IN YOURSELF

The different suit qualities combine in each person to create his or her personality. Examine yourself in light of the four suits. Ask yourself these questions:

Is one suit quality dominant in me?

Is one quality less familiar?

In what situations do I take on each quality?

Do I reflect the so-called positive or negative side most often?

Do I attract people of the same type, or different?

You can repeat this exercise with another person as the subject, if you like.

Card Orientation

All life is energy—currents of force that mix and blend to form the patterns of our lives. Each card in a reading symbolizes a particular energy. Your actions and intentions as you shuffle and cut the cards align certain energies in a way that is meaningful to you. When you lay the cards out, you can see a picture of those energies all in one place.

At any given moment, these energies will be at different levels. Some will be strong and powerful, others less so. Some will be entering your life, others, moving away. It would be useful to be able to assess the energy level each card represents. I use card orientation for this purpose.

The orientation of a card is the direction it faces on the reading surface, or as you hold it. A card can be either *upright* or *reversed*. An upright card appears normal based on its image. A reversed card looks upside-down. When you shuffle the tarot cards, they often end up facing in different directions. (See Part Five, page 333 for a shuffling method that avoids reversed cards.)

PAGE of CUPS.

Card orientation allows us to interpret a card in two different ways. An upright card shows an energy that is developed, available, and active. The energy is strong and clearly present in the situation. A reversed card shows an energy that is not fully developed. It exists in the situation, or it would not have appeared, but it's weak, incomplete, unavailable or in some other way not fully expressed. (Many tarot practitioners interpret card orientation differently. In such systems, a reversed card is viewed as the *opposite* of the card when upright. Tarot methods do differ!)

If you are a beginning tarot student, I recommend that you *not* work with card orientation at first. It's important for you to develop a solid appreciation of the essential nature of each card before you introduce this extra dimension. Later, if you wish, you can add orientation to your practice (see Part Two). Your tarot work will be full and rewarding either way.

The Spread

A tarot reading involves selecting certain cards after shuffling and cutting the deck. When you lay out these cards, you see how certain forces are impacting your life in the moment. Many tarot readers lay out their cards using a spread for greater clarity and insight.

A spread is a preset pattern that defines how many cards to use, where each one goes, and what each one means. A spread is a template guiding the placement of the cards so they can

shed light on a given topic. It is within this template that the meanings of the cards come together so beautifully.

A spread is made up of positions. Each position is a place in the spread for a single card. Positions are numbered to define the order in which cards should be placed. A spread with three cards would have position one for the first card, two for the second, and three for the last.

The most important feature of a spread is the fact that each position has a unique meaning that colors the interpretation of whatever card falls in that spot. For example, the keywords for the Four of Pentacles are possessiveness, control, and blocked change. If this card were to fall in a position meaning "the past," you would look at how these qualities are moving out of your life. In a position meaning "the future," you would instead view them as coming into your life—a quite different interpretation!

When cards are related to each other in a spread, an entirely new level of meaning is created. Combinations appear, and a story line develops with characters, plots, and themes. The weaving of a story from the cards in a spread is the most exciting and creative aspect of a tarot reading. It is an art, but there are many guidelines you can follow. Later, I will explore spreads and the story-making process in more detail.

Learning the Deck

Every beginning tarot student faces a major hurdle. Somehow, you must become familiar with all seventy-eight cards to some degree. This task may seem daunting at first, but it need not be arduous. In fact, it can be fun!

It's tempting to rush into this task. You may try to stuff all the information into your head as quickly as possible, but this method doesn't work well. Nothing sticks for long, and you wind up feeling overwhelmed. In fact, many beginning students give up at this point.

Learning Procedure

The secret is to be patient and take this learning project in small, daily doses. You choose one card a day to study, and you cement that learning by allowing the card to teach you its energy as you go through a twenty-four-hour period. Here's a procedure to try:

Select one card as your card for the day. You can be spontaneous or systematic (first all the Wands, then the Cups, etc.). You can pick a card with an intriguing image, or one that otherwise catches your eye. It doesn't matter as long as you work your way through the deck.

Choose your card at a time that works for you. Mornings are good because you can pick a card during your wake-up routine. You can also select one at night. You will be ready to work with your card the following day as soon as you wake up. Your main goal is to make selections regularly so your tarot work progresses.

1. Look up the card in the Card Descriptions section.

Read the description page for your chosen card at least once. Study the details of the card's image. Write down the keywords, and try to memorize them. They will help you remember the meanings of the card quickly.

If you like, make a copy of the card's pages to refer to during the day. I don't recommend carrying your card around as it could get damaged or lost.

2. Stay aware of your card's energy during the day.

Let's say you draw the Two of Cups. The keywords for this card are connection, truce, and attraction. Watch for signs of these qualities during the day. In the morning, you may notice that a colleague, who has been rather hostile, comes to your office to talk. You sense a *truce*. In the afternoon, while working on a problem, you see the *connection* between two approaches. Later, at a party, you talk to someone who *attracts* you. On each occasion, you have touched the energy of the Two of Cups.

3. Review the card again.

Once the twenty-four hours are over, briefly go over your chosen card again. Consider how its qualities fit into the context of your life. See if you can remember the keywords without checking.

4. Keep a journal of your selections.

Keeping a journal is not necessary, but very rewarding. In your journal, jot down the date, card draw, and a few highlights of the day. This will help you correlate the cards with your moods and activities; but keep it simple, or you will soon tire of the effort.

I wrote my journal entries using five pens of different colors, one for each category:

Wands = Red (Fire, passion)

Cups = Blue (Water, moods, emotion)

Swords = Yellow (Air, mentality)

Pentacles = Green (Earth, growth, plants, nature, money)

Major Arcana = Purple (spirituality, higher purpose)

Color coding helps you see at a glance the shifting tarot patterns of your weeks and months.

Learning the cards in this way takes a minimum of seventy-eight days, but if you stick with it, you will know your deck very well.

Make Your Card Choice a Reading

So far, we have talked about choosing a daily card for learning purposes; however, there is a way to make your card selection even more interesting. You can consider it as an actual daily reading. This change adds a meaningful element, but also alters the tenor of the activity.

A reading is an earnest, even sacred agreement between you and your Inner Guide. You enter into it with the understanding that you are receiving truly meaningful guidance. The card you select is important to you. When you choose a card just for learning, you observe its qualities during the day, but you do not necessarily consider them as personal guidance.

The main disadvantage to doing daily readings for guidance is that the process takes longer because you will repeat cards. On the plus side, you will deepen your knowledge of the cards over time and enjoy the rewards of tarot readings right from the beginning.

If you would like to do daily readings while you learn the deck, you will find more information in Chapter Eight. I recommend that you read Chapter Two first so you understand a little more about readings in general.

Chapter Two

DOING READINGS

The essence of a tarot reading is simple. A reading occurs whenever you use your cards with the intent to receive inner guidance from them. You don't have to lay out your cards in a certain way or interpret them according to fancy principles. You just have to have a desire for understanding and a plan to use your cards in some way that serves that purpose. With this in mind, let's first look at the environment most conducive to receiving inner guidance. The environment includes both the physical setting and your internal state.

The External Environment

The external environment of a tarot reading is the physical setting in which the reading takes place. The ideal setting is one that elicits feelings of quiet, peace, even reverence. You could do a reading in a crowded airport, but the noise and distractions would make inner attunement difficult. Since you will probably be doing most of your readings at home, let's look at how you might create an agreeable environment there.

Set aside a place in your home where you will do your readings. By using the same spot over and over, you build up an energy that reinforces your practice. If you meditate or pray, you can do these activities here as well, as they harmonize with the tarot in spirit and intent.

Try to create a sense of separateness about your spot. When you use the cards, you want to turn away from the everyday world and go into a space that is outside time and the normal flow of events. A separate room is ideal, but a corner set off by a screen, curtain, pillows, or other divider can work well too.

Try to create an atmosphere of beauty and meaning. Place items nearby that are special to you. Objects from nature, such as shells, stones, crystals, and plants are always appropriate. A talisman, figure, or religious icon may help you shift your focus from the mundane to the inspirational. Consider pictures and artwork, especially your own, and appeal to your senses with such items as flowers, incense, candles, textured materials, and quiet, meditative music.

These touches are nice, but all you really need is a space large enough to lay out the cards. You can use a table or the floor. There is a grounded feeling to the floor, but, if that position is uncomfortable, a table is better. The ideal table is made of natural materials such as wood or stone.

If you like, cover the table or floor with a cloth to create a uniform area. The material should be natural, such as silk, cotton, wool, or linen. Choose the color with care as colors have their own energies. Black, dark blue, and purple are good choices. There should be little or no pattern, so the images on the cards stand out from the background.

Store your cards in a container to protect them and contain their energies. Any natural substance is fine, such as wood, stone, shell, or a natural cloth. I know of one woman who sewed herself a silk, drawstring bag and embroidered it with stars, moons, and other designs. Consider keeping your cards wrapped in silk cloth when inside their container. Silk has a luxurious feel that will remind you of the value you place on your cards.

Tarot cards can pick up the energy of those who use them. For this reason, set aside a tarot deck that is just for you, if you can. These cards are going to be your personal tool of communication with your Inner Guide. You want to bond to them closely.

When you do your tarot work in a place of your own, the experience can be quite powerful, but extra preparations are never necessary. All you have to do is use the cards. That's the important part.

CREATING A PLACE FOR YOUR READINGS
Spend some time thinking about where you will do your tarot readings. Consider some of the suggestions in this section, and use your own ideas. Don't feel you have to create a showcase location. Simply see what you can do to create a setting that is pleasing and comfortable.

QUEST FOR A SYMBOL
Read the description of the Fool (page 62). This card often stands for the feeling of joy and freedom that comes from beginning a new adventure. It is in this spirit that you will seek an object that will be a personal symbol of your tarot practice.

Hold the Fool in your hands, and close your eyes. Announce your desire to find or create a tarot symbol. Once you have affirmed your intent, let it go. You will find what you are looking for. When you have your symbol, place it in your tarot spot as an inspiration for your practice.

This exercise will strengthen your faith and commitment to your tarot work. It will also help you learn that hidden within seemingly "foolish" acts is the experience of life as an adventure.

Internal Environment

There are five inner qualities that are beneficial when you do a tarot reading.

1. Being Open: Being open means being receptive. It is an attitude of allowing—being willing to take in what is offered without immediate denial or rejection. By being open, you give yourself the chance to receive what you need to know.

2. Being Calm: It is hard to hear the whispers of your Inner Guide when you are in turmoil. Tarot messages often arrive as gentle hints and realizations that can be easily overwhelmed by a restless mind. When you are calm, you are like a peaceful lake in which every ripple of insight can be perceived.

THE BIG BOOK OF TAROT

3. Being Focused: Focus is very important. I have found that when I feel a question strongly, I receive a direct and powerful message. When I'm scattered and confused, the cards tend to be the same. Your most insightful readings will be those you do when the desire is very strong.

4. Being Alert: When you are alert, all your faculties are alive and awake. A cat is alert when it is watching a bug. Of course, you won't be stalking your cards, but you will find them difficult to read if you are tired or bored.

5. Being Respectful: Being respectful means treating the cards as you would any valued tool. You acknowledge their role in helping you understand yourself better. You honor the choice you have made in deciding to learn the tarot and handle the cards accordingly.

These five qualities are important, but they are not necessary. You can have a meaningful reading without them, but it may be more difficult. The best way to decide if the time is right for a reading is to look inside. Your inner sense will tell you if all is well.

Subjects

The subject of a reading is the person or issue the reading is about. This book is oriented toward readings you do for yourself, so often you will be the subject of your readings. Sometimes, though, you may want to do a reading about a different subject. It's important to recognize that such readings are also *for* you, if not *about* you. The cards are offering you a perspective on the subject that is appropriate for you to absorb at the time.

When someone else asks you for a reading, that person picks the subject. The message of the reading is for him or her, not you. You simply help interpret the cards. Appendix B offers some suggestions for how to do readings for others.

Choosing a Subject

You choose the subject of a reading before you begin. In this way, you pinpoint more exactly what it is you really want to know. You also have a focus to guide your interpretation.

A reading can be about almost anything you can name: your health, a project, a friend, a group, a political issue, or the world itself. It's important to give your chosen subject a name. This label acts as your focus during the reading. It helps you relate all the insights you receive in a meaningful way.

Tarot subjects can be divided into eight categories: self, other, group, area of life, situation, time period, question and open. The overall meaning of a reading is greatly influenced by the subject type.

1. Self: You will often want to be the subject of your own readings. In this way, you make it very clear that all the cards refer to you personally. They may allude to other people and aspects of the environment, but the focus is explicitly you. This is the default subject if you don't name one.

2. **Other:** You can do a reading about another individual—a person, animal, plant, place, object, or idea. These readings can be quite informative, but always remember you explore other individuals from your own perspective, not theirs. The insights you gain are for you.

When your subject is another person, try to view that individual in an evenhanded way. Even if you do not like or admire the subject, respect her right to her own individuality. Try to set aside any preconceived ideas you might have about the subject. Be grateful that this person is giving you a chance to learn and grow despite any challenge she represents.

3. **Group:** You can do a reading about a group with a common identity. Some examples are a marriage, family, class, team, work unit, or organization. The group may or may not include you. The cards in a group reading refer to the group as a whole although some cards may relate to an individual within the group. You can also focus on a very large group such as a country or the Earth, but the message will be very general.

4. **Area of Life:** An area of life is any general category of experience that endures over time and involves situations that come and go. You can explore your own areas or someone else's. Some examples are career, finances, romance, health, and friendships. Areas of life aren't really separate from each other, but it can be useful to look at them this way in a reading. See Part Five for a list of areas.

5. **Situation:** A situation is a unique set of circumstances that exists for a limited period of time—for example, a job opportunity, project, ceremony, or family issue. Unlike areas of life, situations don't endure. They come and go as people and events flow through your life. A disagreement with a neighbor is a "situation" in this sense. Four common subtypes are:

> Problems—challenges or concerns you perceive as troubling
>
> Choices—decisions, either yes/no or among alternatives
>
> Tasks—projects or endeavors with a certain goal
>
> Events—specific happenings with a clear beginning and end

Situations are the grist for life's mill—the concerns that absorb us day to day. Some, such as weddings, are personal. Others, such as political elections, are more general. Readings that address a situation can be especially insightful.

6. **Time Period:** Most time period subjects have a clear beginning and end—for example, a day, week, month, season, or year. Other time periods are more general, such as the past or the future. In readings, cards about the future always show probabilities, not givens.

7. **Question:** You can write a question about any topic and make that question the subject of a reading. A question lets you focus more narrowly on a particular aspect of a subject. You then receive your "answer" by interpreting the cards.

Rather than do a reading about a speech you have to give, you decide to write the question "How can I improve my ability to speak to groups effectively?" Your real concern is not so much the speech event, but your comfort level in public speaking. See Part Five for some suggestions on how to write an effective question.

8. Open: An open reading does not have a subject. These readings give your Inner Guide an open opportunity to communicate what you most need to know at a given moment. You receive a higher level of guidance that embraces the larger patterns that are shaping your everyday experiences.

Open readings can be quite powerful. I try to use them sparingly to preserve their out-of-the-ordinary quality. Consider them for special occasions, such as birthdays, anniversaries, ceremonial days, equinoxes, and first days (new job, date, trip). An open reading is worthwhile whenever an expanse of unknown is opening out before you.

SUBJECT PRACTICE

Knowing how to choose a reading subject and name it quickly is a useful skill. Look for subjects within your own life, but also within the lives of others. In each case, identify the type and give the subject a label. People already have names, but you can also label a person by a relationship (Anne's Mom) or function (Director of Manufacturing). Concentrate on areas of life and situation subjects as well. Try to become clear on the differences between the two.

QUESTION WRITING

Any time you face a problem, take a moment to create a suitable tarot question about it. Work on it while you're doing routine activities, such as riding in a car or doing housework. Writing practice questions helps you learn to analyze a personal problem quickly and recognize what you want in various situations. Also, if you decide to do a reading about the problem, you will have your question handy.

Reading Procedure

Once you decide to do a reading, you need a plan for how to proceed. Here is a complete, step-by-step procedure for doing a tarot reading for yourself. (Part Five includes a summary of this procedure.) The page numbers refer to sections in the text where a topic is covered more completely.

Having a procedure to follow is very helpful in tarot work. When you follow the same steps over and over in a certain way, they help you center yourself in the moment. The details of the steps are not that important; in fact, you can change any of them, if you wish. The goal is to maintain a spirit of mindfulness. Doing a reading with loving concentration will make your tarot practice very powerful.

Choose and Label the Subject

Choose and label the subject of your reading, unless it is open (see above). Consider bringing a picture or memento of your subject to the reading to help you focus.

Assemble Materials

Assemble all your materials in the space you've chosen for the reading. Place your tarot cards nearby in their container. If you are using a spread, bring a sketch if you are concerned you might forget the details. Quickly review the positions, their meanings, and the order of placement. If you have a written opening statement or a question, be sure to have these handy. A pencil and paper or tablet are useful for taking down notes and recording the cards you choose.

Set the Mood

When you are ready, sit down on the floor or at a table leaving some empty space in front of you. At first, a full reading will probably take at least thirty to forty minutes. Try to arrange your affairs so you won't be interrupted. With experience, you will be able to shorten this time, if you wish, but it is always better to feel unhurried.

You now want to create a conducive mood. Begin to relax and still your mind. Put aside your worries and concerns for now. (You can always get them back later!) Settle fully into the present moment. Take a few deep breaths and feel the quiet as you turn away from the outside world. Take as much time as you need for this calming process.

Say an Opening Statement

When you feel centered, take your cards out of their container. Hold them cupped in one hand while you place the other hand on top. Close your eyes and bring the cards into the circle of your energy.

Now, make an opening statement, if you wish. Some possibilities are:

a prayer

an affirmation

a description of how you are feeling

a simple hello to your Inner Guide

You can say the same opening statement every time, or you can speak spontaneously. It is more important to speak from your heart than to mouth an empty formula. Say your statement out loud, as sound adds energy and conviction.

Declare the subject of your reading as well. Request guidance that is in the best interest of all concerned. Set aside any biases or preconceived ideas as much as possible. Try to adopt a curious, but open orientation toward your subject.

If your subject is a question, read it exactly as you wrote it, or say it from memory. This is important because one of the mysteries of the unconscious is that it is very literal; the cards you choose will be keyed to the precise wording of your question.

If your reading is open (no subject), say a general message of intent such as:

I welcome a message of wisdom and open myself to receive the guidance I most need at this time.

Shuffle the Cards

Open your eyes and begin shuffling. It is important to shuffle the cards because this is how you sort through all the forms your reading could take and arrange at a subtle level the one you will receive. There are a number of ways to shuffle the cards. Each method has its pros and cons. Choose one that is comfortable for you. I describe different shuffling techniques in Part Five (page 332).

While you shuffle, keep your mind as open and free of thoughts as possible. If a thought drifts by, let it gently pass without fixing on it. Ideally, you should feel as if you are an empty house with all the windows open to every soft breeze.

Cut the Cards

When you feel you have shuffled long enough, stop and place the cards facedown in front of you with the short edge closest to you. Cut the deck as follows:

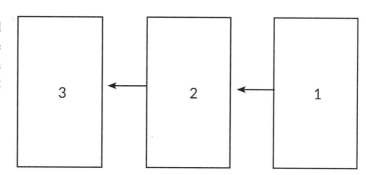

Grab some number of cards from the complete pile.

Drop this smaller pile to the left.

Grab some part of this second pile, and drop the new third pile further to the left.

Regroup the cards into one pile in any fashion.

It's best to regroup the cards in one quick motion. Don't try to figure out which pile should go where. Just let your hand move where it will. The cut is an important finishing step that marks the end of the card-arranging stage. Once you have regrouped the cards, the pattern of the reading is fixed, and all that remains is to lay out the cards and see what they reveal.

Lay Out the Cards

Pick up the deck, and hold it in one hand with the short edge closest to you. With your other hand, turn over the first card as you would the page of a book. Place this card in position 1. The position number corresponds to the placement order of your spread. Turn over the second card, and place it in position 2. Continue in this way until you have placed all the cards for your spread. Set the remainder of the cards to one side.

Turn around any reversed cards if you are not considering card orientation. Do not be concerned about altering the cards in this way. Your Inner Guide knows whether or not reversals are meaningful to you at the time of the reading, and so your actions do not impact the message. See page 333 for a shuffling method that avoids reversed cards.

Respond to the Cards

Pay attention to your reactions to each card as you lay it out. At first, you will not know or remember the usual meaning of a card. Your responses will be based mainly on the images. As you practice, your reactions will become more informed, but also more predictable. Try to keep some of your original openness as much as possible. Pay attention to any responses that seem unusual or out of place.

Remember the cards refer to your subject, but from *your point of view*. This may or may not be related to what the subject actually experiences or believes. The message of any reading you do for yourself is always for you.

When all the cards are laid out, take a moment to respond to them as a whole. Do you get an overall impression? Do you have any new reactions? Jot down some of your thoughts, if you wish. Don't worry if you can't remember all of them. Just as with dreams, you will recall the most important. Try not to get too involved in any notes as that can break the flow of the reading. You simply want to capture a few ideas quickly.

Analyze the Cards

Begin to analyze the individual cards in more depth. See Chapter Three for some hints on interpretation. You can proceed systematically, or go from card to card spontaneously. In the beginning, use the Card Description Section. Later, you can examine the cards on your own, but you may still find this section useful. I use it myself from time to time!

Look up the individual page for the card and read through all the keywords and actions. Look for actions that make you say "Yes, that one really fits!"

I experience a kind of jolt of recognition when I see one. Don't shy away from actions that seem less pleasant. Trust your intuition, and reserve judgment until you've seen all the cards. Note any stray thoughts or "irrelevant" feelings that come to mind.

Consider the Relationships between Cards

Also consider the relationships between the cards. Look for card pairs and card groups (covered in Chapter Three).

For open readings, a detailed analysis is not required. You can instead step back from the minutiae of your life, and let the cards show you larger themes. Concentrate on patterns as revealed in the reading. View everything in a wider context. Open readings are not about the everyday.

You could ponder a reading for hours without running out of insights, but, of course, this isn't practical or desirable. Do try to spend some time, however. Your reward will be equal to your effort.

Create the Story

At some point, you need to pull everything together. I call this creating the story (page 34). Your story will help you understand your subject and give you guidance for the future—what you have been seeking all along.

I recommend that you create your story spontaneously. Once you have finished your card review, let that analytical approach go. Your story will be more authentic if it arises freely from within. When you feel ready, simply begin speaking your story, saying whatever comes to mind. Use any notes you have to help, but don't focus on them too much.

I encourage you to tell your story out loud. Writing is too slow, and just thinking your ideas is too vague. Your story will gather strength as it is spoken. If you begin to ramble or lose your train of thought, don't be concerned. Simply pause, regroup, and start again. As you practice, you will become better at speaking on the fly. You may also want to record your story. When you play it back, you will be amazed at what you hear. You will truly feel you are your own best tarot reader.

Create a Summary Statement

Your story is done when your words slow down and stop naturally. Your next step is to distill the main theme of your story. What is the essence of your guidance? Ask yourself these kinds of questions:

What seems to be the main issue for the subject?

What is my role?

Do I sense any recommendations for action?

What does my Inner Guide want me to understand, and how do I feel about that?

Your Inner Guide has responded to your desire for insight, and now you want to capture that wisdom in a form you can remember. Try to summarize your story in one or two short sentences. Concentrate on the message in the cards and not the mechanics of your interpretation.

Finish Up

The main event is over, but as with any ceremony, there are a few final steps to be taken to end the reading and leave your cards ready for next time.

If you have not yet done so, write down the cards you selected and their positions. It is easy to forget them. Now, clear the deck to remove all traces of the energy patterns of this reading. I clear a deck by scrambling the cards together gently. It reminds me of erasing letters in the sand with a sweep of my hand.

You may enjoy this technique too, but any shuffling method will do. While you clear the deck, try to view only the backs of the cards. Stop when you feel you've shuffled long enough, and gather the cards together. Your deck is ready for your next reading.

Before putting the cards away, hold them again for just a moment. Place your deck in one hand with the other hand on top, and close your eyes. Say what you feel you have learned from this reading. Express your gratitude to your Inner Guide for helping you via the tarot cards. Gratitude is a wonderful sentiment. It provides the ideal frame of mind in which to end your reading.

When you began, you initiated a cycle. You created meaning in the form of a reading, and now you have completed that cycle by returning the cards to their resting state.

Use What You Have Learned

The reading proper is over, but the inner work is just beginning. Your goal is to integrate what you have learned into your life in some way. If you don't, your tarot practice will remain a beautiful pastime with no power to help you.

Decide on one or more appropriate actions you might take to put your guidance to work. You can reinforce what you're doing now or make changes, either radical or minor. Specific actions are usually more helpful than vague plans. If the reading is open, it's not necessary to commit to specific actions. Simply absorb the spirit of the message, and allow it to guide you in a general way.

If you are keeping a journal, write down what you intend to do. Commit only to what you know you will actually carry out. I know how easy it is to lay out some cards, look at them briefly and then never think about that reading again, especially when your reaction is less than positive!

If you were not the subject of the reading, you can consider sharing your insights with the actual subject, but remember the reading was for you. Share from that perspective, not from a desire to inform or lecture the subject about any "facts" he or she should be aware of.

As the days go by, think about your reading and how it meshes with your life. Ask yourself these questions:

How meaningful was my story?

Did I miss anything important?

Did I make a change, and, if so, what happened?

Did something unexpected occur?

Do my daily readings, if any, shed light on this reading?

After your reading, you may wonder if you did everything correctly. Remember there is no one correct approach or interpretation. What you see in the cards is right for you *by definition*, and, no matter what, you will come away with something of value.

You may be tempted to do another reading on the same subject, but it's usually best to wait until there are significant changes. Assume that your reading covers all you need to know. If you are puzzled about certain elements, mine your reading for more insights. By going deeper, you will get closer to the heart of the matter. (Serial readings are an alternative, offering a way to explore a subject through multiple readings in one sitting. See Chapter Eleven.)

Using what you have learned is a vital step, but also perhaps the most difficult. It involves moving beyond playing with the cards. When you actually commit to integrating your tarot insights into your life, you have realized the true and lasting benefit to be gained from the cards.

This is my ideal tarot session, but to be truthful, I don't always follow it. Sometimes I linger over these steps, sometimes I neglect quite a few. I encourage you to adopt whatever procedure best suits your interests and needs at the time. If you don't enjoy the cards, they'll just gather dust on the shelf. The details aren't that important; it's the intention that counts!

A SUBJECT READING ABOUT A NEWS EVENT

Go through today's news, and choose a topic of interest. Look for a topic that is intriguing and somewhat controversial. A short-term media event is a good choice because you will get feedback on the situation quickly.

Read over the facts that are available, and choose an appropriate subject. Follow the guidelines in this section. Later, when the situation has resolved somewhat, go over your reading and relate it to what actually happened. Remember to stay focused on the message for you in the cards about this event.

AN OPEN READING

During the next few weeks, look for an opportunity to try an open reading. I recommend a fairly quiet day when you feel at peace with your life and attuned to the moment. It should be a day when you have the time and inclination to step back a little and look at the larger patterns that are influencing you at this time. If a birthday, anniversary, or other special occasion happens to fall during this period, use it as the basis for your reading.

Chapter Three

INTERPRETING THE CARDS

You're seated in front of your first tarot reading. You've shuffled, cut, and laid out cards in your chosen spread. Your first thought is probably, "Now what do I do?"

When I first began learning the tarot, I sought the answer to this question everywhere—in classes, conversations, books, and practice. I was looking for the *one,* true way to interpret the cards. Of course, I never found such a system because it doesn't exist. Reading the tarot is an art, not a science. There can be no set rules that apply all the time because every person is unique. How could a set of formulas ever provide guidance that honors that uniqueness?

On the other hand, there are some ways to approach the cards that have proven valuable time and again. They work because they bring form and focus to intuitive responses. They provide a framework around which you can build the message of a reading.

In this chapter, I share some of the principles of interpretation that I have discovered. I offer these as guidelines to help you develop a feel for the cards and what they can show you. Take from them what works for you, and use them to create a tarot approach that is uniquely your own.

Interpreting a Single Card

When interpreting a reading, you will go back and forth between sensing all the cards as a whole and examining each one individually. The two approaches reinforce each other, but eventually, you do have to clarify the meaning of each card. You need to understand its unique energy, so you can fit it into the whole picture.

There are three sources of meaning for an individual card:

1. Traditional Meanings

Each card has a set of traditional meanings that have built up around the card over the years. These vary with different tarot writers and teachers. My suggestions for each card are given in the Card Descriptions section.

2. Personal Meanings

Your personal meanings for a card are based on your tarot experience, background, personality, and intuition. This mixture changes over time and from reading to reading, and keeps the meaning of a card fresh.

3. Card Image

Meanings can be triggered by a card's image. Your response to an image can often be quite telling. Details may seem to relate very directly to your subject. For example, in a reading about building a house, the document on the Three of Pentacles may strike you as a set of blueprints. The images on the Rider-Waite deck are particularly evocative. One major benefit of this deck is that there are images on every card.

The context of a card also contributes to its meaning. Context provides a framework and sets an interpretive boundary around the card. It helps you relate a card to a certain person or issue. There are three aspects of context:

1. Actual Situation

The circumstances of your life at the time of a reading always have an influence. You often begin a reading because of something happening at the time, so it is natural that features of the moment impact how you understand a card.

2. Position Meanings

If you are using a spread, the meanings associated with a card's position are key. These meanings are based on tradition, but they too can be affected by your experience and unique point of view. Some examples of position meanings are "the central issue" or "my environment." Part Four on Tarot Spreads provides position meanings for the Celtic Cross and Flex Spreads.

3. Subject of the Reading

Each card reflects some aspect of the subject of the reading. Your interpretation will be guided by that understanding.

To interpret a card, you need to combine all these factors into some composite that makes sense to you. This is a fluid process. These areas seem separate, but in practice, they blend together, and your overall response just happens.

At first, you will probably rely heavily on the traditional card and position meanings, but gradually your personal reactions will become primary. You may not feel any reaction to a card, or perhaps just a mild one. Try to notice any quick thought, feeling, or image that comes to mind, no matter how slight. Here are some questions you can ask yourself to help tease out the meaning of a card:

> *What feeling do I sense in the card scene?*
>
> *What feeling do I sense in myself when I see this card?*
>
> *Am I attracted, repelled, or neutral about this card?*
>
> *What about the subject comes to mind when I see this card?*
>
> *Does this card remind me of anyone?*
>
> *What details seem important in this card, and why?*

Let's say you're doing a reading with your main subject as the question: "How can I improve my chances of receiving a bonus this year?" You have decided to use the popular Celtic Cross spread and have drawn the upright Seven of Cups in position 5. The Celtic Cross is covered in depth in Chapter Nine, but for now, simply use the position 5 meanings on page 292 to follow along with this example.

You first note your reactions. Perhaps your glance fells on the cup filled with jewels. The figure in the foreground seems to be looking directly at this cup. You identify with him as he reaches out for treasure. This fits your question—you're reaching out for a bonus.

Now, look at the keywords for the Seven of Cups. They are wishful thinking, options, and dissipation. When you read through the actions, you are struck by the following:

kidding yourself about the facts

waiting for your ship to come in

lacking focus and commitment

These phrases suggest someone who is passive and unrealistic, who lacks the energy and desire for success. They reinforce the keyword of wishful thinking.

On reading over the meanings for position 5, you feel a pull toward:

your delusions and illusions

what you're obsessed about

what you've set your heart on

The sense of this card is beginning to take shape for you. It seems to be suggesting that you are too busy daydreaming and not acting constructively. The figure now strikes you as awed by the cup dangled in front of him. You decide this card represents for you at this time an attitude of unreasonable hopes and unproductive dreaming. This is your first feeling about the card. You may modify that assessment later when you examine the other cards.

Clearly there are other possibilities. You might have been struck by the array of delights floating in front of the shadowy figure. He seems to have many options, another meaning of the Seven of Cups.

There is never one right answer in tarot work! Both of these interpretations make sense. You may wonder how you can decide on the best meaning when there are so many possibilities. You must trust your intuition.

Your Inner Guide will give you hints that will lead you toward the ideas that are most important for you. An insistent thought may keep popping into your mind. You may circle around a meaning—thinking about it, moving off then finally coming back. When one meaning hits you with particular force, you know you're on the right track. This is the "Aha"

THE BIG BOOK OF TAROT

reaction. An "Aha" reaction may not happen for every card, but when it does, you know it is important. These are the ways that inner knowing manifests.

Part Five contains a step-by-step procedure for interpreting a single card. It summarizes the ideas covered in this section. Try this procedure the next time you encounter a card that is difficult for you to interpret. See if the procedure helps you break through your block.

The benefit of a procedure is that it helps you avoid floundering during interpretation. The disadvantage is that a procedure can cause you to abandon your intuition for a rote system. You don't want your interpretations to become automatic. Practice with this procedure for a while, but don't depend on it.

COMBINING SOURCES OF MEANING

Practice blending card and position meanings. Choose a card from the deck. Read its keywords and actions, and try to get a feel for the card's essential meaning. Now, choose a position to work with from the Celtic Cross (pages 287 to 297). Imagine your card has appeared in that position in a reading. How do the card and position meanings work together to create a composite?

Write one sentence that sums up your interpretation. Select a possibility that appeals to you and makes sense. Your sentence doesn't have to relate to your life in any way as this exercise is simply for practice.

For example, let's say you choose the Emperor. The keywords for the Emperor are fathering, structure, authority and regulation. Some choices for the Emperor in position 1 of the Celtic Cross spread (page 288) might be:

The heart of the matter (position) is that there is too much structure (Emperor) in my life.
My present environment (position) is very regulated and controlled (Emperor).
Becoming a father (Emperor) is the primary factor (position) in my life right now.

These sentences are all different, but each one blends the meanings of the Emperor and position 1. In an actual reading, the most appropriate interpretation for you would become clear as you considered all the many factors of the reading.

Interpreting Major and Minor Arcana Cards

Certain cards in the tarot naturally form into groups. The cards have unique meanings, but they also have a common identity with the other cards in their group. The two largest groups are the major and minor arcanas. The terms major and minor reflect the relative weights of these two groups.

A major arcana card represents an energy that is deep, strong, decisive, or long-term. The minor arcana cards do not carry the same weight, but they are still important. They chart the ups and downs of daily life and register changes in feelings and thoughts. These dramas are gripping while they occur, but they pass with time as new concerns take their place.

Compare the interpretation of two cards with similar meanings, but different weights—the Hermit (major) and the Eight of Cups (minor). The Hermit is the archetypal symbol of one

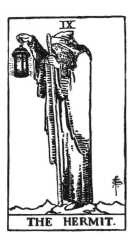

who seeks truth and deeper meaning. He stands for the impulse to renounce superficial pleasures to seek understanding within. In a reading, the Hermit could indicate a strong urge to find answers. This is not a passing fancy, but a major desire that could last for some time.

With the Eight of Cups, your interpretation might be much the same, but, as a minor arcana card, this card implies the search does not have the same force. Maybe you've been a little bored at work, so you feel like chucking everything to make hats on the beach. You are seeking, but the urge is not yet a heartfelt desire.

You could draw a minor arcana card in one reading and then draw a major arcana card with a similar meaning in a later reading. What started as minor has become more important over time. Similarly, a major matter can fade and lose its urgency as circumstances change.

COMMON MEANINGS FOR MAJOR AND MINOR ARCANA CARDS

For every major arcana card, there is at least one minor arcana card with a similar meaning. These correspondences are given as Reinforcing Cards on the description page for each card. Look through the major arcana card descriptions to familiarize yourself with some of the reinforcing minor arcana cards. You will discover other card connections—sometimes surprising ones—as you develop your tarot practice.

Interpreting Aces

Each ace represents the qualities of its suit in their purest form. An ace always adds something special to a reading. It stands out from the other cards as if in a circle of its own light. The images on the aces are all similar. A strong hand, glowing with energy, comes out of

a cloud grasping the token of its suit. An ace "hands" you a gift that comes from some unknown source hidden in the clouds. The nature of the gift is symbolized by the suit token.

Ace of Wands

A wand is a strong, masculine object, alive with potent force. Leaves are growing as new life bursts forth. The wand reminds us of a magic wand used to perform miracles and create wonders. The gift of the Ace of Wands is creativity, enthusiasm, courage, and confidence.

Ace of Cups

A cup is an open, feminine object—a receptacle designed to hold nourishing liquids. Water pours from the cup showing there is a never-ending supply of refreshment flowing into the world. The gift of the Ace of Cups is emotion, intuition, intimacy, and love.

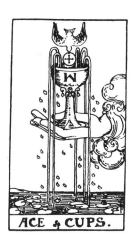

ACE of CUPS.

Ace of Swords

A sword is a weapon—a finely crafted tool to cut through any obstacle or confusion. A sword extends the power of its user to fight and prevail. It can wield a cruel force, but also a clean, sharp one. The gift of the Ace of Swords is mental clarity, truth, justice, and fortitude.

Ace of Pentacles

The pentacle is a magical sign for the mystery of nature and the everyday world. It is stamped on a coin, the token of material exchange. With money and raw materials, we have the wherewithal to make our dreams real. The gift of the Ace of Pentacles is prosperity, practicality, security, and the ability to manifest.

ACE of SWORDS.

Aces are portals between the realms of the major and minor arcanas. They allow powerful, but impersonal forces to come into your everyday life. An Ace in a reading shows that its qualities are becoming available. An Ace is always interpreted as beneficial, positive, and life-enhancing.

An Ace can also represent a window of opportunity that is opening. The Ace tells you to pay attention, so you don't miss it. Think of an Ace as a seed of possibility that will grow given your attention and care. Look for the potential in every situation.

A relative once drew the Ace of Pentacles and the Ace of Wands together in a reading—a dynamic combination that says "Look for a real, creative outlet for your energies that will bring greater prosperity." Several months later, she told me that—encouraged by this sign—she had pursued a challenging opening at her workplace and was now making more money with greater personal satisfaction.

ACE of PENTACLES.

THE ENERGY OF THE ACES

Place the four Aces in a row in front of you. Write the four keywords for each ace on four pieces of paper, and place them below the aces they go with. Concentrate on each ace until you feel you know it well. Look at the details on the cards, especially the suit tokens. Notice how each one captures the qualities of its ace. Try to get to the point where you can see an ace and immediately feel its powerful presence. The first keyword for each ace has force!

Interpreting Court Cards

You probably have noticed that people tend to fall into types. Their traits cluster together in familiar ways. We sometimes give these clusters names, such as "loner," "dreamer," or "workaholic." Psychologists have devised elaborate systems that categorize types of people. The popular Myers-Briggs is one such system.[1]

The tarot has its own system of personalities represented by the 16 court cards—the King, Queen, Knight, and Page of each suit. The key to understanding the personality of each court card is the combination of its suit and rank.

Kings

The King of Wands is creative, inspiring, forceful, charismatic, and bold. These are typical traits of the Wands suit. They are prime examples of its dynamic fire energy, but they also reflect the character of a King. Kings are active and outgoing. They want to make an impact on the world through the force of their personality.

Queens

The Queen of Wands is attractive, wholehearted, energetic, cheerful, and self-assured. These are also Wands qualities. This Queen is upbeat and lively, but she does not wield her personality as a force directed outward. Queens express their suits from the inside, setting a tone without imposing it.

Knights

Knights are extremists; they express their suit qualities to the maximum. Such excessive feelings and behavior can be either welcome or unwelcome depending on the circumstances.

The Knight of Pentacles has an excess of caution—a trait typical of the steady, conservative Pentacles nature. This Knight prefers to check and double-check everything. He always proceeds slowly before committing himself—the kind of person you would ask to fold your parachute or guide you through a minefield.

THE BIG BOOK OF TAROT

On the other hand, you could say the Knight of Pentacles is unadventurous. He will never double his money through a risky investment or propose a surprise trip to Paris on a whim. Such daring moves are not in his nature. You would have to check with the Knight of Wands for that!

The keywords for the Knights are word pairs (cautious/unadventurous). In readings, you must consider both views when interpreting a Knight. Does he represent a beneficial or harmful approach? The other factors (and your own honesty!) will help you decide.

Pages

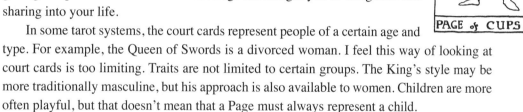

Each page shows a happy child holding the token of his suit. He is fascinated by this plaything. The pages inspire us to enjoy their interests with them. The Page of Swords can represent the thrill of intellectual discovery or other mental challenges.

Pages also encourage you to "Go for it!" Children do not hesitate when they want something. They reach out and grab. If you want what a page is offering, don't be afraid. Seize the day!

If the Page of Cups is your daily reading card, and a fellow student smiles at you, take this opportunity for friendship. Strike up a conversation, or suggest getting a cup of coffee after class. This Page encourages you to bring love and sharing into your life.

In some tarot systems, the court cards represent people of a certain age and type. For example, the Queen of Swords is a divorced woman. I feel this way of looking at court cards is too limiting. Traits are not limited to certain groups. The King's style may be more traditionally masculine, but his approach is also available to women. Children are more often playful, but that doesn't mean that a Page must always represent a child.

A court card in a reading is showing you how a certain approach to life is or could be impacting the situation. There are several possibilities:

Court Cards as Qualities

A court card can show a quality that is being expressed or seeking expression. It may be something that's valued, or something neglected. It may be an approach that's recognized, or one that's denied. The best interpretation depends on the subject, the other cards, and the situation.

Let's say you are trying to decide whether or not to enter into a business partnership and draw the King of Swords. You could interpret this card as a way for you to act in this situation—to be fair and ethical, to review everything carefully, and to articulate your needs.

Court Cards as People

A court card can also represent a particular person. If you look at a court card and say to yourself, "I know who that is!" then it could very well be that person. It may also represent someone of whom you are not yet aware.

KNIGHT of CUPS.

QUEEN of PENTACLES

Let's say you have met someone who is very romantic. You spend long hours together and connect on a deep level. In a reading, the Knight of Cups could represent this new lover, but, since he's a knight, you should look at this relationship closely.

What are you hoping to experience? You may be enjoying the romance, but are you also looking for dependability and commitment? The Knight of Cups is a signal to you that this relationship may be lopsided: abundant in intimate sharing, but deficient in other ways.

Court Cards as the Atmosphere

A court card can also reflect the general atmosphere. Sometimes, an environment seems to take on a personality of its own—one that matches a court card type.

You consult the tarot to find out about the group house you are planning to join. You draw the Queen of Pentacles. This card could be telling you that the atmosphere will be nurturing. Your housemates will be warm and generous with a sensible approach to problems.

On the other hand, you may meet someone in the house who is similar to the Queen of Pentacles, or you may be like her yourself in this situation. Such is the subtle play of the tarot!

SEEING COURT CARD QUALITIES IN PEOPLE

The more you understand your fellow humans, the more you will understand the court cards. Over the next few weeks, observe your relatives, friends, colleagues, and acquaintances. Consider celebrities, historical figures, and characters from books, TV and films. Ask yourself:

What qualities does this person have? Not have?
What qualities are helpful to this person? Not helpful?
What court card is this person most like? Least like?
How is this person unique—unlike any type at all?
What court card types are common in my life? Uncommon?

Interpreting Card Pairs

There is a game called Labyrinth that consists of a square box with a moveable platform inside. On the platform is a maze punctuated by little holes. The object is to move a ball from one end of the maze to the other without letting the ball fall into one of the holes. Knobs on the outside let you guide the ball by rotating the platform in any direction.

A simple game, but difficult in practice! The slightest miscalculation, and the ball goes down. If you lean the platform too far in one direction, you lose control. If you try to compensate too quickly, you lose control in the other direction. The only strategy that works is a patient shepherding of the ball along the path as you maintain a balance of movement and force in all directions.

I see in Labyrinth a metaphor for our navigation along the pathway of life. We travel from birth to death negotiating around the "holes" by continually balancing our approaches. We maintain steady progress forward by making countless life adjustments—first here, then there. Our actions offset each other in a dance that is sometimes delightful, often challenging.

The key is always balance. To achieve balance, we must know how to express all the energies available to us. Personal balance is never static. It comes from the ability to choose dynamically the option that will work in any given moment.

A tarot reading is a map of the counterbalancing tendencies that are operating at any one time. To read this map, you must understand the Law of Opposition—that any quality, once identified, implies its opposite. This is a basic principle of the material universe. The Fool discovers this principle at the very beginning of his journey when he meets both the Magician and the High Priestess. These two archetypes show him that nothing is defined in isolation, only as one pole of a balancing pair.

At the deepest level, opposition does not exist. There is just Oneness, but, in physical life, we perceive Oneness as broken up into countless different energies. These are the forces we navigate in our search for balance.

One way to discover balance issues is by looking for two cards in a reading that oppose each other. One meaning of the Eight of Swords is restriction—being trapped in an oppressive or limiting situation. If you ponder this meaning for a while, you realize that simply by acknowledging the idea of restriction, you imply the opposing idea of freedom—the breaking out of bonds and limitations. This quality is represented by the Four of Wands.

A reading containing these two cards could be showing the importance of the restriction/freedom issue. They define the ends of a continuum of experience from which you can choose the best balance point.

There are three types of opposing card pairs:

Permanent pairs

Certain cards form clear and obvious permanent opposites based on their traditional meanings. The Eight of Swords and Four of Wands are this type. The Magician and the High Priestess are another. The Magician represents action and conscious awareness; the High Priestess, nonaction and unconscious awareness.

Court Card and Ace Pairs

You can create a pair between any two court cards or two aces. These pairs reflect the balance patterns that emerge when you contrast two suits or ranks. Consider the keywords for the King of Pentacles and the Queen of Cups.

enterprising

adept

reliable

supporting

steady

KING of PENTACLES.

emotional

tenderhearted

intuitive

psychic

spiritual

QUEEN of CUPS.

The King of Pentacles acts outwardly (king) in an enterprising, adept way based on his interest in the material world (pentacles). The Queen of Cups has an inner focus (queen) that is emotional and intuitive based on her concern with feelings (cups).

In a reading, this pair could represent a conflict between two people—a can-do type who wants to get the job done, and a dreamer who first wants to see how everyone feels. This pair could also represent dueling qualities within the subject—perhaps a need to focus on worldly concerns vs a desire to concentrate on the spiritual. There are many possibilities. In Part Five I offer some ways in which the suits and ranks interact.

Occasional pairs

You can interpret any two cards as a pair, even if their meanings are not exactly opposites. There is so much meaning in every card that useful comparisons can almost always be made.

Occasional pairs arise by chance in a reading, and their relationship lasts for only that one instance.

The Four of Cups shows a solitary man sitting under a tree. The Ten of Cups shows a happy family celebrating together. If the idea were meaningful to you, you might see these cards as defining the opposites of "being alone" vs "being with others." This understanding might occur to you out of the blue as you think about your reading.

• • •

Two cards do not have to oppose each other to form a pair. They can reinforce each other. Both the Empress and the Nine of Cups suggest pleasure, sensuality, and physical enjoyment. Reinforcing pairs show that a certain energy is or could be having an extra impact. In a sense, the meaning is "doubled." Sometimes we have to face circumstances in an unbalanced way for a while to achieve our goals.

In the Card Descriptions section, I offer some possible opposing and reinforcing pairs for each card. As you do your readings, pay attention to these pair dynamics. Gradually you will begin to appreciate the incredible way the tarot cards work together to reflect balance in the world.

YOUR BALANCE ISSUES

Identify a balance issue that is meaningful to you at this time. Here are some possibilities:

> controlling—letting go
> being free—being restricted
> feeling joy—feeling sadness
> creating peace—creating conflict
> working—playing
> risking—playing it safe
> moving slow—moving fast
> acting—waiting
> coming together—moving apart
> feeling victorious—feeling defeated

Find two cards that represent the opposite ends of your issue. You can use the keyword charts for the card meanings to help (pages 61 and 128–129). In the next few weeks, think about these cards from time to time. Are you closer to one extreme, or somewhere in the middle? Watch for these cards to show up in your readings.

Interpreting Card Groups

A group is any set of cards with some common characteristic. The meaning of a reading is influenced by any groups within it. Here are some groups to look for in a reading:

Major Arcana

The major arcana cards are potent archetypes with extra force and impact. If there are many majors in a reading, this group communicates a sense of heightened energy around the subject.

Aces

The aces represent positive and life-enhancing energies. A reading with more than one ace shows that new possibilities are present. The situation is bursting with potential.

Court Cards

Many court cards in a reading can suggest the involvement of many people or points of view. There are many "cooks in the kitchen" which can be helping or hindering to the subject.

Suits

You can get a sense of the overall energy character of a reading by noticing the number of cards in each suit. This tells you which qualities are dominant (more cards) and which are weak or absent (fewer cards).

Spread Groups

Groups of cards are built into the composition of many spreads. Cards in these groups are placed together physically to emphasize their connection. Spread groups are especially noteworthy because the cards in them are designed to be interpreted according to the group meaning.

Spontaneous Groups

Certain cards in a reading can strike you spontaneously as a group. Let's say you've drawn the Sun, Three of Cups, and Four of Wands in a reading. These three cards all suggest high spirits and the joy of celebration. They form a group because of this common meaning.

EXERCISE: LOOKING FOR CARD GROUPS

Begin looking for groups of cards in your readings. Pay attention to spread groups and the distribution of suits. Consider the number of major arcana cards, aces, and court cards. Look for spontaneous groups of cards that are meaningful.

Creating the Story

This section covers how to pull together the individual elements of a reading to create a tarot story. This is not an easy process to describe because storytelling is an art. Even though you can be shown a few techniques, in the end, you must develop your own style as a tarot artist. This is the challenge (and fun) of card interpretation.

First, I want you to set aside everything you've learned so far! Just disregard all those fancy principles. You've been exposed to much information about the cards, and I've only

THE BIG BOOK OF TAROT

touched on the possibilities. Tarot books contain system after system for relating the cards to each other. This is fascinating stuff, but what is its real purpose? It's to find a way to release your inner knowing through the cards.

The techniques you've learned have been based on the idea that you must figure out what the cards are saying, but this is not really the case. If you think of a tarot reading as an object to be dissected, you will have trouble grasping its full meaning. A tarot story doesn't come from without; it arises from within. Your stories come from a part of you that is seeking expression and conscious realization.

Of course, I don't really want you to discard your tarot learning. The principles are valuable, but not because they hold the key to readings in themselves. They simply help you recognize what you already know. They draw you in so you can set up the circumstances to release your story.

The secret of creating a tarot story is getting from intellectual understanding to knowing, from a piecemeal grasp to a unified vision. To do this, you need to recognize and honor your feelings. Feelings in this sense are not moods or emotions. They are the language of your Inner Guide. They are the outward expression of a knowing that is deeper than thought. The main feature of knowing is a sense of rightness. You know your insights are correct when you feel complete and satisfied with them.

The best way I've found to release inner knowing is through stream-of-consciousness talking—saying your thoughts out loud as they occur, uncensored and uncontrolled. You make no attempt to organize or clean up your speech. You simply let the words come out.

This technique is effective because it bypasses the critical ego. It allows the wisdom of your Inner Guide to come forth spontaneously. You feel as if something within has been set free. Your first attempts will probably be awkward, but your stories will improve with practice. You will develop an ability to guide the flow of words without imposing your will on them. Sometimes insights will surface that completely surprise you!

It's not necessary to rush or talk continually. You can pause whenever you want, but avoid thinking when this happens. Simply wait patiently until you feel the impulse to continue. Sometimes repeating the name of a card a few times can help. Queen of Cups . . . Queen of Cups ... Queen of Cups. After each repetition, wait to see if anything comes to mind in the form of a thought or image.

Sometimes your story will just flow. You will have no trouble fitting everything together. Other times there will be gaps and empty places. Certain cards will stay stubbornly obscure. The moment may not be right for you to fully grasp these cards, or all the pieces of the story may not yet be in place.

Don't be concerned if you can't always create a beautiful narrative. Sometimes knowing comes in fragments. Stay with a reading only as long as the effort seems worthwhile. A partial understanding may be all you need.

I once drew the Ace of Pentacles reversed in a position meaning "key factor." I knew right away that this card was telling me not to focus on money or material concerns. This realization hit me as soon as I saw the card. Everything I needed to know was in that one Ace, so interpreting the other cards was not really all that necessary.

A good spread makes weaving the pattern of the cards easy. By following the spread's built-in structure, your story unfolds naturally. Each spread has its own character based on its history, form, and purpose.

Your tarot story ends when your stream-of-consciousness talking begins to wind down and come to a stop. A few stray thoughts may still occur to you, but the main theme will have been established. You will know the essential message of the reading.

Stream-of-consciousness talking is an effective style for me, but you may not like it. You may prefer to sit quietly and absorb the meaning of the cards. Some people like to write out their reactions or create charts that cross-correlate the cards in a systematic way. Each of us is different, and our approaches to the tarot will be different too.

I'd like to leave you with one final thought about tarot stories. Trust yourself and your intuition completely. Banish right now any concerns you have about reading the cards correctly. You really can't make mistakes. Your tarot realizations are always the right ones for you at a given time and place. They are meaningful because they are yours. Know you are truly connected to all that is. You can access an understanding that is far greater than your everyday awareness. Trust that this is so.

STREAM-OF-CONSCIOUSNESS TALKING

You can practice stream-of-consciousness talking anytime you feel comfortable speaking your thoughts out loud. (For most of us, this means being alone!) Say every thought as it occurs to you. The idea is to "hear" a thought inwardly and then vocalize it. As you finish speaking one thought, listen for the next one.

In the next few weeks, try this exercise whenever you can. Work toward being able to speak naturally with no sense of urgency. Try to get to the point where thoughts about the process don't intrude too much. This is not an easy state to achieve, but it is well worth the effort.

TAROT IMPROVISATION

In theater improvisation, members of the audience call out the names of a few objects, and the actors assemble a skit based on those elements. In this exercise, the cards are the elements, and you are the actor who must bring them together on the fly.

Shuffle and cut the cards in the usual way, and hold the deck facedown in one hand. Turn over the first three cards, and lay them in a row. Now, create a story around the cards. Don't struggle to come up with a clever scenario. Just allow any tale to unfold. In *The Castle of Crossed Destinies* by Italo Calvino,[2] the characters tell their tales to each other using only tarot card images.

Now, if you like, lay out a fourth card. Incorporate this new one into the original tale. Continue developing the story by laying out new cards one at a time. The spirit of this exercise is spontaneous play. Stop if you feel any pressure or strain. If you prefer, you can set aside the first three cards and deal out three more for a new story.

Positive vs Negative Interpretations

You've probably noticed already that you do not feel neutral about your readings. You hope to see cards that are positive and encouraging. This is only natural. In my experience, people respond cheerfully to pleasant cards, but recoil in disappointment if a "nasty" one appears. Indeed, it *is* difficult to look at the Tower and accept it calmly. We don't want something scary to happen; we want the good!

In fact, the good and the bad are so mixed in life that these terms eventually become almost meaningless. If you were to get hurt in an accident, but then develop great inner strength during recovery, could you really say the accident was completely bad? If you were to be fired from your job, but then find a better one on the rebound, where is the positive and negative in this situation?

THE TOWER.

The cards in the tarot are not good or bad in themselves. They only describe certain energies or influences. It is up to you to use this information to make conscious choices about your life. Although the Tower can show a shattering breakup or downfall of some kind, you do not have to view this negatively. Sometimes an explosion of feeling or dramatic shakeup provides welcome relief, clearing the air and freeing up new energy.

It is your concentrated clarity about a situation that gives you the power to mold events along the lines of your choosing. This clarity comes from the wisdom of your Inner Guide paired with the fearless confidence you have in yourself. A reading does not deliver news to you as a passive victim, but as a powerful agent who can use that information creatively. It gives you a picture of the energy patterns in and around you so that you can work with them as you see fit.

Always remember the direction pictured in a reading is the one projected *for now* from all the influences of the present moment. If you can identify those forces, you can alter or encourage them as you wish. The future is never fixed. The outcome of your story is not a certainty, but a possibility. You can always embrace or change a direction provided you have the desire and courage to take the necessary steps. At the deepest level, you know what a situation is all about. Your tarot story simply lets you recognize what you know so you can act consciously.

Perhaps you are concerned that you aren't objective enough when reading the cards. You suspect that you only see in a reading what you want to see and not the "truth." In fact, that's exactly the point! The tarot helps you find out what it is you do believe, so you can acknowledge it. Your unconscious becomes conscious. You can't interpret falsely, but you can fail to perceive all that is there. The tarot is a mirror that reflects your own consciousness back to you. As you learn, that mirror becomes clearer, and you perceive at ever deeper levels.

Part Two

ENERGY AND
CARD ORIENTATION

Chapter Four

UPRIGHT AND REVERSED CARDS AS ENERGY

Y ou have learned that the tarot cards reflect different energies. For our purposes, we will consider an energy as anything that can be named or identified. Energies enjoy a temporary existence in a certain form. They are born, live for a time, and die, all the while contributing to the eternal flow—the animating Spirit that sustains all energies.

All living beings are energies, as are all inanimate objects. Qualities or states of being are also energies—the energy of love or despair can be a palpable force with a life of its own.

Energies often coalesce into groups to form larger energies. Each of us is such a group. Our bodies are made of cells and organs; our personalities are traits and tendencies; our moods reflect thoughts and feelings. A person is a veritable energy vortex!

Every minute of the day, energies of all kinds are flowing in, around, and through you. Some are mild, some strong. Some are new, some old. Some are welcome, some not so welcome. How does this energy flow relate to the tarot?

Energy and the Tarot

In a reading, every card represents a certain energy at a certain moment. A card's energy is not really its energy as a physical object, but the larger archetypal energy it symbolizes. A card's energy is its meaning, but with an added sense of movement and change.

A reading is a snapshot of a personal energy configuration meaningful to you. Just as a snapshot stops the action of a real scene, a reading freezes the flow of your life. But life goes on after a photo is taken, and so do the energies in a reading. Two readings done one after the other rarely contain the exact same cards. The energy pattern changes even in that short time.

In fact, you impact the energies in and around you simply by doing a reading! You alter the flow of events by examining them. This is why working with the cards is so powerful. A reading helps you become aware of the key energies at play in your life so you can work with them creatively.

FEELING ENERGIES IN THE ENVIRONMENT

Take a walk when you are not feeling pressured for time. During your walk, imagine everything you encounter to be a living energy with awareness—even inanimate objects. Sense the two of you as equals encountering each other for a shared purpose. Don't analyze your experience at the time. Just continue as if this way of being is completely natural. Later, think about these questions:

How did I feel during this exercise?

Did this way of being change my interactions? How?

Were some energies easier to feel than others?

Did I notice any answering responses?

FEELING CARD ENERGIES

Choose a card from your deck and look at it for a while. Keep part of your awareness on the card and part near the center of your chest—your heart area. This will help you feel, rather than think. If thoughts do occur, gently set them aside.

After a time, allow words to bubble up that capture the card's energy for you. Don't reach for words, just let them come. The words you receive will be unique to you. Sometimes strong emotions also arise during this exercise. They can be powerful. Repeat this exercise on other days. Some words will repeat, others will be new. Card energies adapt to changes in you and your environment.

The Energy Cycle

Take a moment to become aware of your breathing. Feel how your chest expands as you inhale deeply. You fill your lungs, pause for a moment, then exhale. Your chest slowly contracts as you breathe out.

This is the pulse of life. It's how energies flow within ourselves and our world. A wave builds, peaks, and crashes to the shore. Anger flares up and dies down. Civilizations rise and fall. Figure 1 is a picture of this universal energy cycle over time.

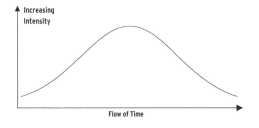

Figure 1

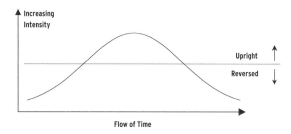

Figure 2

When you do a reading, each card shows an energy at a certain point in its cycle. One energy may be strong, another weak. One may be on the rise, another fading. It would be quite helpful to know the status of each card's energy.

The orientation of a card can give you this information. Orientation is the direction a card faces on the reading surface or as you hold it. A card can be upright (normal view) or reversed (upside-down). If a position is slanted or horizontal, you must decide beforehand how you will interpret cards in these positions for orientation.

Figure 2 shows the energy curve with a horizontal line dividing it in half. The section above the line covers the period when an energy is strong. The section below the line covers the periods when an energy is weak—either just beginning (left) or ending (right).

We can now relate card orientation to energy in this way: an upright card represents an energy in some part of its cycle above the line. Upright energies are strong and well-developed. They have a clear, active presence. You can appreciate their impact in the situation.

A reversed card represents an energy in some part of its cycle below the line. Reversed

energies are weak and less developed. It's not so easy to detect their presence. The energies exist in the situation, but they are not expressing fully.

The Three of Swords represents the energy of heartbreak and betrayal. If this card is upright, hurtful feelings are a strong feature of the situation. Reversed, this card suggests those energies are also present, but reduced. Perhaps the intensity of a painful episode is only beginning or fading.

The Empress reversed once appeared in a reading for a man who wanted to know if he and his wife might have a child. I guessed they had been trying to have a baby for some time. This card showed that the energy of mothering and birth was indeed present, but held down in some way. I told this man that once the block was removed, the chances for a child

were good. Something must have happened to free up that energy because now they have a beautiful baby girl!

An energy does not represent its opposite when reversed. A card's essential nature stays the same no matter what its orientation. A reversed World does not show *unhappiness*—the opposite of happiness. It shows happiness itself is low—a subtle difference! True unhappiness has its own active energy and might appear in a reading as a card such as the Nine of Swords.

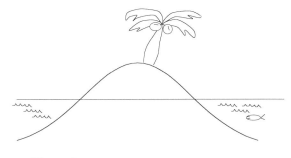

Figure 3

Imagine the energy curve as an island viewed from the side (Figure 3). The horizontal line is the surface of the water. Above the surface is the part of the island we can see; below the surface is the part we can't see. Although this part is hidden, it's still present.

Sometimes a reversed card represents an energy that is hidden, rejected, or ignored. It's not available because it hasn't yet "come to the surface." An upright Devil might show an obsession you acknowledge; a reversed Devil, one you deny. The energy is unconscious, but very real.

Sometimes the meaning of a reversed card comes in the form of subtle wordplay. The Emperor reversed could suggest a powerful authority figure *toppled* from his throne. The Ten of Wands reversed might strike you as a reminder to *get out from under* burdensome responsibilities. Such unusual interpretations keep the tarot fresh and exciting!

NOTICING ENERGY CYCLES

Become aware of energy cycles in your experience—how a feeling, thought, person, or event flows through your life. Notice when an energy first appears. Follow it as it develops over time. Watch it gain and lose power as it goes through its cycle.

See if you can detect when an energy is peaking. At a group event such as a meeting or party, you can sometimes feel the exact moment when the group's energy has reached its crowning moment. As always, don't emphasize intellectual analysis. Concentrate on how an energy feels as you experience it.

THE BIG BOOK OF TAROT

Energy Phases

An energy cycle is made up of three distinct phases—early, middle, and late—as shown in Figure 4. Each phase has its own unique character:

Early-phase energy is just beginning. It's not yet developed, but it's poised to grow. It's moving toward full expression in the future.

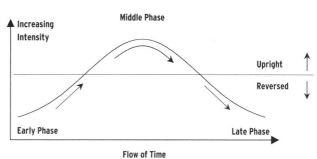

Figure 4

Middle-phase energy is strong and developed. It's clear, immediate, and obvious in the present.

Late-phase energy is on the decline. It's losing power and clarity. The energy's full expression is in the past.

An upright card represents an energy in the strong, middle phase of its cycle (above the line). Interpreting upright cards is fairly straightforward because there's only one possible phase. The energy is well-developed, active, and at or near full strength.

A reversed card is not so easy to interpret because its weak energy can be in either of two phases: early or late (below the line). To interpret the card, you need to know why its energy is weak. The best clue comes from an awareness of timing.

A reversed card is early phase if you haven't experienced its energy much or at all as yet. It may be new or tied to some upcoming event. A reversed Five of Swords is in the early phase if you know you're heading into some contest or battle. The "warfare" has not yet occurred.

A reversed card is late phase if you've already experienced its energy. It's been active in the situation in some way you can easily recognize, but you sense that era is now past. A reversed Five of Swords is in the late phase if you've gone through some battle that is now winding down.

You can also identify phase by sensing the "feel" of an energy. Is it growing or fading? A growing energy is developing, expanding, or moving toward you. You sense it's going to get stronger and more noticeable. A fading energy is contracting or moving away. It's getting weaker and less noticeable.

The reversed Knight of Wands can represent a low level of passion. The passion is early phase if you feel it's going to get stronger and more compelling. It's late phase if it's been present, but has lost most of its drive and power.

Sometimes a reversed card shows an energy that seems to be completely absent. Its level is so low that, to all intents and purposes, it doesn't seem to exist, but appearances can be deceiving! If a card appears in a reading, you can assume its energy is playing some kind of role. The energy may be so new, you can't perceive it yet. It may only seem absent because you're unconscious of it, but it's still having an impact. Knowing an energy's phase can help you deal with the energy effectively. You can anticipate what to expect from it.

PHASES OF A CARD'S ENERGY

Pick a card to work with, and choose one of its keywords. Imagine that keyword energy as you might experience it in each of the three phases—early, middle, and late. One meaning of the Five of Pentacles is illness. For this card, you might say:

> *Early Phase—I'm feeling a little off today. I wonder if I'm getting sick.*
> *Middle Phase—I feel really lousy. I'm staying home from work.*
> *Late Phase—Thank goodness that flu is over. I'm feeling better today.*

You can do this exercise for the other keywords, or you can move on to another card. As you practice, you will become better at recognizing energy phases.

Repeating Cycles

Usually when one energy fades, a new one takes its place. As we finish one breath, we begin another. A love affair ends and a new one begins. Figure 5 shows the rise and fall of energies as they engage our attention.

Figure 6 shows what happens when instead of moving on to a new energy, we get caught up again in an existing one. The late phase energy turns back to become the early phase of a repeat cycle. We reexperience the same energy for better or worse. How often have you said to yourself, "Here I go again—doing the exact same thing!"

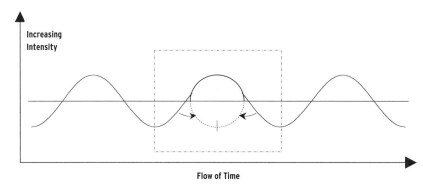

Figure 5

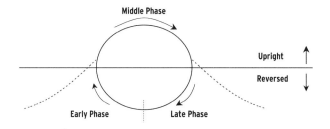

Figure 6

THE BIG BOOK OF TAROT

You will experience a card's energy energy differently if you sense it's in a new or repeating cycle.

Early Phase

A new energy in the early phase has a fresh quality. You respond to it spontaneously. It may be delightful or unnerving, but the past is not dictating your response. You have little experience of its energy to guide you.

A repeating energy in the early phase is familiar. It triggers old patterns. Your responses are more predictable, but also more assured. Assumptions from the past color your experience, but you have more knowledge to go by.

You can recognize a pattern that is starting to repeat, and change your habitual response. Awareness helps you break the pattern. The Nine of Swords reversed can show a familiar worry beginning to trouble you again. You can choose to avoid that old thought pattern if it's not helping.

You can check if an early phase energy is repeating by asking yourself the following questions:

Is this energy familiar?

Have I been in this situation before?

Are my reactions predictable?

Do I feel compelled to act in certain ways?

Is it hard for me to change my behavior?

Can others predict my actions?

Late Phase

Late-phase energy is fading, but you can experience it as complete or incomplete. A completed energy brings peace and closure. You can let go with little doubt or hesitation. You know the energy has been resolved, so you can put it to rest. It's not likely to repeat.

An incomplete energy is only temporary. The energy is probably going to return to be resolved. This is especially likely if the energy faded because it was neglected, mishandled, or the timing wasn't right for it to remain strong.

A reversed Justice can show a legal matter is coming to an end. If the case hasn't been resolved to your satisfaction, you may feel the need to relitigate—start the cycle again. Or, you may decide to accept the ruling and move on.

You can check if a late phase energy is repeating by asking yourself the following questions:

Am I dissatisfied with what's happened?

Do I feel compelled to hold on?

Is something keeping me from releasing?

Am I sorry this energy is fading?

Was this energy cut off prematurely?

Will I want to revisit this energy again?

Knowing energy tends to repeat helps you appreciate the subtle shifts that occur at the reversed card stages. You can watch for past influences affecting new energies. You can make sure fading energies are resolved satisfactorily.

NOTICING REPEATING CYCLES

Examine your life for repeating cycles. Are there any patterns that seem to recur over and over? Can you identify when such patterns begin? Have you been able to resolve any repeating patterns successfully? Think about how you were able to break free of the repetition and move forward.

Pay attention to cards that show up over and over in your readings. These cards often represent energies that are part of repeating cycles in your life.

Chapter Five

UPRIGHT AND REVERSED CARDS IN READINGS

O ne day you feel adventurous. You drive to a new beach, take a swim, and return home, tired and happy. The next day you venture out again, but this time your car breaks down, and you cut your foot on a shell. You decide to forget adventure and stay home. You want security.

Opposing Energy Pairs

It's common for energies to swing back and forth between their opposites. Figure 7 shows the relationship between two opposite energy cycles. The top circle represents the single energy pattern we've been working with so far. Now, we're adding a second cycle linked to it.

Let's see how the beach trips fit into this pattern. Your first trip began in the energy of adventure (top cycle). You initiated a trip and then returned home—one successful turn around the circle. Because the trip was fun, you stayed in the energy of adventure and repeated the cycle the next day.

This time the trip was not fun, so you left the energy of adventure and moved to the energy of security (bottom cycle). Your unpleasant adventure led you to seek the opposite. If the appeal of security stays strong, you may remain in the security cycle for a while. Or you may forget your bad trip at some point and desire adventure again.

If an energy is strong, it's as far away as possible from its opposite. An energy shifts when it's at a low level and, more particularly, in its late phase. Instead of ending or repeating, it moves to the early phase of its opposite.

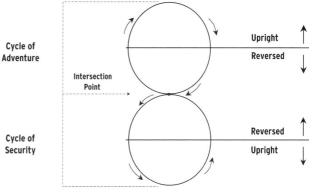

Figure 7

In the tarot, linked energies are represented by two cards with opposite meanings. Some cards are natural opposites such as the Fool (beginning) and Death (ending). Aces and court cards can also be opposites. The emotional Queen of Cups and practical Queen of Pentacles are poles apart in some circumstances.

Once you've identified an opposing pair in a reading, the orientation of the cards can help you understand their energy relationship in more detail.

The orientation of two opposing cards shows the strengths of the energies in relation to each other. The King of Wands and King of Pentacles could represent you and your partner in a reading. If the cards have the same orientation, you are both at about the same energy level. If one card is upright and one reversed, there's an energy imbalance—one of you is stronger or more dominant in some way for now.

The orientation of two opposing cards can also suggest whether or not there might be change in a situation and what direction it might take.

 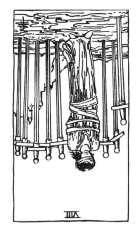

Both Cards Are Upright

When two opposing cards are both upright, their energies are not changing at the moment. There is balance in the situation because both approaches are strong, but there also could be struggle and tension. It's difficult to keep two contrary tendencies in play at the same time. You may be absorbed in one, while someone is resisting you from the other. You may be trying to balance both tendencies in yourself simultaneously. The upright Ten of Wands paired with the upright Seven of Swords can show a struggle between wanting to meet responsibilities (Ten) and wanting to run away from them (Seven).

Both Cards Are Reversed

If both opposing cards are reversed, the situation is balanced, but flexible. Neither energy is dominant for the moment. Little may seem to be happening, but it's a time of opportunity. The two energies may stay in this uncommitted state for a time, or one may become more prominent. A reversed Two of Wands and a reversed Eight of Swords can indicate an unclear power issue. Feelings of power (Two) and powerlessness (Eight) are trading off with neither one more important than the other as yet.

One Card Is Upright, One Reversed

Different orientations show a swing in progress. The upright energy may be strong at the moment, but the seed of its opposite energy is present. There may be a shift from one energy to the other.

The Sun and Moon are opposites in the area of clarity—the Moon is confusion, the Sun, enlightenment. An upright Moon/reversed Sun can show that even if uncertainty is dominant right now (Moon), a seed of certainty (Sun) exists in the situation.

If a reversed energy is growing (early phase), it's on its way to replacing the upright energy, which will likely fade. The upright Six of Wands (pride) and reversed Tower (downfall) are a perfect symbol for the saying, "Pride goeth before a fall!"

If the reversed energy is fading (late phase), it's possibly being replaced by its upright opposite. An upright Five of Wands paired with a reversed World

can show that competition (Five) has replaced a diminishing spirit of cooperation (World).

OPPOSING ENERGIES IN LIFE

Become aware of the play of opposing energies in your life. As you go about your daily activities, notice how often energies come in pairs, one force balancing another. Can you sense how the lessening of one energy corresponds to the growth of another, though not always immediately? Look for examples both within and without. You will find them everywhere.

Mismatches

We humans have an endless capacity to fool ourselves. We misperceive motivations and actions. We read into a situation what we wish were true and fail to recognize tough realities we would like to deny. This is why the tarot is such a valuable tool. The cards act as a mirror reflecting truths about our experience. They let us know when our perceptions are not aligned with the energies of the moment and our own best interests.

When a card's orientation matches your sense of its strength, you can feel fairly confident you are seeing your situation realistically. But what if a card's orientation doesn't match? You think an energy is strong, but it shows up as reversed. Or, you think it's weak, but the card is upright. In these cases, you have an excellent opportunity to become more aware!

A general rule of thumb is: When a card's orientation doesn't match your expectation, you're misperceiving the strength of the card's energy.

Card Is Reversed, You Expect Upright

If you feel a reversed card should be upright, you're experiencing the energy as stronger than it really is. You're giving it more weight than is justified for the moment. Sometimes

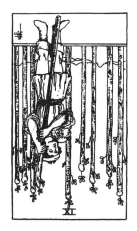 

an energy is rather humble, but you think it's grand. Sometimes the energy is not yet as developed as you think it is. It may be in the early phase, but you see it as further along in its cycle.

You've been preparing diligently for a major exam, but you draw the Nine of Wands reversed. This card shows your perseverance, but the reversal implies you're still not working hard enough. The energy is low. You need to step up the pace if you want to succeed.

Sometimes a reversed energy is no longer as strong as you think it is. It's in the late phase, but you still see it as active. In a reading about a game your team lost, you draw Judgement reversed. You sense this card refers to the fact that your coach was critical of your performance. You thought he was still judging you harshly, but the reversal suggests otherwise. His negative judgment has been much reduced.

Card Is Upright, You Expect Reversed

If you feel an upright card should be reversed, you're underestimating the strength and presence of the energy. It's having a more immediate impact than you realize.

You and your partner have been trying to adopt a child. None of your attempts have worked, so you're about to give up. You're surprised and delighted when you draw the upright Six of Cups. This card can sometimes represent a baby. The upright orientation tells you something concrete is happening even though you don't know what it is.

Sometimes you think an energy is almost gone, but it's actually still in play. You may not be aware of the effects, but they're real nonetheless. You've drawn the Ace of Swords in a reading about your youngest child. This card sometimes shows a challenge testing you in some way. You recognize the challenge with your child, but you thought you'd resolved the problem. The upright orientation suggests it's still active!

A card's orientation offers a way to catch misperceptions and denials. The tarot reflects energy patterns without bias or judgment. The cards show you the energetic reality of a situation. It's up to you to accommodate that truth.

MISMATCHES IN YOUR READINGS

Watch for occasions in your readings when a card's orientation doesn't seem to match your expectation. Such a discrepancy is easy to miss, as it often comes in a flash when you first see a card. You may have a quick feeling of disappointment if you expect an energy to be strong. You may feel a rush of pleasure if an energy you don't like is weak.

If you perceive a mismatch, take the time to explore the card's energy and your expectations a little deeper than usual. These occasions have great potential for exposing areas of denial and resistance in your life.

Orientation and Card Groups

Orientation is meaningful for groups of cards. In a reading, you can determine the energy status of a group by comparing the number of upright and reversed cards in it. Usually there is a mixture, showing balance in the group's energy. When there is balance, orientation is less important for the group as a whole.

It's rare for all or nearly all cards in a group to have the same orientation. This gives the group a definite energy character. When the cards are mostly upright, the group energy is very strong and well-developed. When mostly reversed, the group energy is weak and less developed. The larger the group, the more pronounced the effect.

Major Arcana

If all the majors in a group are upright, their combined energies make a very powerful force indeed. If they are all reversed, their strong effect is reduced, but still important. Something is keeping this potent group from achieving its full potential.

You draw the Chariot, Moon, and Empress in a three-card reading. Getting three out of three major arcana cards is striking enough, but if they are all upright, they make quite a powerful group. The overall energy level is high. If the cards are all reversed, the group energy is suppressed in some way, but major effects are simmering just below the surface.

Court Cards

If all the court cards in a group are upright, there are a lot of powerful players in the situation. If they are all reversed, people are more hesitant and uncertain. The energy of the situation is low because people are not participating fully.

Suits

If all the cards of one suit in a group are upright, that suit's qualities are well-developed and pronounced. If they are all reversed, the suit's qualities are less developed, but still important in potential. If all the cups in a reading are reversed, the energy of love and emotion is at a low level, but there is still the possibility for those qualities to grow.

Spread Groups

Orientation in spread groups tells you much about the energy of what that group represents. Some relationship spreads have two sets of cards that mirror each other—one for each person. If all the cards for one person are upright, you can guess that person has a very strong, dominant presence in the relationship.

Spontaneous Groups

Certain cards in a reading can strike you spontaneously as a group. The orientation of those cards describes the energy state of whatever feature brings the group together.

The Entire Reading

The distribution of upright and reversed cards in the entire reading often provides a clue to the energy of the overall situation.

If most cards are upright, the situation is well-developed. Abundant energy is available. The time is right for action, or actions are already being taken. There are few hidden agendas or unrecognized problems. The focus is on the present, not the past or future. The situation is straightforward, open, and obvious.

If most cards are reversed, the overall energy is low. There may be a lack of direction or a sense of restriction. There is little momentum toward goals. Actions, if any, are low-key and tentative. Much is unexpressed or unexposed. The focus is on the past or future, not the present, but the situation is flexible. New directions are possible because choices have not been fixed. Since energies are not well-developed, they are free to go in new directions.

Life is a constant energy flow—a marvelous dance guided by Spirit. When we understand that flow and move with it creatively, all things are possible. We can direct energy consciously or just let it take us where it will. In either case, reversed cards add an extra dimension to a reading that will help you appreciate the play of energy in your life.

INTUITIVE SCANNING

Shuffle and cut your deck, then lay out between four to ten cards. Now, scan the cards for orientation. Try to get an impression of the distribution of upright and reversed cards without slipping into detailed analysis. Imagine how you might interpret these cards as a group based simply on orientation. You can repeat this exercise with another set of cards, perhaps of a different size.

SUMMARY

Imagine standing on a train track with a train approaching in the distance. This train is "your future." From your perspective, all you can see is the engine bearing down. The only information you have is what is directly in front of you.

But now imagine rising up and looking in all directions. You can see where the train has come from and where it's going. You can pick out the path you took to the track and see other possible paths as well. You have much more knowledge about the whole situation.

A tarot reading is one way to rise above the track of your life so you can see forward and backward at the same time. As you deepen your communication with your Inner Guide through the cards, your present moment gradually becomes all-encompassing. You begin to see your life in a more expansive way.

With the information in this book, you now have a firm foundation of knowledge about the tarot that will sustain you in the days ahead. If you continue to practice, you'll find the techniques become more and more invisible as your intuition takes over. Eventually you will reach a point where you can rely on your tarot abilities consistently.

A tarot practice is based on the understanding that wisdom from some Source will come to you through the cards. At first, you may have to accept this on faith, but after a while you will receive the "proof" you need in the results you experience in your life. If you can approach the cards with trust, your tarot practice will take off!

Part Three

CARD DESCRIPTIONS

INTRODUCTION TO
THE CARD DESCRIPTIONS

This section contains information about every card in the tarot deck. Here are the features you will find:

Name and Picture

The name of the card with a small picture of its image from the Rider-Waite deck.

Keywords

Keywords are three to five words or phrases that capture the main themes of the card. They are listed at the top of each card's page. There is a keyword summary chart for all the major arcana cards (page 61) and two charts for the minor arcana cards (pages 128–129).

Actions

Actions are phrases describing some ways the energy of each keyword manifests. Two sample actions for the High Priestess are "looking beyond the obvious" and "sensing the secret and hidden." These are ways to experience *mystery*. The active form is used to emphasize how a card represents dynamic energy.

Reversed

A card's energy is conveyed by its keywords and actions. When a card is reversed, that same energy is present, but at a low level. It's not expressing strongly and freely. It is blocked, restricted, incomplete, or otherwise reduced in some way. The energy may be just beginning (early phase) or losing power (ending phase). As a rule of thumb, an energy is in the early phase if it hasn't been noticeably present as yet. It's in the late phase if it has been present and is now fading.

For each keyword, some examples are given of how that energy might express if the card is reversed. There are examples for early and late phases. Think of these examples as applying to whatever a reversed card represents in a reading.

Description

The description offers a few paragraphs of extra information about a card and what it implies in a reading. The major arcana descriptions tend to be more general and philosophical. The minor arcana descriptions are more concrete and everyday.

Opposing Cards

Some cards are listed that might form an opposing pair with the given card when it appears in a reading. See Chapters Three and Five for more about opposing pairs. Some suit and court card rank pair combinations are listed in Part Five, page 336.

Reinforcing Cards

Some cards are listed that might form a reinforcing pair with the given card when it appears in a reading. See Chapter Three for more on reinforcing cards.

Court Card Pairs

Court cards form natural pairs because of their distinctive personalities. The pairs are based on the ranks and suits of the two court cards. See Chapters Three and Five. Some suit pair combinations and court card rank pair combinations are listed in Part Five.

Ace-Ace Pairs

An Ace-Ace pair indicates a unique chance to grow in a new direction that taps the energy of both suits.

Fool's Journey

You can discover more about the major arcana cards in Appendix A: The Fool's Journey.

Major Arcana

Tarot Keywords Major Arcana

FOOL (0)	MAGICIAN (1)	HIGH PRIESTESS (2)	EMPRESS (3)
Beginning	Action	Nonaction	Mothering
Spontaneity	Conscious Awareness	Unconscious Awareness	Abundance
Faith	Concentration	Potential	Senses
Apparent Folly	Power	Mystery	Nature
EMPEROR (4)	**HIEROPHANT (5)**	**LOVERS (6)**	**CHARIOT (7)**
Fathering	Education	Relationship	Victory
Structure	Belief Systems	Sexuality	Will
Authority	Conformity	Personal Beliefs	Self-Assertion
Regulation	Group Identification	Values	Hard Control
STRENGTH (8)	**HERMIT (9)**	**WHEEL OF FORTUNE (10)**	**JUSTICE (11)**
Strength	Introspection	Destiny	Justice
Patience	Searching	Turning Point	Responsibility
Compassion	Guidance	Movement	Decision
Soft Control	Solitude	Personal Vision	Cause and Effect
HANGED MAN (12)	**DEATH (13)**	**TEMPERANCE (14)**	**DEVIL (15)**
Letting Go	Ending	Temperance	Bondage
Reversal	Transition	Balance	Materialism
Suspension	Elimination	Health	Ignorance
Sacrifice	Inexorable Forces	Combination	Hopelessness
TOWER (16)	**STAR (17)**	**MOON (18)**	**SUN (19)**
Sudden Change	Hope	Fear	Enlightenment
Release	Inspiration	Illusion	Greatness
Downfall	Generosity	Imagination	Vitality
Revelation	Serenity	Bewilderment	Assurance
	JUDGEMENT (20)	**WORLD (21)**	
	Judgment	Integration	
	Rebirth	Accomplishment	
	Inner Calling	Involvement	
	Absolution	Fulfillment	

0

THE FOOL

BEGINNING
SPONTANEITY
FAITH
APPARENT FOLLY

Actions

BEGINNING

entering a new phase

striking out on a new path

expanding horizons

starting something new

beginning an adventure

going on a journey

heading into the unknown

Reversed

Early Phase: You're getting ready to start. The journey may be about to begin. A new phase may be coming up. You're thinking of initiating a novel plan. The unknown may start to beckon.

Late Phase: A chance to begin is disappearing. A new opportunity is no longer available. An initiative is less likely now. A start date has passed. An unknown is losing its appeal.

BEING SPONTANEOUS

living in the moment

letting go of expectations

doing the unexpected

acting on impulse

feeling uninhibited

surprising someone

feeling carefree

Reversed

Early Phase: The atmosphere may become freer. You may let go of expectations. It may get easier to act on the spur of the moment. You may start to feel more uninhibited.

Late Phase: The carefree times are ending. You're no longer willing to improvise. Impromptu decisions are less effective now. Someone is becoming less impetuous. The free and natural mood is fading.

HAVING FAITH

trusting the flow

staying open

letting go of worry and fear

feeling protected and loved

living in joy

recapturing innocence

believing

Reversed

Early Phase: Your faith may return. It may get easier to believe. You may gain more confidence. The situation may start to feel secure. Someone may become more willing to believe.

Late Phase: You're losing faith. Hope is fading. You're not as confident as you were. Someone is no longer trusting. The time of innocence is past.

EMBRACING FOLLY

accepting your choices

taking the "foolish" path

pursuing a pipe dream

being true to yourself

taking a "crazy" chance

trusting your heart's desire

Reversed

Early Phase: You may start to pursue a dream. You may become involved in some foolishness. You're getting ready to take a wild chance. You may decide to go for it, even if you fail.

Late Phase: The time to be wild and crazy has passed. You're more disillusioned now. It's no longer possible to pursue your dream. A bit of foolishness is behind you.

Description

As Card 0, the Fool lies at the beginning of the major arcana, but also somewhat apart from the other cards. In medieval courts, the court jester was someone who was not expected to follow the same rules as others. He could observe and then poke fun. This makes the Fool unpredictable and full of surprises. He reminds us of the unlimited potential and spontaneity inherent in every moment. There is a sense with this card that anything goes—nothing is certain or regular. The Fool adds the new and unfamiliar to a situation.

The Fool also represents the complete faith that life is good and worthy of trust. Some might call the Fool too innocent, but his innocence sustains him and brings him joy. In readings, the Fool can signal a new beginning or change of direction—one that will guide you onto a path of adventure, wonder, and personal growth. He also reminds you to keep your faith and trust your natural responses. If you are facing a decision or moment of doubt, the Fool tells you to believe in yourself and follow your heart no matter how crazy or foolish your impulses may seem.

Some Possible Opposing Cards

Emperor—structure, regulation
Hierophant—following convention, routine
Death—ending, closing down
Devil—feeling cynical, lacking faith
Two of Swords—blocking off experience, feeling tense, holding back
Four of Pentacles—order and regularity

Some Possible Reinforcing Cards

Hanged Man—having faith in what is, going with the flow
Star—innocence, faith, trust
Judgement—rebirth, new starts
Three of Wands—expanding horizons, going into unexplored territory

1

THE MAGICIAN

ACTION
CONSCIOUS AWARENESS
CONCENTRATION
POWER

Actions

TAKING ACTION.

doing what needs to be done

realizing your potential

making what's possible real

practicing what you preach

carrying out plans

producing magical results

using your talents

Reversed

Early Phase: The time for action may be approaching. You're getting ready to make your move. The plan may begin to go forward. You may have a chance to do what you have to do. There may be more activity in the future.

Late Phase: The time for action is ending. The activity level is decreasing. There's less support for your exploits now. Someone is using less force. People are no longer carrying out the plan.

ACTING CONSCIOUSLY

knowing what you are doing and why

acknowledging your motivations

understanding your intentions

examining the known situation

Reversed

Early Phase: You may begin to catch on. You may grow more aware. The true nature of the situation may become clear. People may start to speak openly. You may need to stay on top of things in the future.

Late Phase: You're becoming less aware. You're no longer sure what's happening. Your clarity of purpose is disappearing. It's not as easy to defend your position now. Understanding is fading.

CONCENTRATING

having singleness of purpose

being totally committed

applying the force of your will

feeling centered

setting aside distractions

focusing on a goal

Reversed

Early Phase: You may start to concentrate better. It may get easier to stay focused. Your sense of purpose may return. Dedication may grow. You may begin to commit to your goal.

Late Phase: You're no longer able to avoid distractions. Your commitment is not as strong. People are less dedicated now. The period of concentration is ending. Your energies are no longer focused.

EXPERIENCING POWER

making a strong impact

having vitality

creating miracles

becoming energized

feeling vigorous

being creative

Reversed

Early Phase: You may become more powerful. You may start to make your presence known. Strength may increase. Your influence may grow. Potency may return.

Late Phase: Your power is decreasing. You're no longer as vigorous. The ability to sway the group is fading. Someone's prestige is declining. There's less energy available.

Description

The Magician is the archetype of the active, masculine principle—the ultimate achiever. He symbolizes the power to tap universal forces and use them for creative purposes. Note his stance in the picture. He acts as a lightning rod—one arm extended up into the Divine for inspiration, the other pointing toward Earth to ground this potent energy.[3] His abilities appear magical at times because his will helps him achieve what seem to be miracles.

What makes the Magician so powerful? First, he is not afraid to act. He believes in himself and is willing to put that belief on the line. He also knows what he intends to do and why. He doesn't hesitate because he understands his situation exactly. The Magician can focus with single-minded determination. As long as he remembers the divine source of his power, the Magician remains the perfect conduit for miracles.

In a reading, the Magician implies that the primal forces of creativity are yours if you can claim your power and act with awareness and concentration. This card is a signal to act and act now, provided you understand exactly what you want and are committed to getting it.

Some Possible Opposing Cards

High Priestess—nonaction, intuition, accessing the unconscious
Hanged Man—suspending action, not doing
Seven of Cups—lacking focus and commitment
Four of Swords—resting quietly, storing energy
Eight of Swords—confused and uncertain, powerless

Some Possible Reinforcing Cards

Chariot—focusing, concentrating, being forceful
Two of Wands—personal power, wielding a strong force
Eight of Wands—quick action, making your move
Eight of Pentacles—focus and concentration

2

THE HIGH PRIESTESS

NONACTION
UNCONSCIOUS AWARENESS
POTENTIAL
MYSTERY

Actions

STAYING NONACTIVE

withdrawing from involvement

allowing events to proceed without intervention

being receptive to influence

becoming calm

being passive

waiting patiently

Reversed

Early Phase: You may begin to withdraw. You may have to lay low for a while. A quiet time may be approaching. You may be idle in the future. Someone may start to show more patience.

Late Phase: The time of nonaction is ending. You can no longer stand by and watch. You're less inclined to remain passive now. The waiting is over. People are no longer willing to be quiet.

ACCESSING THE UNCONSCIOUS

using your intuition

seeking guidance from within

trusting your inner voice

opening to dreams and the imagination

being aware of a larger reality

Reversed

Early Phase: You may begin to look within. Someone may open to inner truths. Unconscious material may start to surface. You may become aware of different realities.

Late Phase: You're no longer exploring the unconscious. Doors to the inner realms are closing. People are less willing to face hidden truths. It's getting harder to hear your inner voice. Interest in other realities is fading.

SEEING THE POTENTIAL

understanding the possibilities

opening to what could be

seeing your hidden talents

allowing development

letting what is there flower

Reversed

Early Phase: You may begin to recognize your potential. A talent may develop. People may open to what could be. The possibilities may get clearer.

Late Phase: Your potential is no longer being recognized. The latent possibilities were not realized. People are less open to growth now. A talent is fading. An opportunity has passed.

SENSING THE MYSTERY

looking beyond the obvious

approaching a closed-off area

opening to the unknown

remembering something important

sensing the secret and hidden

seeking what is concealed

acknowledging the Shadow

Reversed

Early Phase: A mystery may come to light. You may start to look at what's been concealed. You may approach a closed-off area. Someone may be on the point of remembering. The unknown may beckon.

Late Phase: You're moving away from the mystery. The secret has been revealed or covered up. Someone has opened up a can of worms. Interest in the unknown is fading. The shadow-side is less exposed.

Description

The High Priestess is the guardian of the unconscious. She sits in front of the thin veil of un-awareness which is all that separates us from our inner landscape. She contains within herself the secret of these realms and offers us the silent invitation, "Be still and know that I am God.'

The High Priestess is the feminine principle that balances the masculine force of the Magician. The feminine archetype in the tarot is split between the High Priestess and the Empress. The High Priestess is the mysterious unknown that women often represent, especially in cultures that focus on the tangible and known. The Empress represents woman's role as the crucible of life.

In readings, the High Priestess poses a challenge to you to go deeper—to look beyond the obvious, surface situation to what is hidden and obscure. She also asks you to recall the vastness of your potential and to remember the unlimited possibilities you hold within yourself. The High Priestess can represent a time of waiting and allowing. It is not always necessary to act to achieve your goals. Sometimes they can be realized through a stillness that gives desire a chance to flower within the fullness of time.

Some Possible Opposing Cards

Magician—acting consciously, thinking, the known and obvious
Two of Wands—acting boldly
Seven of Wands—being aggressive
Eight of Wands—putting plans into action

Some Possible Reinforcing Cards

Hermit—looking inward, withdrawing, seeking guidance
Hanged Man—suspending activity, waiting
Four of Swords—resting quietly, contemplating

3

THE EMPRESS

MOTHERING
ABUNDANCE
SENSES
NATURE

Actions

. . . .

MOTHERING

giving birth

nourishing life

nurturing and caring for others

cherishing the world

expressing tenderness

working with children

Reversed

Early Phase: Mothering may become more important. A birth may be approaching. A desire to nurture may grow. You may start to care for someone. A link with a child may come up. A mother may become more involved.

Late Phase: A time of mothering is ending. A birth has past. There is less nurturing now. A mother is not as close. You're becoming separated from a child. The feeling of being cherished is fading.

WELCOMING ABUNDANCE

enjoying extravagance

receiving lavish reward

luxuriating in plenty

having more than enough

feeling rich

Reversed

Early Phase: You may start to experience more abundance. An ample supply may be forthcoming. You may move toward plenty. There may be more than enough in the future. A surplus may become possible.

Late Phase: The time of profusion is past. People can no longer be extravagant. Wealth is decreasing. There is less to go around now. The coffers are emptying.

EXPERIENCING THE SENSES

giving and receiving pleasure

focusing on the body

appreciating beauty

feeling vibrantly healthy

being earthy

doing physical activity

Reversed

Early Phase: You may start feeling more sensual. Pleasure may become more important. Your vigor and energy may return. One of the senses may improve. You may start to focus on your body.

Late Phase: An experience of pleasure is past. You're no longer enjoying your senses. Physical activity is declining. There's less interest in the body now. One of the senses is failing.

RESPONDING TO NATURE

relating to plants and animals

embracing the natural

feeling connected to the Earth

going outdoors

harmonizing with natural rhythms

Reversed

Early Phase: A relationship with nature may develop. You may start to feel more natural. Environmental protections may increase. Being outdoors may become more important. An experience with nature may occur in the future.

Late Phase: You're no longer involved with animals or plants. A focus on the environment is decreasing. People are feeling less connected with the Earth. There's less support for a natural approach.

Description

The Empress and the High Priestess are the two halves of the female archetype in the major arcana. The Empress represents the fertile, life-giving Mother who reigns over the bounty of nature and the rhythms of the Earth. From her comes all the pleasures and joys of the senses and the abundance of new life in all its forms. The Empress encourages you to strengthen your connections with the natural world which is the ground of our being. Too often false sophistications and pleasures take us far from our roots. Let the Empress remind you to keep your feet firmly planted in the Earth.

In readings the Empress can refer to any aspect of Motherhood. She can be an individual mother, but as a major arcana card, she also goes beyond the specifics of mothering to its essence—the creation of life and its sustenance through loving care and attention.

The Empress can also represent lavish abundance of all kinds. She offers a cornucopia of delights, especially those of the senses—food, pleasure, and beauty. She can suggest material reward, but only with the understanding that riches go with a generous and open spirit. The Empress asks you to embrace the principle of life and enjoy its bountiful goodness.

Some Possible Opposing Cards

Emperor—fathering, order and discipline, regularity
Death—less life-affirming
Four of Pentacles—miserly possessiveness
Nine of Pentacles—refinement, sophistication

Some Possible Reinforcing Cards

Lovers—sexual fulfillment, pleasure
Star—generosity, free-flowing love
Nine of Cups—enjoying the senses
Seven of Pentacles—material reward
Ten of Pentacles—affluence, luxury, physical comfort

4

THE EMPEROR

FATHERING
STRUCTURE
AUTHORITY
REGULATION

Actions

. . . .

FATHERING

establishing a family line

setting direction and tone

protecting and defending

guiding growth

bringing security and comfort

offering explanations

Reversed

Early Phase: Fathering may become more important. You may begin to provide support. You may develop a connection to a child. A relationship with a father may improve. Someone may start to guide growth.

Late Phase: A time of fathering is ending. You're no longer supporting a child. A father is becoming less involved. The need for protection is decreasing. Being head of the family is no longer an issue.

EMPHASIZING STRUCTURE

creating order out of chaos

categorizing

being systematic

providing shape and form

being organized

applying reason

coordinating

sticking to a plan

Reversed

Early Phase: Order may return. A plan may begin to take shape. You may start to coordinate activities. The environment may become more structured. Loose ends may be tied up in the future.

Late Phase: The structure is falling apart. Organization is declining. You're no longer following a plan. The period of order is ending. Fixed relationships are breaking up.

   ▧

EXERCISING AUTHORITY

taking a leadership role

commanding

exerting control

representing the establishment

being in a position of strength

coming in contact with officials

setting direction

Reversed

Early Phase: You may start to exert control. An authority figure may become involved. Direction may be imposed. Respect may grow. You may have a chance to become a leader.

Late Phase: You're no longer in authority. You're losing your position of strength. Control is passing to someone else. Leadership is no longer strong. Officials are stepping aside.

REGULATING

establishing law and order

operating from sound principles

applying rules or guidelines

working within the legal system

setting standards of behavior

following a regimen

Reversed

Early Phase: You may begin to establish rules. A legal matter may become important. Contacts with the law may increase. Regulations may be enforced.

Late Phase: A legal matter is being concluded. Rules are decreasing. The monitoring period is over. There's less support for the program now. Regulations are no longer respected.

Description

The figure of the Emperor says much about the essential qualities of this card. We see a stern, commanding figure seated on a stone-slab throne. His back is straight, and his eyes meet ours directly. He is confident of his complete authority to rule.

The Emperor represents structure, order, and regulation—forces to balance the free-flowing, lavish abundance of the Empress. He advocates a four-square world where trains are on time, games are played by rules, and commanding officers are respected. In chaotic situations, the Emperor can indicate the need for organization. Loose ends should be tied up, and wayward elements, harnessed. In situations that are already overcontrolled, he suggests the confining effect of those constraints.

The Emperor can represent an encounter with authority or the assumption of power and control. As the regulator, he is often associated with legal matters, disciplinary actions, and officialdom in all its forms. He can also stand for an individual father or archetypal Father in his role as guide, protector, and provider.

Some Possible Opposing Cards

Empress—mothering, free-flowing abundance
Seven of Cups—dissipation, lack of order
Five of Swords—bending the rules, breaking the law

Some Possible Reinforcing Cards

Hierophant—conforming to rules
Justice—concerns of justice and legality
Two of Wands—having authority
Three of Wands—assuming leadership
Four of Pentacles—control, structure, order

5

THE HIEROPHANT

EDUCATION
BELIEF SYSTEMS
CONFORMITY
GROUP IDENTIFICATION

THE HIEROPHANT

Actions

. . . .

GETTING AN EDUCATION

pursuing knowledge

becoming informed

increasing understanding

studying and learning

seeking a deeper meaning

finding out more

Reversed

Early Phase: You may begin your studies. Someone may enter school. A thirst for knowledge may grow. You may need more information. A learning session may be about to start.

Late Phase: A time of learning is ending. Your studies are over. Getting an education is no longer a priority. You found out what you needed to know. Understanding is decreasing.

. . . .

HAVING A BELIEF SYSTEM

sharing a cultural heritage

learning a religious tradition

honoring ritual and ceremony

identifying a worldview

following a discipline

knowing where to put your faith

Reversed

Early Phase: You may be forming a worldview. You're getting ready to follow a discipline. A ritual may be coming up. You may decide to learn a set of beliefs. Traditions may become more important.

Late Phase: You're losing your beliefs. The traditional ways are no longer appealing. A way of life is disappearing. Your faith has been shaken. The old assumptions are less valid.

CONFORMING

following the rules

taking an orthodox approach

staying within conventional bounds

adapting to the system

fitting in

going along with the program

doing what's expected

being part of the Establishment

Reversed

Early Phase: You may begin to go along with the program. You may start to be more conventional. People may become more orthodox. Someone may fall in line in the future.

Late Phase: There's less conformity now. People are no longer abiding by the rules. The need to blend in is decreasing. The party line is losing its appeal. Someone is less obedient.

IDENTIFYING WITH A GROUP

being committed to a cause

devoting energy to a group

joining an organization

working as part of a team

feeling loyal to others

being in an institutionalized setting

Reversed

Early Phase: You're thinking of joining a group. You may become part of a team. A spirit of community may be forming. Like-minded people may start coming together. You may decide to add your voice to others.

Late Phase: You're separating from a group. The time of togetherness is ending. Your commitment to the mutual cause is fading. The team is dissolving. There's less commonality.

Description

Except in rare cases, every human grows and develops within a culture. We learn by living with others. The Hierophant represents such official learning, especially in groups. A Hierophant is someone who interprets secret knowledge. On Card 5 we see a religious figure in a formal church setting. He is wearing the elaborate vestments of his office. His task is to bring the two initiates into the church so they can take up their appointed roles.

Besides churches, there are schools, clubs, teams, companies, and societies. The Hierophant represents all of these because his realm is structured groups with rules and assigned roles. Such environments emphasize belief systems—facts, rules, procedures, and ritual. Members are rewarded for following conventions. They develop a group identity. The Hierophant is one of three cards that focuses on the group. (The Three of Cups and the Three of Pentacles are the others.)

In readings, the Hierophant often represents learning with experts or knowledgeable teachers. This card also stands for institutions and their values. The Hierophant is a symbol of the need to conform to rules or fixed situations. His appearance in a reading can show that you are struggling with a force that is not innovative, free-spirited, or individual. Groups can be enriching or stifling, depending on circumstances. Sometimes we need to follow a program or embrace tradition; other times we need to trust ourselves.

Some Possible Opposing Cards

Fool—being "crazy" and unorthodox
Lovers—personal beliefs
Two of Wands—diverging from the crowd, being a pioneer
Seven of Swords—being a lone wolf
Two of Pentacles—being flexible, changing with the times

Some Possible Reinforcing Cards

Emperor—following rules
Three of Cups—focusing on the group
Three of Pentacles—working in a team or group
Eight of Pentacles—learning, studying
Ten of Pentacles—conforming, following rules, conservative

6

THE LOVERS

RELATIONSHIP
SEXUALITY
PERSONAL BELIEFS
VALUES

Actions

. . . .

RELATING TO OTHERS

establishing bonds

feeling love

forming a union or marriage

acknowledging kinship

sympathizing with another

getting closer

making a connection

being intimate

BEING SEXUAL

seeking union

experiencing desire

making love

opening to another

responding with passion

feeling a physical attraction

tapping inner energy

Reversed

Early Phase: You may begin a relationship. Love may grow. A connection may develop. You may be drawn closer to someone. A marriage or union may occur in the future.

Late Phase: A relationship is ending. There's less intimacy now. You no longer feel love for someone. A family tie is loosening. Communication is decreasing. A partnership is dissolving.

Reversed

Early Phase: You may begin to feel a sexual attraction. Desire may grow. You may become more passionate. Life-force energy may increase. A sexual relationship may be initiated in the future.

Late Phase: There are few opportunities to be sexual now. You're losing your desire. The passionate phase is ending. The atmosphere is no longer sexually charged. The life-force energy is not as strong.

4erliptIlrt

ESTABLISHING PERSONAL BELIEFS

questioning received opinions

figuring out where you stand

staying true to yourself

setting your own philosophy

going by your own standards

making up your own mind

Reversed

Early Phase: You may begin to think for yourself. You may come to your own conclusions. Someone may question the group consensus. A maverick thinker may get involved.

Late Phase: Your personal views are no longer involved. Your belief system has been challenged. The chance to make up your own mind is ending. It's harder to stay true to yourself at this point.

DETERMINING VALUES

struggling with temptation

choosing between right and wrong

facing an ethical or moral choice

refusing to let ends justify means

finding out what you care about

Reversed

Early Phase: You may become more concerned with values. A moral or ethical dilemma may come up. You may have to choose between right and wrong. You may rediscover your ideals.

Late Phase: A code of ethics is no longer in place. Values are being discarded. Integrity is less of an issue now. The moment of temptation has passed. Your struggle with your ideals is ending.

Description

The Lovers is one card that is easy to remember. Love and sex are riveting subjects, and, as you'd expect, this card represents both. The urge for union is powerful and, in its highest form, takes us beyond ourselves. That is why an angel is blessing the bond between the man and woman on this card.

In readings, Card 6 often refers to a relationship that is based on deep love—the strongest force of all. The relationship may not be sexual, although it often is or could be. More generally, the Lovers can represent the attractive force that draws any two entities together in a relationship—whether people, ideas, events, movements, or groups.

Card 6 can also stand for tough value choices and the questioning that goes with them. In some decks,[4] the Lovers shows a man torn between two women—a virgin and a temptress. This rather old-fashioned triangle symbolizes the larger dilemmas we face when we are tempted between right and wrong.

The Lovers can indicate a moral or ethical crossroads—a decision point where you must choose between the high road or the low road. This card can also represent your personal beliefs because to make such a decision you must know where you stand. Following your own path can mean going against those who are urging you in a direction that is wrong for you.

Some Possible Opposing Cards

Hierophant—established beliefs
Hermit—being alone, not relating, less sexuality
Five of Cups—loss in relationships
Three of Swords—rejection, separation

Some Possible Reinforcing Cards

Empress—sexual fulfillment, pleasure
Two of Cups—union, marriage, connection
Nine of Cups—sexual pleasure
Ten of Cups—family relationships, bonding
Ten of Pentacles—permanent unions, family ties

7

THE CHARIOT

VICTORY
WILL
SELF-ASSERTION
HARD CONTROL

Actions

ACHIEVING VICTORY

reaching your goal

winning

being successful

dominating

coming out on top

beating the competition

Reversed

Early Phase: You may begin to be successful. A victory may become possible in the future. You may triumph in the end. The path to the top may begin soon. A mood of conquest may develop.

Late Phase: The victory is behind you. Your string of wins is ending. A moment of triumph is in the past. You're no longer dominating. The battle is winding down.

USING YOUR WILL

being determined to succeed

focusing your intent

rising above temptation

letting nothing distract you

sustaining an effort

concentrating your energies

fixing on a goal

Reversed

Early Phase: You may start to get focused. Your determination may grow. The desire for success may become stronger. Someone may show more discipline.

Late Phase: Your concentration is decreasing. You can no longer sustain an effort. The will to achieve is fading. You're less intent now. Your strength of purpose is weakening.

ASSERTING YOURSELF

being ego-focused

establishing an identity

knowing who you are

feeling self-confident

having faith in yourself

looking out for your interests

Reversed

Early Phase: You may become more assertive. You may start to stand up for yourself. Self-confidence may grow. You're getting ready to ask for what you want.

Late Phase: You're less assertive now. You're no longer making your presence felt. Your desire to be first is decreasing. Selfish needs are losing importance. It's no longer necessary to grab the attention.

ACHIEVING HARD CONTROL

mastering emotions

curbing impulses

maintaining discipline

holding in anger

getting your own way

assuming the reins of power

showing authority

Reversed

Early Phase: Strong controls may begin to be implemented. You may need to be firm in the future. Strict measures may become necessary. You may start to master your emotions.

Late Phase: The rigid controls are loosening. You're no longer in control. The reins of power are slipping away. The need to be strict is decreasing. You're putting an oppressive environment behind you.

Description

Picture Julius Caesar riding his chariot triumphantly into Rome. He has defeated his enemies and conquered vast, new lands. This is the spirit of the Chariot. Card 7 represents the victories that are possible through willpower and self-mastery. A military image is appropriate for the Chariot because this card stands for the strengths associated with combat—discipline, grit, determination, and assertiveness.

The Chariot represents the positive aspects of the ego. A healthy ego is one that is strong and self-assured. It knows what it wants and how to get it. We can get annoyed with someone whose ego is *too* healthy, but we often turn to that person to lead us through difficult moments. We know he or she won't be wishy-washy.

In readings, the Chariot often appears when hard control is or could be in evidence. At its best, hard control is not brutal, but firm and direct. It is backed by a strong will and great confidence. The Chariot can mean self-control or control of the environment. This card also represents victory. There are many types of wins; the Chariot's is of the win-lose type. Your success comes from beating the competition to become number one. Such moments are glorious in the right circumstances.

Some Possible Opposing Cards

Strength—soft control
Hanged Man—accepting the flow of Spirit, putting others first
Tower—defeat, humbling experience
Eight of Swords—confusion, self-doubt
Ten of Swords—feeling powerless, in the pits, putting others first

Some Possible Reinforcing Cards

Magician—using your will, concentrating
Two of Wands—being in authority, dominating
Six of Wands—triumph, self-confidence
Four of Pentacles—control
Nine of Pentacles—self-control, discipline

8

STRENGTH

STRENGTH
PATIENCE
COMPASSION
SOFT CONTROL

Actions

SHOWING STRENGTH

knowing you can endure

having a gallant spirit

feeling an unshakable resolve

taking heart despite setbacks

having stamina

being a rock

Reversed

Early Phase: You may begin to feel stronger. Energy may return. You may become more determined. The will to survive may grow. Your power may build.

Late Phase: Your strength is declining. You're no longer feeling vigorous. You've lost heart. Energy is draining out of the situation. People are losing resolve. The peak of power is past.

BEING PATIENT

dealing calmly with frustration

accepting others

taking time

maintaining composure

refusing to get angry

showing forbearance

Reversed

Early Phase: You may become more patient. It may get easier to wait. You may develop calm endurance. You may need to bide your time. People may become more accepting.

Late Phase: You're losing patience. You can't wait any longer. The period of resigned acceptance is over. Suffering in silence is no longer an option. You're losing your composure.

THE BIG BOOK OF TAROT

BEING COMPASSIONATE

giving others lots of space

tolerating

understanding what others are feeling

accepting

forgiving imperfection

being kind

Reversed

Early Phase: You may start to feel sympathy. Tolerance may grow. People may show more kindness. A mood of good will may develop. You may begin to feel sorry for someone.

Late Phase: Compassion is fading. You no longer feel kindly disposed. The era of good intentions is ending. Well-meaning gestures are becoming less frequent.

ACHIEVING SOFT CONTROL

persuading

working with

guiding indirectly

being able to influence

tempering force with benevolence

demonstrating the strength of love

Reversed

Early Phase: You may start to guide indirectly. You're considering a delicate approach. People may become more accommodating. A lighter touch may be applied in the future.

Late Phase: The period of benevolent control is ending. You're no longer open to influence. Attempts to persuade are decreasing. People are less willing to go along gracefully.

Description

Usually we think of strength in physical terms—big arms, powerful legs—but there is also inner strength. Inner strength comes from an exercise of the heart muscle. It is perseverance, courage, resolve, and composure—qualities that help us endure when times are tough. In the past, a person with inner strength was said to have character; he or she could be counted on in the darkest moments. Card 8 represents this energy of quiet determination. Strength is not a flashy card, but one that is solid and reliable.

   Card 8 also represents patience and compassion. Getting angry is easy when events turn sour, but dealing calmly with frustration takes great strength. So does accepting others and forgiving mistakes. We need strength to mold situations softly. The Chariot controls through mastery and authority. Card 8 is more subtle, even loving. Notice how the lion (itself a symbol of strength) is being guided and tamed by the woman's gentle hands.

   Card 8 will appear in a reading when its qualities are needed. It can be a reminder not to despair or give up. You have the inner strength to endure and triumph. If you are pushing too hard, you need to withdraw for the moment and be patient. If other people or circumstances are driving you crazy, remember the strength that comes with love and forbearance. These will see you through the hardest moments.

Some Possible Opposing Cards

Chariot—hard control
Eight of Cups—weariness, lack of strength
Six of Swords—being listless, lacking heart
Five of Pentacles—ill health, weakness

Some Possible Reinforcing Cards

Hanged Man—taking time, patience
Nine of Wands—stamina, strength to endure

9

THE HERMIT

INTROSPECTION
SEARCHING
GUIDANCE
SOLITUDE

Actions

BEING INTROSPECTIVE

thinking things over

focusing inward

concentrating less on the senses

quieting yourself

looking for answers within

needing to understand

Reversed

Early Phase: You may start to look within. You may begin to question your identity. You may have more time to think in the future. Quiet time may become important. An inner journey may be approaching.

Late Phase: Your period of soul-searching is past. You're less inclined to focus inward now. You had a significant inner experience. Self-analysis is no longer necessary.

SEARCHING

seeking greater understanding

looking for something

wanting the truth at all costs

going on a personal quest

needing more

desiring a new direction

Reversed

Early Phase: You may begin to look for answers. You may need to learn more. People may initiate a search. A quest may begin. Someone may start looking below the surface.

Late Phase: The search is ending. You're no longer curious to learn more. A period of questioning is behind you. The hunger for truth is fading. The desire to look around is decreasing.

RECEIVING/GIVING GUIDANCE

going to/being a mentor

accepting/offering wise counsel

learning from/being a guru

turning to/being a trusted teacher

being helped/helping

Reversed

Early Phase: You may decide to seek guidance. An outside opinion may become useful. An encounter with a teacher or guru may occur in the future. You may begin a therapeutic program.

Late Phase: You're losing a source of guidance. Your counsel is no longer desired. There's less help available now. Someone is rejecting supervision. Suggestions are dwindling.

SEEKING SOLITUDE

needing to be alone

desiring stillness

withdrawing from the world

experiencing seclusion

giving up distractions

retreating into a private world

Reversed

Early Phase: You may become more private. A need for solitude may grow. Someone may decide to live alone. You may be more isolated in the future. Quiet time may gain appeal.

Late Phase: Your period of solitude is ending. You're no longer on your own. The feelings of separation are fading. There's less need to be apart now. Someone is leaving a private world.

Description

The traditional hermit is a crusty, bearded character who has withdrawn from the company of men to live a life of seclusion and hardship. Card 9 supports this understanding. The Hermit represents the desire to turn away from the getting and spending of society to focus on the inner world. He seeks answers within and knows that they will come only with quiet and solitude.

There comes a point in life when we begin to question the obvious. We sense there is a deeper reality and begin to search for it. This is mainly a solitary quest because answers do not lie in the external world, but in ourselves. The hermit on Card 9 reminds us of Diogenes, the Greek ascetic who is said to have gone out with a lantern in hand to search for an honest man. Diogenes is a symbol of the search for truth that the Hermit hopes to find by stripping away all diversions.

In readings, the Hermit often suggests a need for time alone—a period of reflection when distractions are limited. In times of action and high energy, he stands for the still center that must be created for balance. He can also indicate that withdrawal or retreat is advised for the moment. In addition, the Hermit can imply seeking of all kinds, especially for deeper understanding or the truth of a situation. "Seek, and ye shall find," we have been told, and so the Hermit stands for guidance as well. We can receive help from wise teachers, and, in turn, help others as we progress.

Some Possible Opposing Cards

Lovers—being in a relationship, sexuality
World—involvement with the world
Two of Cups—making connections, partnerships
Three of Cups—being in a group, being with others
Nine of Cups—sensual pleasure

Some Possible Reinforcing Cards

High Priestess—looking inward, withdrawing
Four of Cups—withdrawing, being introverted
Eight of Cups—searching for deeper meaning
Four of Swords—contemplating, being quiet
Seven of Swords—being alone, staying away from others

WHEEL of FORTUNE.

10

WHEEL OF FORTUNE

DESTINY
TURNING POINT
MOVEMENT
PERSONAL VISION

Actions

FEELING A SENSE OF DESTINY

using what chance offers

seeing life's threads weave together

finding opportunity in an accident

opening to luck

sensing the action of fate

witnessing miracles

Reversed

Early Phase: You may begin to sense the action of fate. A chance encounter may become important. The threads of your life may come together. A surprise twist may be possible in the future.

Late Phase: The moment of destiny has passed. You're no longer open to the fortunes of fate. An unexpected event is behind you. The role of chance is decreasing. The karmic moment has played itself out.

BEING AT A TURNING POINT

reversing

moving in a different direction

turning things around

having a change in fortune

altering the present course

being surprised at a turn of events

Reversed

Early Phase: A turning point may be coming up. You're considering a change of direction. A surprising turn of events could occur. The situation may reverse itself in the future.

Late Phase: The turning point is behind you. Change is less likely at this point. You're no longer open to a new direction. Options are narrowing. A course has been set, one way or the other.

FEELING MOVEMENT

experiencing change

feeling the tempo of life speed up

being swept up in new developments

rejoining the world of activity

getting involved

Reversed

Early Phase: The pace may pick up. You may start to notice more activity. People may move around more. The agitation may become more obvious. Everyone may begin to hurry.

Late Phase: There's less activity now. The pace is slowing. You're no longer moving around much. The number of changes is decreasing. There's less switching around.

HAVING A PERSONAL VISION

seeing how everything connects

becoming more aware

uncovering patterns and cycles

expanding your outlook

gaining greater perspective

discovering your role and purpose

Reversed

Early Phase: You may become more aware. You may begin to understand yourself. Patterns may start to make sense. Your outlook may expand. An epiphany may occur in the future.

Late Phase: Your personal vision is behind you. You're moving beyond a moment of clarity. Your perspective is no longer all-encompassing. There's less understanding now. You're losing touch with your dream.

Description

In Greek mythology, there are three women known as the Fates. They are responsible for spinning the destiny of each person at his or her birth. It is not surprising that the Fates are spinners because the wheel of fortune is an apt image for the elusive turns of a man's fate. This is the theme of Card 10.

The Wheel of Fortune is one of the few cards in the major arcana that does not have a human figure as a focal point. This is because its center is above the realm of man—in the higher levels (clouds) where the destinies of all are woven together in the tapestry of life. The tarot recognizes that each person sets his own path in life, but is also subject to the larger cycles that include him. We experience chance events that appear to be accidents although they are part of the great plan.

In readings, the Wheel of Fortune can indicate a vision or realization that strikes with great force. If you've been struggling with a problem or tough situation, this card can signal that you will find the answer if you stand back and view everything from a larger perspective.

The Wheel of Fortune also represents unexpected encounters and twists of fate. You can't predict surprises; you can only be aware when one is circling around. Indeed, Card 10 often suggests wheel-like actions—changes in direction, repeating cycles, and rapid movement. When the energy of the Wheel arrives, you will feel life speed up. You are caught in a cyclone that may deposit you anywhere. "Round and round and round she goes, and where she stops, nobody knows."

Some Possible Opposing Cards

Two of Swords—being stuck, at an impasse
Four of Swords—rest, quiet, slow pace
Four of Pentacles—blocked change, no movement
Seven of Pentacles—assessment before direction change

Some Possible Reinforcing Cards

Eight of Wands—rapid pace, quick developments

11

JUSTICE

JUSTICE
RESPONSIBILITY
DECISION
CAUSE AND EFFECT

Actions

RESPECTING JUSTICE

insisting on fairness

acting on ethical principles

being involved in legal concerns

committing to honesty

seeking equality

being impartial

trying to do what is right

Reversed

Early Phase: You're thinking of seeking justice. Questions of fairness may come up. Principles may become important. Someone may seek equal treatment. You may get involved with the law.

Late Phase: The time for justice has passed. You're no longer concerned with a legal matter. The focus on equality is decreasing. Principles are being abandoned. Fair play is less of an issue now.

ASSUMING RESPONSIBILITY

settling old accounts and debts

being accountable

acknowledging the truth

admitting involvement

handling the situation

doing what has to be done

Reversed

Early Phase: You may start to assume responsibility. You're thinking of taking charge. Someone may admit involvement. People may become more reliable. You may need to answer for your deeds.

Late Phase: The conscientious period is ending. People are less willing to meet obligations. You no longer have to bear the brunt. The finger-pointing is behind you. Someone is not as trustworthy now.

PREPARING FOR A DECISION

weighing all sides of an issue

setting a course for the future

balancing all factors

determining right action

choosing with full awareness

Reversed

Early Phase: You may be approaching a decision. A need for resolution may develop. You may start to explore options. Someone may need to weigh all sides. The verdict may be on the way.

Late Phase: The period of deciding is past. A choice has been made, or the time for choosing is ending. A verdict was rendered. Someone is less decisive now. Resolution is no longer important.

UNDERSTANDING CAUSE AND EFFECT

accepting the results you created

seeing how you chose your situation

recognizing the action of karma

knowing that what is makes sense

making connections between events

Reversed

Early Phase: You may begin to see patterns. The impact of the past may become obvious. The situation may start to make sense. You may be causing future effects now.

Late Phase: The cause and effect connections are less clear. You no longer understand why. A fateful result has occurred, and you don't recognize the cause.

Description

On Card 11 we see the familiar figure of Justice. She has the scales of equality and impartial judgment in one hand, and the sword of decision in the other. In the tarot, Justice represents the understanding that life is ultimately fair and just. Even though the vagaries of day-to-day life can make us doubt this fact, Justice reminds us that there is divine balance. Notice the similarity between the Emperor and Justice. Both cards stand for universal order; the Emperor in its underlying structure, Justice in the action of karma—cause and effect.

There is a serious feel to Card 11—the tone of the courtroom. This card refers to legal matters of all kinds, but is not restricted to them. The courts are where judgments are made and decisions rendered. Our legal system is the official arena in which we explore the principles of Justice—fairness, impartiality, and the quest for truth.

In readings, Justice often appears when you are concerned with doing what is right or making sure you receive your due. This card can also appear when you are feeling the impact of a past mistake or good deed. The *cause* you set in motion is now returning to you as an *effect*.

Sometimes Justice is a signal to do what needs to be done. A time comes when responsibilities must be accepted and accounts settled. The past will continue to haunt you if you do not recognize your mistakes and make amends for them. You will need to weigh matters carefully and perhaps make important decisions about your future course.

Some Possible Opposing Cards

Two of Swords—avoiding the truth, disavowing your role
Five of Swords—lack of integrity, not doing what is right
Seven of Swords—shirking responsibility

Some Possible Reinforcing Cards

Emperor—justice, regulations, legal issues
Judgement—deciding, accepting past actions/mistakes
Ten of Wands—accepting responsibility, being accountable
Nine of Swords—guilt over the past, acknowledging mistakes
Seven of Pentacles—assessing where you are, deciding a future course

THE HANGED MAN.

12

THE HANGED MAN

LETTING GO
REVERSAL
SUSPENSION
SACRIFICE

Actions

LETTING GO

having an emotional release

accepting what is

surrendering to experience

ending the struggle

being vulnerable and open

giving up control

REVERSING

turning the world around

changing your mind

overturning old priorities

seeing from a new angle

upending the old order

doing an about-face

Reversed

Early Phase: You may begin to relinquish control. You may become more vulnerable. You may need to surrender in the future. Someone may be getting ready to yield. You may have to renounce a claim.

Late Phase: The time for letting go is over. The release is behind you now. Someone or something was set free. The mood is less open now. The moment for capitulation has passed.

Reversed

Early Phase: A change of direction may be approaching. You may be thinking of switching. Someone may be going to flip. You may need to turn the situation around. A ruling may be overturned.

Late Phase: The moment for reversal is behind you. The situation is less likely to change now. You're no longer thinking of switching. The urge to revoke or recant is decreasing.

SUSPENDING ACTION

pausing to reflect

feeling outside of time

taking time to just be

giving up urgency

living in the moment

waiting for the best opportunity

Reversed

Early Phase: You may begin to feel cut off. An interruption may be approaching. An event may be put on hold. The chance of delay may grow. Activity may cease in the future.

Late Phase: The period of suspension is past. You're no longer on hold. The feeling of timelessness is fading. There's less chance for a pause now. The break is ending.

SACRIFICING

being a martyr

renouncing a claim

putting self-interest aside

going one step back to go two steps forward

giving up for a higher cause

putting others first

Reversed

Early Phase: You're thinking of making a sacrifice. You're considering putting someone else's needs first. You may start to devote yourself to a cause. The need to do without may increase.

Late Phase: A time of sacrifice is behind you. You no longer need to deny yourself. There's less call for selfless service now. The need to do without is decreasing. The mood of martyrdom is fading.

MAJORS

Description

The Hanged Man is one of the most mysterious cards in the tarot deck. It is simple, but complex. It attracts, but also disturbs. It contradicts itself in countless ways. The Hanged Man is unsettling because it symbolizes the action of paradox in our lives. A paradox is something that appears contradictory, and yet is true. The Hanged Man presents to us certain truths, but they are hidden in their opposites.

The main lesson of the Hanged Man is that we "control" by letting go—we "win" by surrendering. The figure on Card 12 has made the ultimate surrender—to die on the cross of his own travails—yet he shines with the glory of divine understanding. He has sacrificed himself, but he emerges the victor. The Hanged Man also tells us that we can "move forward" by standing still. By suspending time, we can have all the time in the world.

In readings, the Hanged Man reminds us that the best approach to a problem is not always the most obvious. When we most want to force our will on someone, that is when we should release. When we most want to have our own way, that is when we should sacrifice. When we most want to act, that is when we should wait. The irony is that by making these contradictory moves, we find what we are looking for.

Some Possible Opposing Cards

Magician—acting, doing
Chariot—self-assertion
Seven of Wands—defiance, struggling against
Ten of Wands—struggle
Four of Pentacles—holding on, control

Some Possible Reinforcing Cards

Fool—faith in what is, going with the flow
High Priestess—suspending activity, waiting
Strength—patience, taking time
Four of Swords—rest, suspended activity
Ten of Swords—sacrifice, martyrdom

13

DEATH

ENDING
TRANSITION
ELIMINATION
INEXORABLE FORCES

Actions

ENDING

closing one door to open another

bringing something to a close

completing a chapter

concluding unfinished business

putting the past behind you

having a parting of the ways

Reversed

Early Phase: You may be approaching an ending. A parting of the ways may be coming up. You may be entering the end game. A task may be nearing completion. Someone may decide to call it a day.

Late Phase: The time of ending is past. The completion is behind you. Unfinished business is no longer an issue. The old ways are fading. The urge to terminate is decreasing.

GOING THROUGH TRANSITION

changing status

moving from the known to the unknown

being cast adrift

waiting in an in-between state

being in the middle

Reversed

Early Phase: You may enter a period of transition. A change of condition may be on the horizon. The tide may begin to shift. Someone may be nearing an in-between state. A major transformation may become possible.

Late Phase: A transition is behind you. You're no longer moving from one state to another. A passage is almost completed. People are less interested in change now. The need for conversion is decreasing.

ELIMINATING EXCESS

cutting out what isn't necessary

shedding old attitudes

getting down to bare bones

concentrating on essentials

getting back to basics

Reversed

Early Phase: You may start to get rid of baggage. Something may be jettisoned in the future. Non-essentials may be on the way out. A dismissal may be in the works. You may begin to simplify.

Late Phase: The period of elimination is behind you. A paring down is less likely now. You're no longer concerned about a removal. The cut has been made. The need to do away with is fading.

EXPERIENCING INEXORABLE FORCES

being in the path of sweeping change

being caught in the inescapable

going through what cannot be avoided

being part of a powerful movement

riding your fate

accepting the inevitable

Reversed

Early Phase: An irresistible event may be on the horizon. An earthshaking experience may be coming up. Powerful happenings may be building strength. You may get drawn into a compelling scenario.

Late Phase: A powerful moment is behind you. You've gone through a fateful encounter. A larger-than-life experience has passed. You're no longer at the mercy of forces. The situation is less unyielding now.

Description

Death! A powerful energy indeed. Who can look at the dark, skeletal figure on Card 13 and not feel uneasy? Here we see the face of our deepest fear—our greatest unknown. We recoil from Death because we think of it as annihilation. In the tarot (and in life I would suggest) Death is not a permanent end, but a transition into a new state. Life is eternal in its essence, if not in its form. To grow, to move, to live—we must "die' to the old to give birth to the new.

It is a truism in tarot work that Card 13 *rarely* has anything to do with physical death. A responsible card reader never interprets Card 13 in this way because this view is too limiting. Death is not something that happens once to our bodies. It happens continually, at many levels and not just in the physical. Each moment we die to the present so the future can unfold.

In readings, Death often represents an important ending that will initiate great change. It signals the end of an era, a moment when a door is closing. At such times, there may be sadness and reluctance, but also relief and a sense of completion. Death also suggests getting down to basics. Dying has a way of making you concentrate on what's important. This card

THE BIG BOOK OF TAROT

reminds you to cut out the unnecessary. Death can also mean you will experience an inexorable force. Death is inevitable, and sometimes there are events that are inescapable as well. When these moments occur, the best approach is to ride your fate and see where it takes you.

Some Possible Opposing Cards

Fool—beginning
Empress—birth
Judgement—rebirth, fresh start

Some Possible Reinforcing Cards

Tower—sweeping impact, powerful forces
Eight of Wands—conclusion, ending
Five of Cups—loss, goodbyes
Eight of Cups—moving on, finishing up

14

TEMPERANCE

TEMPERANCE
BALANCE
HEALTH
COMBINATION

Actions

BEING TEMPERATE

finding the middle ground

showing moderation

avoiding excess

mitigating a harsh position

looking for the golden mean

reaching a compromise

offsetting an extreme

Reversed

Early Phase: You may start to be more moderate. You're thinking of abstaining. Someone may look for the middle ground. A centrist position may gain momentum. Forbearance may increase.

Late Phase: The period of moderation is ending. There's less restraint now. You're no longer feeling temperate. The urge to be low-key is fading. Discretion is disappearing.

MAINTAINING BALANCE

experiencing harmony

achieving equilibrium

bringing together opposites

recognizing all sides

fostering cooperation

feeling centered and secure

Reversed

Early Phase: The situation may grow more balanced. Equilibrium may become a goal. You may start to feel more composed. A focus on equality may begin. You may keep your cool in the future.

Late Phase: The period of balance is ending. Sides are no longer equal. There's less harmony now. A stable situation is breaking up. You're losing composure.

EXPERIENCING HEALTH

renewing energy and vigor

healing

enjoying well-being

recovering

flourishing

Reversed

Early Phase: Vitality may return. A recovery may begin. You may start to concentrate on your health. More energy may become available. Physical conditioning may improve.

Late Phase: Health is declining. You're feeling less vigorous. The energetic phase is ending. Someone is no longer well. The period of comfort and ease is passing.

COMBINING FORCES

gathering together what is needed

joining with others

consolidating

finding the right mix

creating synthesis

getting it all together

Reversed

Early Phase: A merger may occur in the future. A union may become possible. You may start to blend in. An alliance may form. Elements may come together.

Late Phase: An association is breaking up. Parties are no longer joined. There's less consolidation now. The mixture is dissolving. Bonds are not as strong.

Description

There are certain people who exude a kind of quiet composure. They may not say much, but they go about their business with an air of calm deliberation. Their presence is comforting because they are so centered. For me, this is the energy of Temperance.

To be temperate is to show moderation and self-restraint. In a world full of enticing indulgences, it is often necessary to find the middle ground. Sensible, maybe, but also a bit boring? The energy of Temperance may seem unexciting on the surface, but it is the calm of a hurricane's eye. All around are swirling winds, but in the center is a still point that brings everything into balance.

In readings, Temperance can represent a need for moderation, especially when extreme cards are present (such as the Knights). This card can also indicate a need for balance. In conflict situations, Temperance suggests that compromise and cooperation are vital. Look for any opportunity to bring opposing parties together. In fact, to *temper* can mean to modify by adding a new component. By combining and recombining, we come up with the ideal mixture or solution. Temperance is the card of good health in all areas—physical, mental, and emotional. When illness or dis-ease is a concern, Temperance holds out the promise of vitality and well-being.

Some Possible Opposing Cards

Tower—extremes, exploding apart
Five of Wands—disagreement, competition, imbalance
Seven of Cups—excess, overindulgence
Five of Swords—discord, lack of harmony
Five of Pentacles—ill health

Some Possible Reinforcing Cards

World—integration, synthesis, combination
Two of Cups—connection, working together
Three of Cups—joining forces, working together
Two of Pentacles—balance, finding the right mix
Three of Pentacles—teamwork, combining

15

THE DEVIL

BONDAGE
MATERIALISM
IGNORANCE
HOPELESSNESS

Actions

EXPERIENCING BONDAGE

accepting an unwanted situation

being obsessed

feeling tied down against your will

losing independence

allowing yourself to be controlled

being addicted and enslaved

submitting to another

Reversed

Early Phase: You may begin to feel controlled. An obsession may form. Someone may get hooked. The walls may start to close in. You may be heading into a limiting situation.

Late Phase: The period of bondage is ending. You're putting an obsession behind you. An addiction is less powerful now. You no longer need to submit. A fixation is decreasing.

FOCUSING ON THE MATERIAL

being caught up in appearances

believing only in the physical

forgetting the spiritual

getting and spending

overindulging the senses

Reversed

Early Phase: You may begin to focus on the material. Acquiring may become important. A desire for physical pleasure may grow. You may start to wish for more comfortable surroundings.

Late Phase: You're losing interest in material possessions. Your desire to spend is decreasing. Surface appearances are less important now. You're no longer focused on the senses.

STAYING IN IGNORANCE

being unaware

operating within a narrow range

experiencing limitation

choosing to stay in the dark

fearing the unknown

being taken in by appearances

Reversed

Early Phase: You may become uninformed. The truth may start to be obscured. You may get out of touch. Someone may begin to look the other way.

Late Phase: The time of not knowing is over. You're no longer ignorant of the truth. Being unenlightened is less desirable now. Your lack of awareness is ending.

FEELING HOPELESS

believing the worst

despairing

lacking faith

seeing a cold world

thinking negatively

foreseeing a bleak future

doubting

Reversed

Early Phase: You may begin to lose hope. Doubts may grow. The future may seem less promising. Your faith may be challenged. A mood of pessimism may develop.

Late Phase: A hopeless period is behind you. Feelings of despair are fading. The world seems less hostile now. You're no longer consumed by doubt. The atmosphere of gloom is lifting.

Description

Lucifer. Mephistopheles. Satan. The Prince of Darkness. No matter what we call him, the Devil is our symbol for what is bad and undesirable. From our human perspective, we see the world as a struggle between light and dark. We want to vanquish the bad so the good can prevail. In fact, good and bad cannot be separated, just as you cannot separate a shadow from its source. Darkness is simply the absence of light, and it is caused by errors that hide the truth. Card 15 shows us these errors.

First is ignorance—not knowing the truth and not realizing we do not know. Second is materialism—the belief that there is nothing but the physical. As spiritual beings, we long for the Divine, but we lose contact with this source of truth if we trust only our senses. There is also hopelessness, which robs us of our joy and movement toward the light.

Traditionally the Devil stands for evil, but it does not have this rather frightening meaning in a reading. This card lets you know that you are caught in an unhealthy, unproductive situation. You may be in the dark about something—ignorant of the truth and its implications. You may be obsessed by a person, idea, substance, or pattern that you know is bad for you (or maybe you don't!). Sometimes this card reflects back the negativity that has made you doubt yourself and your future. We are prone to many errors in life. Card 15 lets us know when they are serious enough to require attention. When you see the Devil, examine your assumptions carefully. Make sure you are not working from a false picture of yourself and the situation. Hold fast to the highest vision of who you are.

Some Possible Opposing Cards

Fool—having faith, believing
Star—hope, faith, optimism
Four of Wands—freedom, release
Six of Cups—goodwill, innocence, simple joys
Ten of Cups—joy, peace, blessings

Some Possible Reinforcing Cards

Seven of Cups—overindulgence, dissipation
Eight of Swords—confusion, restriction
Nine of Swords—despair, lack of joy

16

THE TOWER

SUDDEN CHANGE
RELEASE
DOWNFALL
REVELATION

Actions

GOING THROUGH SUDDEN CHANGE

experiencing upheaval

having plans disrupted

being surprised

undergoing a crisis

having routines shaken up

being in chaos

Reversed

Early Phase: A crisis may be developing. A major shake-up may be coming. A revolution may be in the works. You may experience a disruption. A drastic change may occur in the future.

Late Phase: The crisis is behind you. The period of upheaval is ending. You're no longer caught in chaos. There's less chance of a surprise now. The disruption is diminishing.

RELEASING

exploding

having an emotional outburst

erupting in anger

crashing through ego defenses

breaking through pretense

letting everything go

Reversed

Early Phase: Anger may be building. You're getting ready to explode. You may need to let it all out. The dam may break in the future. A release of energy may become necessary.

Late Phase: The release is behind you. An emotional explosion occurred. You no longer want to lash out. Loss of control is less likely now. The anger is decreasing.

FALLING DOWN

being humbled

experiencing a crash

toppling from the heights

having a downturn in fortune

suffering a blow to the ego

Reversed

Early Phase: A downfall may be in the works. A humbling experience may occur in the future. Someone may topple from the heights. You may be heading toward a collapse.

Late Phase: The downfall is behind you. A period of ruin is over. The breakdown is in the past. You're no longer concerned about failing. The plunge has already occurred.

HAVING A REVELATION

suddenly realizing the truth

exposing what was hidden

having a burst of insight

seeing through illusions

getting the answer

seeing everything in a flash

Reversed

Early Phase: You may be heading toward a revelation. The truth may be revealed. You may be able to see everything in a flash. An eye-opener may be on the horizon.

Late Phase: A surprise disclosure has occurred. The truth has been divulged. You experienced a burst of awareness. A revelation is behind you. Someone is no longer exposing the truth.

Description

The Tower is an unsettling card. Fire, lightning, falling on jagged rocks—definitely looks like trouble! Card 16 will not be welcomed by those who dislike change. It represents a sudden, dramatic upheaval or reversal in fortune. Usually change is gradual, giving us time to adapt, but sometimes it is quick and explosive. This is the action of the Tower.

In films, the hero sometimes slaps someone who is groggy or babbling. Having tried everything else, he finally resorts to a sharp sting to snap him out of it. Sudden crises are life's way of telling you to wake up. Something's wrong, and you're not responding. Are you too full of pride? Expect a blow to the ego. Are you holding back your anger? Expect the dam to burst. Are you stuck in a rut? Expect a surprise.

How you respond to the Tower's change makes all the difference in how uncomfortable the experience will be. Recognize that the disruption occurred because it was needed. Perhaps embracing the change is too much to ask, but try to find the positive in it. In fact, you may feel tremendous release that you have finally been forced in a new direction. You may have a burst of insight about your situation and reach a new level of understanding about it.

Some Possible Opposing Cards

Chariot—victory, control
Temperance—middle ground, staying together, contained
Star—serenity, calm
Six of Wands—acclaim, pride
Ten of Cups—peace, serenity

Some Possible Reinforcing Cards

Death—sweeping impact, powerful forces
Sun—enlightenment, revelation
Five of Pentacles—hard times

17

THE STAR

HOPE
INSPIRATION
GENEROSITY
SERENITY

Actions

REGAINING HOPE

having faith in the future

thinking positively

believing

counting your blessings

seeing the light at the end of the tunnel

feeling great expectation

looking forward to success

Reversed

Early Phase: Hope may grow. You may start to feel more confident in the future. The chance for success may improve. Expectations may rise.

Late Phase: Hope is fading. You no longer have faith in a positive outcome. The light at the end of the tunnel is disappearing. Belief is not as strong now. Your spirits are sinking.

BEING INSPIRED

regaining motivation

realizing an inner strength

seeing the way clear

being stimulated to a higher level

creating

receiving the answer

Reversed

Early Phase: You may begin to get inspired. The creative impulse may grow. Someone may become motivated. A positive example may spur you on. You may be stimulated to a higher level.

Late Phase: The period of inspiration is fading. You're less motivated now. The way is no longer clear. The call to greatness is fading. Encouragement is harder to come by.

BEING GENEROUS

wanting to give or share

spreading the wealth

opening your heart

giving back what you have received

letting love flow freely

offering with no reservations

holding nothing back

Reversed

Early Phase: You may start to feel generous. A gift may be on the horizon. A spirit of sharing may develop. Someone may extend love and forgiveness. You may contribute openly in the future.

Late Phase: A time of generosity is ending. You're no longer willing or able to offer support. Your heart is not as open now. The charitable impulse is fading. There's less desire to spare no expense.

FEELING SERENE

experiencing peace of mind

relaxing

finding your still center

remaining untroubled

savoring perfect calm

being tranquil amid trouble

enjoying harmony

Reversed

Early Phase: The environment may become peaceful. You may start to feel calmer. Tranquility may be restored. A period of serenity may be approaching.

Late Phase: You're no longer feeling calm. The mood of serenity is fading. You're losing your ability to stay centered. People are less in harmony now. The moment of peace is behind you.

Description

People have always looked to the stars as a source of inspiration and hope. There is something about their twinkling light that draws us out of ourselves and up into a higher plane. When we turn our eyes heavenward, we no longer feel the distress of Earth. The Star reminds me of the clear, high voice of a soprano. There is something otherworldly about it. All the harshness and density of everyday life has been refined away leaving only the purest essence. After being exposed to the Star, we feel uplifted and blessed.

In readings, the Star is most welcome when grief and despair have overwhelmed us. In our darkest moments, we need to know that there is hope, that there is light at the end of the tunnel. The Star is the opposite of the Devil who strips us of our faith in the future. Card 17 holds out the promise that we can eventually find peace of mind. The Star also reminds us to open our heart and release our fears and doubt. If you have been holding back in any way, now is the time to give generously.

It is important to remember that the Star is inspiring, but it is not a card of practical solutions or final answers. Without hope we can accomplish nothing, but hope is only a beginning. When you see Card 17, know that you are on the right track. Your goals and your aspirations are blessed, but to realize them, you must take positive action. Use the light of the Star to guide you in your efforts.

Some Possible Opposing Cards

Devil—hopelessness, lack of faith, pessimism
Tower—upheaval, chaos
Moon—being troubled, disturbed, anxious
Two of Swords—blocked flow of feelings
Nine of Swords—guilt, anguish

Some Possible Reinforcing Cards

Fool—innocence, faith, trust
Empress—generosity, free-flowing love
Six of Cups—goodwill, sharing
Ten of Cups—joy, positive feelings, blessings

18

THE MOON

FEAR
ILLUSION
IMAGINATION
BEWILDERMENT

Actions

FEELING FEAR

releasing inner demons

feeling a nameless apprehension

suffering from phobias

giving in to the shadow self

lacking courage

being overcome by anxieties

Reversed

Early Phase: You may start to feel anxious. A mood of uncertainty may develop. Someone may become apprehensive. A hidden fear may surface. You may begin to feel some qualms.

Late Phase: Fears are diminishing. An inner demon is less powerful now. You're no longer intimidated. The anxious moments are behind you. The mood of foreboding is disappearing.

BELIEVING ILLUSIONS

accepting a false picture

deceiving yourself

having unrealistic ideas

misapprehending the truth

experiencing distortions

chasing after a fantasy

Reversed

Early Phase: You may get drawn into an illusion. A false picture may develop. You may start to deceive yourself. The truth may become elusive. Hallucinations may get stronger.

Late Phase: An illusion has been revealed. Appearances are no longer deceiving. The false reality is losing its hold. You're less susceptible to fantasy. Someone has stopped trying to fool you.

THE BIG BOOK OF TAROT

STIMULATING THE IMAGINATION

having vivid dreams or visions

opening to fantasy

plumbing the unconscious

entertaining unusual thoughts

being outlandish and bizarre

Reversed

Early Phase: You may begin to use your imagination. You may open to what is strange and bizarre. Unconscious material may surface. Someone may start to indulge in make-believe.

Late Phase: A fantasy is no longer strong. You're less imaginative now. Someone is losing interest in dreams. Fanciful notions are decreasing. The strange happenings are decreasing.

FEELING BEWILDERED

losing direction and purpose

having trouble thinking clearly

becoming confused

being easily distracted

feeling disoriented

wandering aimlessly

Reversed

Early Phase: You may start to get disoriented. Uncertainty may grow. The way may become unclear. Someone may begin to get lost. You may lose your bearings.

Late Phase: The period of bewilderment is behind you. You're no longer confused. The aimless wandering is over. The mental fog is lifting. Someone is less disoriented now.

Description

If you look around the room right now, you will (probably!) see people and objects that are comforting in their familiarity. Everything is exactly as you expect it to be. You *know* that if you closed your eyes and opened them, the room would be the same. But . . . have you ever lost the familiar to find, in its place, a world so extraordinary you can't even grasp it? This is the experience of the Moon.

Most of the time we live in a tiny pocket of normality that we wrap around us like a security blanket. We turn our backs on the mysterious universe that waits outside. From time to time we may sneak a peek with our imagination or venture out through fantasy or expanded awareness. We can be thrust out there unprepared through drugs, madness, or intense experiences such as battle.

The Moon is the light of this realm—the world of shadow and night. Although this place is awesome, it does not have to be frightening. In the right circumstances, the Moon inspires and enchants. It holds out the promise that all you imagine can be yours. The Moon guides you to the unknown so you can allow the unusual into your life.

Sadly, we are usually afraid of the Moon. In readings, this card often stands for fears and anxieties—the ones that come in the darkest part of the night. Card 18 also stands for illusions. It is easy to lose our way in the moonlight. Be careful not to let deceptions and false ideas lead you astray. Sometimes the Moon is a signal that you are lost and wandering aimlessly. You must find your way back to the path and your clarity of purpose.

Some Possible Opposing Cards

Star—being serene, untroubled, at peace
Sun—assurance, clarity, enlightenment

Some Possible Reinforcing Cards

Seven of Cups—illusions, unrealistic ideas, fantasy
Two of Swords—self-deception, not seeing the truth
Eight of Swords—confusion, lack of clarity

19

THE SUN

ENLIGHTENMENT
GREATNESS
VITALITY
ASSURANCE

Actions

BECOMING ENLIGHTENED

understanding

finding the sense behind the chaos

attaining a new level of insight

having an intellectual breakthrough

getting to the heart of the matter

realizing the truth

Reversed

Early Phase: You may begin to understand. Insights may start to come. You may get closer to a breakthrough. Someone may have an epiphany. An expanded vision may become possible.

Late Phase: The moment of enlightenment is behind you. You experienced an epiphany. There's less awareness now. You're losing your grasp of the truth. The sun is going behind a cloud.

EXPERIENCING GREATNESS

achieving prominence

being singled out for notice

having a personal moment of glory

setting an outstanding example

shining forth brilliantly

demonstrating distinction

becoming the center of attention

Reversed

Early Phase: You may start to be noticed. Your light may get brighter. Your talent may develop. A glorious moment may be approaching. Someone may show great promise.

Late Phase: A period of renown is ending. You're no longer standing out. The height of success is behind you. Fame is slipping away. Your time as leader is winding down.

FEELING VITALITY

becoming radiantly energized

bursting with enthusiasm

experiencing joy

feeling invigorated

getting charged up

enjoying great health

Reversed

Early Phase: You may begin to feel animated. The mood may pick up. Your vigor may return. Enthusiasm may grow. People may start to get charged.

Late Phase: Your vitality is decreasing. You no longer have much energy. The life force is diminishing. The dynamic period is behind you. There's less zip in your step now.

HAVING ASSURANCE

feeling free and expansive

honoring your true self

knowing you can succeed

being confident

believing in your worth

trusting your abilities

forgiving yourself

Reversed

Early Phase: You may gain some assurance. You may start to trust your abilities. Confidence may return. You may become free and expansive.

Late Phase: You're less confident now. You're no longer certain. People are losing their nerve. Your faith in yourself is fading. Convictions are not as strong now.

Description

Brilliant. Radiant. Sparkling. So many of our words reflect (!) the power and glory of light. When we turn on the light in a room, we *illuminate* it so all the dark corners are visible. When we turn on the light in our minds, we are *enlightened*. We see clearly and understand the truth. Both within and without, the energy of light expands our limits and makes us shine.

Throughout history, people have honored the Sun as the source of light and warmth. In the myths of many cultures, the Sun is a prominent god—full of vigor and courage. He is the vital energy center that makes life on Earth possible. In the tarot the Sun also symbolizes vitality and splendor. The Sun is definitely not a meek and retiring card.

In readings, you will understand Card 19 if you imagine yourself to be a sun god. How do you think and feel? You have total confidence in yourself. You are not cocky, but profoundly sure of your power. You have unlimited energy and glow with health. You have a greatness about you and stand out brilliantly. Finally, you see and understand all that is happening within your sphere. When you see this card, know that you will be successful at all you undertake. Now is the time to let your light shine.

Some Possible Opposing Cards

Moon—confusion, disorientation, illusion
Eight of Cups—weariness
Six of Swords—depressed, listless
Five of Pentacles—being run-down, tired

Some Possible Reinforcing Cards

Tower—enlightenment, revelation
World—accomplishment, great achievement
Two of Wands—personal power, vitality, brilliance
Six of Wands—acclaim, prominence

20

JUDGEMENT

JUDGMENT
REBIRTH
INNER CALLING
ABSOLUTION

Actions

MAKING A JUDGMENT

having a day of reckoning

separating the wheat from the chaff

making an honest appraisal

getting off the fence

using critical faculties

taking a stand

making hard choices

Reversed

Early Phase: You may have to judge. You're preparing to make a choice. An opinion may be rendered. Someone may get off the fence. A conclusion may be reached.

Late Phase: There's less judging now. Your actions are no longer under scrutiny. A decision has been made. A day of reckoning is behind you. The period of criticism is ending.

FEELING REBORN

awakening to possibilities

transforming

enjoying renewed hope

making a fresh start

seeing everything in a new light

discovering joy

Reversed

Early Phase: Someone may start over. A renewal may be in progress. A time of awakening may be coming. You may see everything differently in the future.

Late Phase: The fresh start is ending. A transforming experience is behind you. The bright new beginning is past. Your newfound hope is fading. You're less joyful now.

HEARING A CALL

recognizing your true vocation

feeling inner conviction

feeling an impulse to act

deciding to make a difference

feeling drawn in a new direction

knowing what you must do

answering a need

Reversed

Early Phase: You may begin to see your path. You may become drawn in a new direction. Self-confidence may be growing. The way forward may get clearer.

Late Phase: You're losing your sense of purpose. You no longer feel committed to a chosen field. Your certainty is draining away. Someone has failed to heed a call.

FINDING ABSOLUTION

feeling cleansed and refreshed

releasing guilts and sorrows

forgiving yourself and others

atoning for past mistakes

unburdening yourself

feeling sins washed away

Reversed

Early Phase: You may start to seek forgiveness. You may begin to unburden yourself. It may become possible to wipe the slate clean. Someone may be getting ready to atone.

Late Phase: You experienced absolution. Your guilt has been washed away. The desire to atone is fading. A reprieve is less likely now. Someone is no longer willing to overlook an offense.

Description

On Card 20, we see people rising up at the call of an angel. It is Judgment Day, when the faithful are brought to heaven, but what about those who are not saved? Have they been judged and found wanting? For their sins, will they be denied the presence of the Divine? It is this aspect of judgment that is unsettling. How can judgment be reconciled with forgiveness?

In fact, judgment comes in two forms. The hurtful kind says, "What you did is wrong, and you are bad and worthless for having done it." This type of judgment separates and leaves no room for redemption. It is possible to judge without condemning. We assess the matter, weigh all sides, and try to discern the truth. We recognize the need to choose and hope for the courage to do so wisely—but without blame.

In readings, Card 20 can be a reminder that judgments are necessary; sometimes you *must* decide. At such moments, it is best to consider the matter carefully and then commit yourself without censure. If you are being judged yourself, learn from the process. Take what is of value, correct what needs correcting, but never lose sight of your worth.

Card 20 also stands for the feelings that come with salvation. When the angel calls, you are reborn—cleansed of all guilts and burdens. The past and its mistakes are behind you, and you are ready to begin anew. You may feel a calling—a personal conviction of what you are meant to do. If you are in a low period, in need of hope and absolution, Judgement can show that renewal is at hand.

Some Possible Opposing Cards

Death—endings
Five of Cups—regret, mistakes
Nine of Swords—guilt, blame, feelings of sinfulness

Some Possible Reinforcing Cards

Fool—rebirth, new starts
Justice—deciding, accepting past mistakes/actions
Seven of Pentacles—decision point

21

THE WORLD

INTEGRATION
ACCOMPLISHMENT
INVOLVEMENT
FULFILLMENT

Actions

INTEGRATING

experiencing wholeness

bringing parts together

achieving dynamic balance

combining

creating synthesis

joining together

working in unison

Reversed

Early Phase: You may begin to feel whole. Everything may start coming together. A spirit of unity may develop. A synthesis may become possible. You may be approaching a time of togetherness.

Late Phase: A combination is coming apart. People are no longer united. You're losing your sense of completeness. The parts are separating. There's less coordination now.

ACCOMPLISHING

realizing your goals

prospering

achieving your heart's desire

seeing dreams come true

flourishing

finding a beautiful solution

Reversed

Early Phase: You may be moving toward your goals. Achievements may become possible. A dream may start to be realized. You may start taking your first steps toward success. Prosperity may be returning.

Late Phase: An accomplishment is behind you. A period of achievement is over. You're no longer meeting your goals. The chance to realize your dream is fading. The era of prosperity is ending.

BECOMING INVOLVED

contributing

healing

rendering a service

using a gift or talent

sharing what you have

giving of yourself

feeling engaged

being active

Reversed

Early Phase: You may begin to get involved. Someone may join the effort. You're getting ready to contribute. A desire to serve may grow. Connections may be forged in the future.

Late Phase: There's less involvement now. You're no longer feeling engaged. Someone is pulling away. A period of intense activity is ending. The focus on serving is decreasing.

FEELING FULFILLED

savoring the present

taking pleasure in life

enjoying peace of mind

getting satisfaction

finding contentment

counting your blessings

Reversed

Early Phase: You may become more contented. Moments of happiness may start to happen. A feeling of satisfaction may grow. A time of fulfillment may be approaching.

Late Phase: There's less satisfaction now. You're not as content as you were. The mood of happiness is fading. You no longer have peace of mind.

Description

It's Thanksgiving Day. You've just finished a delicious meal, and there's a hot mug of coffee in your hand. Friends and family are arguing about the latest fiasco, the baby's cooing at you from across the table, and your feet are rubbing the belly of a devoted mutt. You're happy, fulfilled, and truly thankful (at least until you have to start the dishes!). For this moment, the World and everything in it is yours.

We all recognize this feeling. It can come at any time or place and is always welcome. We can feel it at home raking the leaves or on the world stage accepting the Nobel Prize. It can seem quiet and simple, or wild and glorious. What is this feeling, and where does it come from? Card 21 can help us find out.

A major element of happiness is wholeness—the sense that everything is working together in harmony. Not in a static way, but with dynamic balance. Involvement is also important. To be happy, we must feel connected—engaged with what is around us. There is also accomplishment—knowing that we have goals and are moving toward them successfully. When all these elements come together, we feel fulfilled and blessed.

The World represents these moments and all that goes into them. In readings, it is a very positive sign that you are in a position to realize your heart's desire. What that is for you depends on the situation, but it will always feel great. Remember, though, that Card 21 is a symbol of active contribution and service. To hold the World in our hands, we must give of ourselves to it. That is the source of true happiness.

Some Possible Opposing Cards

Hermit—isolation
Four of Cups—lack of involvement, apathy, withdrawal
Five of Wands—working at cross-purposes, lack of integration

Some Possible Reinforcing Cards

Temperance—integration, synthesis, combination
Sun—accomplishment, achievements
Nine of Cups—achieving your heart's desire
Ten of Cups—happiness, emotional fulfillment
Ten of Pentacles—affluence, material fulfillment

Minor Arcana

Tarot Keywords Minor Arcana—Ace to Ten

	WANDS	CUPS	SWORDS	PENTACLES
ACE	Creative Force Enthusiasm Confidence Courage	Emotional Force Intuition Intimacy Love	Mental Force Fortitude Justice Truth	Material Force Prosperity Practicality Trust
TWO	Personal Power Boldness Originality	Connection Truce Attraction	Blocked Emotions Avoidance Stalemate	Juggling Flexibility Fun
THREE	Exploration Foresight Leadership	Exuberance Friendship Community	Heartbreak Loneliness Betrayal	Teamwork Planning Competence
FOUR	Celebration Freedom Excitement	Self-Absorption Apathy Going Within	Rest Contemplation Quiet Preparation	Possessiveness Control Blocked Change
FIVE	Disagreement Competition Hassles	Loss Bereavement Regret	Self-Interest Discord Open Dishonor	Hard Times Ill Health Rejection
SIX	Triumph Acclaim Pride	Good Will Innocence Childhood	The Blues Recovery Travel	Having/Not Having: Resources, Knowledge, Power
SEVEN	Aggression Defiance Conviction	Wishful Thinking Options Dissipation	Running Away Lone-Wolf Style Hidden Dishonor	Assessment Reward Direction Change
EIGHT	Quick Action Conclusion News	Deeper Meaning Moving On Weariness	Restriction Confusion Powerlessness	Diligence Knowledge Detail
NINE	Defensiveness Perseverance Stamina	Wish Fulfillment Satisfaction Sensual Pleasure	Worry Guilt Anguish	Discipline Self-Reliance Refinement
TEN	Overextending Burdens Struggle	Joy Peace Family	Bottoming Out Victim Mentality Martyrdom	Affluence Permanence Convention

Tarot Keywords Minor Arcana—Court Cards

	WANDS	CUPS	SWORDS	PENTACLES
PAGE	Be Creative Be Enthusiastic Be Confident Be Courageous	Be Emotional Be Intuitive Be Intimate Be Loving	Use Your Mind Be Truthful Be Just Have Fortitude	Have an Effect Be Practical Be Prosperous Be Trusting/ Trustworthy
KNIGHT POSITIVE	Charming Self-Confident Daring Adventurous Passionate	Romantic Imaginative Sensitive Refined Introspective	Direct Authoritative Incisive Knowledgeable Logical	Unwavering Cautious Thorough Realistic Hardworking
KNIGHT NEGATIVE	Superficial Cocky Foolhardy Restless Hot-Tempered	Overemotional Fanciful Tempermental Overrefined Introverted	Blunt Overbearing Cutting Opinionated Unfeeling	Stubborn Unadventurous Obsessive Pessimistic Grinding
QUEEN	Attractive Wholehearted Energetic Cheerful Self-Assured	Loving Tenderhearted Intuitive Psychic Spiritual	Honest Astute Forthright Witty Experienced	Nurturing Bighearted Down-to-Earth Resourceful Trustworthy
KING	Creative Inspiring Forceful Charismatic Bold	Wise Calm Diplomatic Caring Tolerant	Intellectual Analytical Articulate Just Ethical	Enterprising Adept Reliable Supporting Steady

ACE OF WANDS

CREATIVE FORCE
ENTHUSIASM
CONFIDENCE
COURAGE

Actions

USING CREATIVE FORCE

inventing a better way

expanding your potential

opening to greater possibilities

conceiving a dream

expressing yourself

stimulating your imagination

allowing a talent to unfold

coming up with a solution

Reversed

Early Phase: You may have a chance to be creative. An original idea may materialize. Someone may come up with a novel approach. A venue for your talent could open up.

Late Phase: The opportunity to use creative force is fading. The chance to do something new is past. The support for original ideas is disappearing. Creative moments are less frequent.

SHOWING ENTHUSIASM

feeling fired up and eager

creating an aura of excitement

being ready to tackle the world

inspiring others

sustaining optimism

giving 100 percent

Reversed

Early Phase: You may have a chance to be enthusiastic. An inspiring occasion may occur. Someone may present an exciting proposal. You may back a winner. Support may start building.

Late Phase: The opportunity to be enthusiastic is fading. You're less eager to take part. The ride seems to be over. You're no longer up for the challenge. There are fewer reasons to be optimistic now.

HAVING CONFIDENCE

believing in yourself

feeling assured of your abilities

being sure of success

having high self-esteem

having faith in your path

knowing things will work out

Reversed

Early Phase: You may have a chance to show confidence. An opportunity to prove yourself may be on the way. A test of your skills may be coming up. Your belief in yourself may be put on the line.

Late Phase: The opportunity to show confidence is fading. The moment to convince someone has passed. You can't demonstrate your certainty now. People are no longer focused on your performance.

PROCEEDING WITH COURAGE

tackling a challenging task

going beyond your limits

being true to your beliefs

daring to take a stand

facing your fears

going for it

Reversed

Early Phase: You may have a chance to show courage. You may have to face a challenge. A time of testing may be approaching. You may be asked to take a stand.

Late Phase: The opportunity to show courage is fading. You're no longer being challenged. The test of your mettle is past. The fearful situation is ending.

Description

The Ace of Wands is a symbol of possibility in the area of creativity, excitement, adventure, courage, and personal power. In readings, it shows that a seed of bold enthusiasm has been planted in your life although you may not yet recognize it. When the seed sprouts, it could take almost any form. It might be a creative idea, surge of optimism, or need to act boldly. On the outside, it could be an offer, gift, opportunity, encounter, or synchronistic event.

When you see this Ace, examine your life to see how its potent, confident energy could work for you. Be daring and brave. Sometimes you have to risk to get what you want. Look for the path that will excite you and push you beyond your limits. Seize the initiative, and let your enthusiasm take you to new heights. Wands are the suit of individual power and fulfillment. This Ace tells you that a time of passion is beginning. You will be able to assert your best for all to see.

The Ace of Wands is also the card of creativity. Under its influence, you can become a conduit for inspiration and invention. Forget tired, worn-out solutions. You have the chance to be original. Trust your own creative potential, and there will be no end to what you can achieve.

WANDS

Ace-Ace Pairs

An Ace-Ace pair shows that a new spirit is entering your life. It draws on the energy of the Ace of Wands—creativity, excitement, adventure, courage, personal power—plus one of these:

Ace of Cups—deep feelings, intimacy, attunement, compassion, love

Ace of Swords—intelligence, reason, justice, truth, clarity, perseverance

Ace of Pentacles—prosperity, abundance, trust, security, groundedness

TWO OF WANDS

PERSONAL POWER
BOLDNESS
ORIGINALITY

Actions

HAVING PERSONAL POWER

commanding attention and respect

directing those around you

holding the world in your hands

wielding influence

calling the shots

having authority

swaying others to your position

being able to achieve your goals

BEING BOLD

daring to do what you want

taking a risk

gambling events will go your way

confronting the situation head-on

taking the initiative

speaking your mind

facing fear directly

seizing the day

Reversed

Early Phase: You may gain more power. Others may start paying attention to you. Your position may get stronger. You may be able to seize control. You may be put in charge in the future.

Late Phase: Your power is fading. It's no longer as easy to assert authority. People are not paying as much attention to you. The reins are slipping out of your hands.

Reversed

Early Phase: You may become bold. You may need to take a risk. Daring gestures may become necessary. You may have to seize the initiative. A chance to make your move may open up.

Late Phase: You're feeling less daring. Your courage is slipping. The chance to take a risk has passed. You're pulling back from a dangerous situation. The urge to gamble is fading.

SHOWING ORIGINALITY

doing what no one else has done

creating your own style

being a pioneer

taking a different approach

inventing something new

diverging from the crowd

marching to a different drummer

Reversed

Early Phase: You may become more creative. It may get easier to diverge from the crowd. A novel path may open up. You may have a unique experience. Something new may occur.

Late Phase: You're feeling less creative. There are fewer novel approaches now. It's no longer easy to adopt your own style. You had a unique experience that is now ending.

Description

The Two of Wands glorifies individual courage and greatness. This card taps the same energy as the Magician, but with one important difference. The Magician represents the archetype of power—the impersonal energy of creativity and strength. The Two of Wands stands for that power brought down to Earth and made personal. Personal power is an invigorating force that fills you up and lends you the courage to be great. A powerful person is like a magnet that attracts all those within a certain area.

True power always comes from the Divine. It passes through us and then flows out into the world. When we understand this relationship, we are blessed because this flow brings with it a tremendous feeling of expansion and fulfillment. We feel as if we can accomplish anything. Problems develop when we forget that we are not the *source* of power, only its conduit. We must be careful not to let the intoxicating feelings that come with power overwhelm our good sense and blind us to our true desires and intentions.

In readings, the Two of Wands indicates that power is a major issue in the situation. You or someone else has it or wants it. When you see this card, look carefully at your goals and activities to make sure you are using power wisely. Don't support power for its own sake, but enjoy it when it serves your worthwhile purposes. Take this gift and use it to mold your environment in positive ways.

The Two of Wands can also stand for an extra dose of daring and inventiveness. When you see this card, trust that the time is right for the bold, creative move that will knock their socks off. Forget subtlety and old, tired approaches. Allow yourself free rein and you'll be amazed at the results.

Some Possible Opposing Cards

High Priestess—being passive, staying in the background
Hierophant—conforming, going along with the group
Eight of Swords—powerlessness, fear of action
Ten of Swords—victim mentality, powerlessness
Ten of Pentacles—going by the rules, being conventional

Some Possible Reinforcing Cards

Magician—personal power, wielding a strong force
Emperor—authority
Chariot—personal power, command
Sun—vitality, brilliance, greatness

THREE OF WANDS

EXPLORATION
FORESIGHT
LEADERSHIP

Actions

EXPLORING THE UNKNOWN

seeking out uncharted areas

going in quest of new adventure

expanding horizons

leaving the secure behind

tackling something different

Reversed

Early Phase: You're thinking of exploring new possibilities. An adventure may begin. The future may be more open. You may move into unfamiliar territory. Someone may decide to test uncharted waters.

Late Phase: A period of adventure is ending. The desire to explore is fading. You're no longer interested in dealing with unknowns. There's less need to seek novelty now.

HAVING FORESIGHT

being visionary

looking for greater possibilities

planning ahead

knowing what to expect

getting a premonition

anticipating obstacles

taking the long view

Reversed

Early Phase: You may need to plan for the future. People may begin taking the long view. It may be possible to foresee problems. You may get premonitions of what's to come.

Late Phase: Attempts to plan for the future are fading. You're no longer showing foresight. There's less focus on looking ahead. People are less interested in the big picture.

DEMONSTRATING LEADERSHIP

showing others the way

taking the main role

providing needed direction

rallying the group behind you

assuming a responsible position

setting an example

serving as a representative

Reversed

Early Phase: You may be moving into a leadership position. A chance to take command may open up. You may need to set an example. The main role may fall to you. You may be chosen as a representative.

Late Phase: The opportunity to take command is fading. Your leadership role is behind you. You're no longer setting an example. There's less direction than before. A commander is stepping down.

Description

On the Three of Wands, we see a figure standing on a cliff looking out over the sea to distant mountains. From this height, he sees all that lies ahead. This is a card of vision and foresight. By climbing higher, we increase our range. We detach and gain perspective.

In readings, the Three of Wands can tell you to take the long view. Don't react to the heat of the moment, but step back and consider how the present fits into the greater picture. This card asks you to be a visionary—to dream beyond current limitations. It can indicate premonitions or other intuitions about what is to come.

Taking the long view is an aspect of leadership—another meaning of the Three of Wands. Someone who knows the way can show it to those who follow. The Three of Wands tells you that now is the time to accept your vision and be confident that you can lead others to it.

A leader not only sees far, but he is willing to go there first. This is a card of exploration. Compare this figure to the Fool who is also on a cliff edge. The Fool steps out in innocence, not realizing he is going to fall to his fate. The adventurer on the Three of Wands is also willing to step out, but with full awareness of what he is doing. His courage is more informed, if less spontaneous. The Three of Wands encourages you to move fearlessly into new areas.

Some Possible Opposing Cards

Two of Swords—avoiding the facts, staying stuck
Ten of Pentacles—being conservative, focusing on security

Some Possible Reinforcing Cards

Fool—expanding horizons, going into unexplored territory
Emperor—leadership, providing direction
Eight of Cups—going on a trip, starting a journey
Three of Pentacles—planning, preparing for the future

FOUR OF WANDS

CELEBRATION
FREEDOM
EXCITEMENT

Actions

CELEBRATING

rejoicing over a happy event

recognizing a success

observing an anniversary, milestone, or special time

congratulating on a job well done

reflecting on accomplishments

enjoying some well-deserved rewards

taking part in a ceremony or rite

Reversed

Early Phase: A major celebration may be approaching. You may experience a joyous occasion. A milestone may be reached. You may receive some congratulations.

Late Phase: The event or ceremony is behind you. The festivities are ending. A milestone was reached and passed. The mood of rejoicing is fading. You no longer have much reason to celebrate.

SEEKING FREEDOM

getting out of an oppressive situation

breaking free of bonds

cutting loose

opening to new possibilities

escaping unhappy circumstances

claiming self-determination

letting go of limitations

Reversed

Early Phase: You may decide to claim your freedom. You may let go of inhibitions. You may need to plan an escape. You may cut some cords. Delivery may be at hand.

Late Phase: The break for freedom is behind you. You made your escape. The cords have been cut. You no longer need to assert your independence. A period of unlimited possibility is ending.

FEELING EXCITED

bubbling over with delight

feeling thrilled

looking forward expectantly

getting caught up in the moment

feeling jubilant

being surprised

Reversed

Early Phase: You may start looking for excitement. You may begin seeking thrills. A big adventure may be approaching. Enthusiasm may grow. A surprise may occur.

Late Phase: The mood of excitement is fading. You're not as enthusiastic as you were. Thrills are not as important now. The spirit of adventure is not as strong. The commotion is dying down.

Description

Do you remember the thrill you felt as a child seeing your birthday cake alight with candles? Or waiting to get on a roller coaster? Or slow dancing with your first love? This bubbly, high-as-a-kite feeling lies at the heart of the Four of Wands. As a toddler, my son expressed it through his "happy dance." He'd run in place faster and faster, barely able to control his delight. Of course, as mature (!) adults, we contain this feeling, but it never leaves completely. Each of us still has an excited, little kid inside waiting to come out.

In readings, the Four of Wands often represents the events and experiences that generate excitement. These vary from person to person, but the stirring feelings are the same. The Four of Wands can signal a surprise or spontaneous thrill. Other times this card represents planned celebrations, such as weddings, anniversaries, birthdays, and victory parties. These events have their solemn side, but they are also a chance to feel the joy of living.

The Four of Wands often means freedom. Freedom can take many forms, but it always brings with it an exhilarating feeling. When we break the bonds that bind us, whether physical, mental, or emotional, we feel triumphant and able to move on to a new period of growth and happiness. If you feel trapped or restricted right now, use the energy of the Four of Wands to launch you into freedom. Do not be afraid to claim the open vistas that are rightfully yours.

Some Possible Opposing Cards

Devil—bondage, lack of freedom
Ten of Wands—burdens, being in an oppressive situation
Four of Cups—apathy, lack of excitement, flat feeling
Six of Swords—mild depression, little to celebrate
Eight of Swords—restriction, lack of freedom

Some Possible Reinforcing Cards

Three of Cups—excitement, high spirits, celebration
Two of Pentacles—fun, excitement, parties

WANDS

FIVE OF WANDS

DISAGREEMENT
COMPETITION
HASSLES

Actions

DISAGREEING

feeling everyone is at cross-purposes

being torn by dissension

quarreling, arguing, and bickering

becoming embroiled in a debate

being at odds with others

quibbling over details

Reversed

Early Phase: You may begin to disagree. Arguments may break out. The lack of consensus may become obvious. People could start quibbling over details.

Late Phase: Disagreements are decreasing. People are no longer arguing much. The period of contention is ending. Differences are not as obvious now. The debate is coming to a close.

EXPERIENCING COMPETITION

feeling the thrill of the contest

going against an opponent

rising to the challenge

being involved in a game or sport

trying to outdo yourself

going for the gold

looking for a fight

having a rival

Reversed

Early Phase: Competitive elements may increase. A rivalry may develop. You may have a run-in with an opponent. A match may be coming up. A challenge may occur in the future.

Late Phase: The competition is ending. There's less opposition now. You no longer have to deal with a rival or challenger. The match is behind you. People are not as concerned with outdoing each other.

EXPERIENCING HASSLES

getting annoyed by demands

having minor setbacks

needing to take care of details

suffering from irritations

being bothered by trivialities

Reversed

Early Phase: You may experience a few set-backs. Minor irritations may increase. Some hassles may develop in the future. You may have to deal with some annoying problems.

Late Phase: The hassles are decreasing. You've worked through the worst problems. Resistance is no longer slowing you down. The demands are not as bothersome now.

Description

You wake up and stub your toe going to the bathroom. You're in the shower and find out there's no soap. At breakfast, you get juice on your shirt. When you get to the car, your battery is dead. It's going to be a terrible, horrible, no good, very bad day.[5] You're beset by hassles—those petty annoyances that are infuriating *because* they are so minor.

The Five of Wands stands for times when your environment seems to be fighting you. Nothing flows smoothly; everyone is working at cross-purposes. The figures on this card show no coordinated effort, no agreement. When this card shows up, be prepared for a bumpy ride—extra patience and perseverance will be needed to accomplish something. The Five of Wands does not represent major blockages, just many small, irritating ones.

This card also stands for competition. In the right circumstances, competition is useful. It fosters extra effort, generates excitement, and encourages the best. When the Five of Wands appears in a reading, check for competitive elements. You may be involved in a contest, race, or game. You may discover you have rivals who are opposing you or challenging your position. You may feel disheartened (or invigorated!) by the dog-eat-dog environment you find yourself in. At its heart, competition is divisive. Make sure it is helping you and others reach your true goals. Otherwise, work toward cooperation.

Some Possible Opposing Cards

Temperance—balance, agreement, working together
World—integration, working together
Two of Cups—truce, agreement, coming together
Two of Pentacles—working smoothly, getting people together
Three of Pentacles—teamwork, cooperation

Some Possible Reinforcing Cards

Seven of Wands—opposition, fighting
Ten of Wands—struggle, hassles, meeting resistance
Five of Swords—discord, people set against each other

SIX OF WANDS

TRIUMPH
ACCLAIM
PRIDE

Actions

TRIUMPHING

having your day in the sun

being vindicated

walking away with the prize

prevailing against all comers

coming out on top

achieving success

Reversed

Early Phase: You may see signs of success. Victory may be getting closer. Your day of vindication may be approaching. Someone may start winning.

Late Phase: The victory is behind you. The time for success has passed. People are losing their concern with the contest. Chances for vindication are decreasing. You're no longer focused on winning.

RECEIVING ACCLAIM

being acknowledged

getting a pat on the back

receiving some honor or award

getting praise or a compliment

earning applause

achieving recognition

Reversed

Early Phase: You may receive an award or acknowledgement. Hard work may begin to pay off. Your efforts may be recognized. Fame may become important. People may start taking notice.

Late Phase: Praise and acclaim are fading. Your efforts are no longer being recognized. The prize or reward is behind you. Someone received a compliment or pat on the back.

FEELING PRIDE

enjoying healthy self-esteem

strutting your stuff

holding your head up high

feeling worthy of notice

having a high opinion of yourself

putting yourself above others

being arrogant

condescending

feeling self-important

Reversed

Early Phase: You may become more confident. Arrogance may become a problem. Someone may be condescending. Healthy pride may change to overconfidence.

Late Phase: Your pride has taken a blow. You went through a humbling experience. You're feeling less confident. There's less arrogance now. People are no longer sure of themselves.

Description

The Six of Wands is the minor arcana counterpart of the Chariot. Both of these cards represent moments of victory and triumph. Sometimes in life, all we want to do is win—to be number one. You can see this dream in the faces of athletes, politicians, and other champions as they step into the winner's circle. It's all been worthwhile. I'm the best. I've won!

In readings, the Six of Wands appears when you have been working hard toward a goal, and success is finally within reach. The recognition you have sought so long is yours. You can receive the acclaim, honor, and reward you deserve. If you do not feel close to victory now, know that it is on its way provided you are doing all you can to make it happen. The victory of this card does not have to involve beating someone else. You can triumph over yourself, the environment, or the odds.

The Six of Wands also represents a healthy self-esteem. Feeling good about your accomplishments is an important part of success, but too much pride can lead to arrogance and self-inflation. When you see this card, check that you are not feeling superior to others. It is easy to forget that individual achievement is not really individual at all. Our talents begin in the Divine, develop with the love and support of others, and only in the end express *through* us. How can we indulge in excess pride?

In the *Purgatorio* Dante considers pride the first and greatest sin that must be overcome by souls reaching toward heaven. When the Six of Wands appears, enjoy your triumph, feel good about yourself, but remember Dante's words:

O gifted men, vainglorious for first place, how short a time the laurel crown stays green

A breath of wind is all there is to fame here upon earth: it blows this way and that, and when it changes quarter it changes name.[6]

Some Possible Opposing Cards

Tower—humility, loss of acclaim
Five of Cups—loss, defeat
Ten of Swords—self-deprecating, in the pits
Five of Pentacles—rejection, lack of recognition

Some Possible Reinforcing Cards

Chariot—triumph, self-confidence
Sun—acclaim, prominence
Nine of Cups—self-satisfaction, achieving what you want

SEVEN OF WANDS

AGGRESSION
DEFIANCE
CONVICTION

Actions

BEING AGGRESSIVE

going after what you want

asserting yourself

taking the offensive

firing the first shot

fighting

making your point forcefully

seizing the advantage

Reversed

Early Phase: Aggression may increase. Hostilities may break out. You may be thinking of a fight. A chance to seize the advantage may come up. You may need to make your point forcefully.

Late Phase: The period of aggression is ending. You're no longer involved in a fight. There's less chance to state your case now. The advantage is no longer yours. Someone has already fired the first shot.

BEING DEFIANT

holding out against pressure

defending your position

opposing all challengers

combating criticism

refusing to yield

saying "no!"

resisting authority

Reversed

Early Phase: You may become more defiant. Resistance may increase. You may need to defend your position. Someone could decide to hold out. People may get their back up.

Late Phase: You're no longer resisting. Defiance is decreasing. Opposition is not as strong now. Challengers are backing off. Refusals are no longer a problem.

SHOWING CONVICTION

being sure, knowing you are right

having a fixed position

demonstrating strong character

standing up for what you believe

acting resolutely

being firm

Reversed

Early Phase: Conviction may grow. You may gain confidence. You may decide to stay the course. Someone may speak out forcefully. Character may become important.

Late Phase: You're becoming less certain. You're no longer convinced you're right. Someone is giving up. Firm resolutions are getting broken. People are losing the courage to speak out.

Description

The Seven of Wands is about taking a stand. Taking a stand is a forceful act that changes the energy flow of the world for good or ill. Most of the time we flow with our lives as if on a river. Events and feelings carry us forward with little effort. Sometimes, though, we are not content to drift. We want to resist the flow, or change its course entirely!

The figure on the Seven of Wands appears to be in a battle. He's either attacking or under attack, probably both. When we decide to take a stand, we set in motion an energy of resistance. When we take up a firm position, others do the same. The Seven of Wands stands for aggression *and* defiance because they are two sides of the same coin.

Some battles are worth fighting, others just cause trouble. If you are involved in a conflict, ask yourself if it's worth the struggle. Is it important? Will the outcome serve you or others? If so, be bold and aggressive. Defend your position. Refuse to yield! If not, then consider letting the conflict go. Be honest with yourself about this. You will be tempted to hold onto your position, especially if you have invested much time and energy into it.

The Seven of Wands can also indicate strong convictions. In order to take a firm stand, you must believe in your position and yourself. You'll need integrity and strength of character to see you through. For a just cause, the energy of the Seven of Wands makes a difference.

Some Possible Opposing Cards

High Priestess—being passive, holding back
Hanged Man—waiting, letting go
Three of Pentacles—teamwork

Some Possible Reinforcing Cards

Five of Wands—opposition, fighting
Nine of Wands—defending your position, refusing to yield
Five of Swords—conflict, "me-against-them" mentality

EIGHT OF WANDS

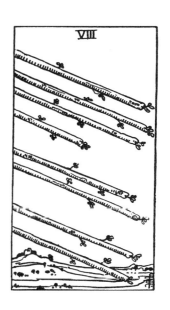

QUICK ACTION
CONCLUSION
NEWS

Actions

TAKING QUICK ACTION

making your move

striking while the iron is hot

declaring yourself openly

putting plans into action

rushing into a new area

moving into high gear

getting caught up in change

Reversed

Early Phase: You're thinking of declaring yourself openly. The pace may pick up. People may decide to act. Changes may become obvious. The time to strike may be coming. Events may start taking off.

Late Phase: The rapid changes are behind you. The pace is slowing. The time for action is past. You no longer have to rush around. You're dealing with the aftermath now.

COMING TO A CONCLUSION

culminating an effort

having all elements come together

closing out an activity

experiencing a grand finale

finding a successful resolution

completing unfinished business

Reversed

Early Phase: You're thinking of concluding matters. The last act may begin. A final resolution may be approaching. You may be heading toward a culmination.

Late Phase: The situation has been resolved. Everything has been completed. The final act is ending. You're closing out some activity. The last word has nearly been spoken.

RECEIVING NEWS

getting an important message

obtaining a needed bit of information

finding the missing puzzle piece

discovering the truth

having a meaningful conversation

learning more

Reversed

Early Phase: Some news may be on the way. You may hear an important announcement. You may be getting closer to the truth. Someone may initiate a meaningful conversation.

Late Phase: The news has been delivered. You found out what you needed to know. The truth came out. Less news is getting through. You're no longer in the loop. You have fewer opportunities to be informed.

Description

In the film *The Ten Commandments,* Moses touches his staff to water to set a plague in motion. His staff is the agent of power that initiates events. Moses' staff reminds me of the wands on this card. They are a symbol of the onset of action and its effects. Before acting, we think, imagine, speculate, talk, and dream. This is the realm of air—the sky. Then, finally, we make our move. We bring our ideas down to Earth and put them into action.

In readings, the Eight of Wands is often a sign that *now* is the time to declare yourself. All the elements are ready and will work for you as long as you don't hesitate. If events are in motion, they will proceed rapidly. You may feel caught in a whirlwind, but soon the dust will settle, and you will see how your plans have fared.

The Eight of Wands also stands for the arrival of news or information, which may show up in a disguised form, so stay alert. You may see or hear something important. Pay attention to everything.

This card also signifies endings. Sooner or later, all activities run their course. The eight wands on this card not only symbolize putting events into motion, but also bringing them to a close, down to Earth. The Eight of Wands in a reading may indicate it is time to conclude whatever you have been doing. Celebrate the past, but prepare to move on to something new.

Some Possible Opposing Cards

High Priestess—waiting, holding off
Four of Swords—not rushing in, preparing
Seven of Pentacles—assessment, taking stock before action

Some Possible Reinforcing Cards

Magician—taking action, carrying out plans
Wheel of Fortune—rapid pace, quick developments
Death—conclusion, endings
Eight of Cups—finishing up, ending a chapter

NINE OF WANDS

DEFENSIVENENSS
PERSERVERANCE
STAMINA

Actions

DEFENDING YOURSELF

assuming ill will

expecting the worst

taking extra precautions

being paranoid

feeling wary and guarded

protecting others

remembering past attacks

Reversed

Early Phase: You may become wary. You may need to defend yourself. Someone may start getting paranoid. The atmosphere may become guarded. Protection may be necessary.

Late Phase: You're no longer defensive. The need to be guarded is ending. There's less chance of an attack now. The mood of paranoia is decreasing. Extra precautions are no longer required.

PERSEVERING

persisting despite all setbacks

refusing to take "no" for an answer

seeing something through to the end

getting knocked down, then standing up

keeping your resolve

trying repeatedly

Reversed

Early Phase: Your resolve may grow. You may get more committed. People may show more determination. You may decide to keep going. Multiple attempts may become necessary.

Late Phase: Commitment is weakening. You're not trying as hard now. Your resolve is fading. You got knocked down and don't want to get up again. The effort no longer seems worth it.

SHOWING STAMINA

continuing despite fatigue

holding fast

drawing on hidden reserves

holding together through force of will

demonstrating physical strength

keeping up the pace

Reversed

Early Phase: Your strength may return. It may get easier to keep up the pace. You may develop more stamina. You may need to hold fast. A test of staying power may be coming up.

Late Phase: Your energy is decreasing. Your strength is wearing out. It's no longer possible to keep going. Your endurance is not what it was. You're letting up a bit. The test of your staying power is ending.

Description

The figure on the Nine of Wands has definitely been through tough times. His head and arm are bandaged, and he's leaning on a "crutch." This fighter has seen some battles, but he's still standing! He's hurt, but he's not down. When we have had a bad experience, we feel weary and battle-scarred. Even if we aren't hurt physically, our psyches are wounded. Our openness, innocence, and trust are gone, replaced by wary defensiveness.

In readings, the Nine of Wands can be a warning that you must proceed carefully. Keep a watchful eye because there is the possibility that you will be hurt. Life's lessons can be hard sometimes, especially when hopes have been dashed. It is natural to feel defensive at such times, but try to avoid becoming bitter. What wounded you is also a source of strength.

Strength is the other aspect of the Nine of Wands. This fighter is tough. He has the physical stamina and the inner drive to persist despite all setbacks. In *The Terminator,* Arnold Schwarzenegger plays an android from the future who never gives up. In the end he is nothing but a wire framework with glowing eyes, but he still keeps coming—dragging himself along the floor to his goal. This is the spirit of the Nine of Wands (without the evil intent!). This card tells you to keep going no matter what. Even if everyone and everything seems to be against you right now, don't give up. Within you are the hidden reserves you need to prevail.

Some Possible Opposing Cards

Three of Cups—friendship, trusting someone
Six of Cups—innocence, believing the best
Eight of Cups—weariness, fatigue

Some Possible Reinforcing Cards

Strength—endurance, resolve, heart
Seven of Wands—defending a position, holding out
Two of Swords—being defensive, closing yourself off
Eight of Pentacles—persistence

TEN OF WANDS

OVEREXTENDING
BURDENS
STRUGGLE

Actions

OVEREXTENDING

trying to do too much

refusing to say "no"

taking all the blame

assuming another's debt

doing the lion's share

having to work overtime

shouldering all the work

being saddled with an extra load

Reversed

Early Phase: You may become overextended. It may get harder to say "no." The lion's share may fall to you. There may be extra work in the future. You may have to delegate.

Late Phase: Demands are decreasing. You no longer have to shoulder the responsibility. There's less overtime now. You've passed on some of the work.

FEELING BURDENED

never having time to relax

feeling tied to a treadmill

being taxed to the limit

assuming responsibility

being held accountable

carrying out an unpleasant duty

cleaning up a messy situation

being left holding the bag

Reversed

Early Phase: You may start to feel burdened. The work may increase. You may get in over your head. A taxing problem may be looming. Worries may become more oppressive. Accountability may become an issue.

Late Phase: The burdens are decreasing. The unpleasantness is behind you. You've managed to get off the treadmill. You're no longer the main one responsible. The load is lighter now.

STRUGGLING

fighting uphill

doing everything the hard way

experiencing resistance

pushing against the current

having to work for every gain

finding that nothing comes easily

laboring

Reversed

Early Phase: A struggle may begin. Resistance could develop. You may need to fight for every gain. The path ahead may be steep. The opposition could make your work harder.

Late Phase: The struggle is ending. There's less resistance now. You no longer need to work so hard. The path is heading downhill. The tough times are behind you.

Description

On the Ten of Wands, we see a bent figure trying to carry ten heavy poles. They are ranged so closely in front of him that he can't even see where he's going. Nothing exists for this man except his burdens and responsibilities. How true this is for so many today! We take on so much, trying to do all the things that need to be done. We think that if we can hang on until the weekend (or vacation, or end of the semester) then we can finally relax. The weekend comes, and the overload continues.

In readings, the Ten of Wands can be a sign that you are pushing yourself too hard. If your days are an endless round of duties and tasks, you need to lighten up for the sake of your health and well-being. Cut back, and take on only those activities that give you pleasure. If you love your work, but it's all-consuming, you may be too narrowly focused in one area. Balance your life with other interests.

The Ten of Wands can also stand for times when you have to assume the lion's share of responsibility. You may be blamed or left holding the bag. On the other hand, you may have to step forward and take charge because you are the only one capable enough. Rightly or wrongly, the cleanup will fall to you.

The Ten of Wands indicates that your life is going to be tougher than usual for a time. You will have to fight uphill for every little gain. Each step will feel like a struggle. When you see this card, be kind to yourself. Lighten the load wherever you can, and let others help you. You don't have to handle everything yourself.

Some Possible Opposing Cards

Fool—carefree, living in the moment
Hanged Man—letting go
Four of Wands—free of burdens, escaping oppression
Four of Swords—relaxing, resting
Seven of Swords—avoiding responsibility

Some Possible Reinforcing Cards

Justice—accepting responsibility, being accountable
Five of Wands—struggle; hassles, resistance
Six of Swords—getting by, struggling along
Nine of Swords—worrying
Five of Pentacles—struggling, hard times

WANDS

PAGE OF WANDS

BE CREATIVE
BE ENTHUSIASTIC
BE CONFIDENT
BE COURAGEOUS

Actions

. . . .

BE CREATIVE

take a novel approach

be original

invent

find a new area of self-expression

use your art

come up with a solution

go in a new direction

Reversed

Early Phase: You may have a chance to be creative. Someone may show originality. The time to take a novel approach is approaching. You make be called on to go in a new direction.

Late Phase: A creative period is fading. There are fewer chances to do your art now. An opportunity to change direction was taken. There is no longer much interest in the new.

. . . .

BE ENTHUSIASTIC

jump in wholeheartedly

get excited

show optimism

be the first to volunteer

be passionate

get your blood flowing

Reversed

Early Phase: You may be called on to volunteer. An opportunity for passion may present itself. A chance to commit yourself wholeheartedly may be on the way. Someone is developing greater optimism.

Late Phase: A period of enthusiasm is ending. You are less passionate now. There is less opportunity for excitement. Someone was all-in, but has lost interest.

▓

BE CONFIDENT

tackle a challenge

say "yes, I can"

believe in yourself

stretch your envelope

move beyond doubts

focus on success

know where there's a will, there's a way

Reversed

Early Phase: You may be challenged. An opportunity to be confident may arise. Someone may need to let go of doubt. A chance to be successful may present itself.

Late Phase: A confident moment is behind you. A challenging event is over. There are fewer opportunities to be successful now. Someone was able to demonstrate self-assurance.

BE COURAGEOUS

take a risk

be daring

have an adventure

avoid the sure thing

take assertive action

be a leader

overcome a fear

Reversed

Early Phase: The time for assertive action may be approaching. You may be called on to lead. An opportunity to overcome fear could present itself. An adventure is brewing.

Late Phase: Daring moves are not as necessary now. The opportunities to show courage are fading. Assertive action is not as necessary now. The chance to lead is behind you.

Description

The Page of Wands is a messenger bringing you opportunities for passion. He delivers real chances to experience creativity, courage, charm, and inspiration—the wonders of the Wands suit. In readings, this Page suggests that an opening may appear that excites you, feeds your talents, or dares you to be great. When you see such a chance, act on it!

The Page of Wands can also stand for a child or young-at-heart adult whose interactions with you involve independence, high energy, risky behavior, or shared enthusiasms. Sometimes the Page of Wands implies that your entire situation is suffused with the spirit of excitement and adventure. At such times, feel free to express your individuality and power with lighthearted abandon.

Court Card Pairs

The Page of Wands can form a pair with any other court card. Compare the ranks and suits of the two cards to see what such a pair might mean.

KNIGHT of WANDS.

KNIGHT OF WANDS

CHARMING/SUPERFICIAL
SELF-CONFIDENT/COCKY DARING/FOOLHARDY
ADVENTUROUS/RESTLESS
PASSIONATE/HOT-TEMPERED

Actions

CHARMING/SUPERFICIAL

is physically attractive/focuses on style and appearance

disarms opposition with a smile/can be thoughtless and insensitive

sexy and seductive/pursues sexual conquests

generates glamour and excitement/ avoids deep or serious matters

is honey-tongued/may say or do what's expedient

Reversed

Early Phase: You may be becoming more charming, but also more superficial. Someone who likes excitement, but not seriousness may be entering the picture. A mood of easy convincing, but also expediency may be developing.

Late Phase: You are becoming less attractive, but also less thoughtless. Someone sexy, but manipulative is leaving the picture. A mood of glamour with insensitivity is ending.

SELF-CONFIDENT/COCKY

totally lacks self-doubt/overestimates abilities

a can-do attitude/may boast and brag

is convinced of his or her talent/ exaggerates accomplishments

self-assured at all times/brash and nervy

doesn't sweat the small stuff/is sometimes presumptuous

Reversed

Early Phase: You may be becoming more self-assured, but also more brash. Someone who is can-do, but also cocky may be entering the picture. A mood of confidence, but also boasting may be developing.

Late Phase: You are becoming less self-confident, but also less nervy Someone who lacks self-doubt, but also reflection is leaving the picture. An assertive, but overly casual mood is ending.

🞘

DARING/FOOLHARDY

will risk anything without fear/is reckless and rash

will tackle what others avoid/will endanger self and others

is the first to volunteer for danger/ doesn't give danger due respect

loves being a hero/is impetuous

boldly goes where no one has gone before/is a daredevil

Reversed

Early Phase: You may be becoming more daring, but also more foolhardy. Someone who likes risk, but not being careful may be entering the picture. A heroic, but reckless mood may be developing.

Late Phase: You are becoming less bold, but also less rash. Someone who readily volunteers, but perhaps foolishly is leaving the picture. A fearless, but impetuous mood is ending.

ADVENTUROUS/RESTLESS

loves travel and new experiences/is never content to be still

seeks novelty and change/can't set down roots or make ties

makes things happen/lacks inner peace and serenity

rises to every challenge/won't stop to smell the roses

is footloose and fancy-free/must have constant stimulation

Reversed

Early Phase: You may be becoming freer, but also more footloose. Someone who likes novelty, but not serenity may be entering the picture. A mood of change, but also rootlessness may be developing.

Late Phase: You are becoming less restless, but also less fancy-free. Someone who loves travel, but can't sit still is leaving the picture. A mood of adventure, but without stability is ending.

PASSIONATE/HOT-TEMPERED

is easily roused to action/angers easily

feels strong loyalties/is too ready for a fight

feels everything powerfully/lashes out when riled

takes a vocal stand/often acts without thinking

jumps in with both feet/may have a chip on his or her shoulder

Reversed

Early Phase: You may be becoming more passionate, but also more hot-tempered. Someone who takes a stand, but without much thought may be entering the picture. A mood of action, but also irritation may be developing.

Late Phase: You are becoming less jumpy, but also less committed. Someone with powerful but angry feelings is leaving the picture. A mood of strong loyalties when riled is ending.

Description

On the positive side, the Knight of Wands is full of energy and life. He's never afraid to try something new and will reach for all the gusto he can. Others may shake their heads at his crazy stunts, but they still admire his courage and passion. He's sexy and irresistible ... always the charmer.

On the negative side, this Knight is a little too sure of himself and his abilities. He tends to be shallow and thoughtless. Don't expect a deep commitment from him. He's also reckless and irresponsible. He acts without thinking and constantly gets in trouble because of his temper.

In readings, a Knight of Wands shows that his confident, passionate style is involved in the situation as an aspect of you, someone else, or the atmosphere in general. You need to ask yourself "Is this Knight's energy helping or hurting?"

If his style is evident, then balance is needed. Is your confidence really cockiness? Are you angry and impatient all the time? Are you crazy about someone whom you know is going to break your heart? Is your company rushing into something risky with no preparation? It may be time for a change.

If this Knight's energy is missing, a dose of passion and daring may be called for. Are you in a rut? Try something new. Are you always planning every last detail? Wing it next time. Are you working too hard? Go out and have some fun. Let the Knight of Wands introduce you to his world of adventure, excitement, and risk.

Court Card Pairs

The Knight of Wands can form a pair with any other court card. Compare the ranks and suits of the two cards to see what such a pair might mean.

QUEEN OF WANDS

ATTRACTIVE
WHOLEHEARTED
ENERGETIC
CHEERFUL
SELF-ASSURED

Actions

ATTRACTIVE

is appealing and popular

creates a powerful first impression

makes friends easily

has great sex appeal

is warm and outgoing

Reversed

Early Phase: You are beginning to be more out-going and popular. Someone sexy and attractive may enter the picture. A mood of friendliness may develop.

Late Phase: You are becoming less warm and outgoing. Someone is no longer making a powerful impression. A sexy mood is less in evidence.

WHOLEHEARTED

is loaded with enthusiasm

tackles a task with total dedication

gives the utmost in any situation

is open and sincere

doesn't hold anything back

Reversed

Early Phase: You are becoming more open and sincere. Someone wholehearted may enter the picture. A mood of dedication may be developing.

Late Phase: You are becoming less dedicated. Someone is more likely to hold back. A mood of sincerity is less in evidence.

ENERGETIC

leads a busy and active life

is vigorous and strong

radiates health and vitality

has an inner vibrancy

is a natural athlete

Reversed

Early Phase: You are beginning to be more healthy and vibrant. Someone athletic may become involved. A busy, active mood may become more prevalent.

Late Phase: You are becoming less vigorous and strong. Someone is not as energetic as before. A mood of constant activity is ending.

SELF-ASSURED

quietly demonstrates self-confidence

handles any situation with aplomb

can't be easily rattled or provoked

is spontaneous and gracious in defeat

has faith in his/her abilities

Reversed

Early Phase: You are beginning to feel confident in yourself. Someone who can't be rattled may enter the picture. A mood of easy faith in abilities is developing.

Late Phase: You are becoming less self-assured. Someone who was handling the situation is leaving. A confident mood is ending.

CHEERFUL

is optimistic and upbeat

has an encouraging word for everyone

brightens whatever room he/she is in

has a warm and sunny disposition

can shake off the blues easily

Reversed

Early Phase: You are beginning to move out of the blues. Someone warm and sunny may become important. An upbeat mood may be on the horizon.

Late Phase: You are becoming less cheerful. Someone is not as encouraging as before. A bright and lively mood is less in evidence.

Description

The personality of the Queen of Wands combines the positive fire energy of the Wands suit with the inward focus of a Queen. She is the one voted most popular in her class. She is always attractive and often good-looking. Her warm smile and easygoing manner bring her lots of friends and admirers. Her energy is contagious, and her enthusiasm, total. No matter what the task, she tackles it with wholehearted dedication and commitment. Nothing gets her down. She is always upbeat and cheerful—ready to look for the positive in the situation.

Her life is full and busy, and she prefers it that way. She loves to be going and doing. She keeps up this pace because she is radiantly healthy and fit. She is often a good athlete, being naturally strong and coordinated. Although she's never arrogant, the Queen of Wands has a deep faith in her own abilities. Her quiet self-assurance comes from the knowledge that she can accomplish whatever she sets her mind to.

In readings, the Queen of Wands asks you to *think and feel* as she does. For example: Do you feel attractive? Do you believe in yourself? Are you full of energy? Can you shake off the blues? Are you gung-ho about life?

This Queen can also represent a man or woman who is like her, or an atmosphere of cheerful and confident enthusiasm. In a reading, she tells you that her special energy has meaning for you at this time. Let yourself be inspired by this Queen in whatever form she appears in your life.

Court Card Pairs

The Queen of Wands can form a pair with any other court card. Compare the ranks and suits of the two cards to see what such a pair might mean.

KING OF WANDS

CREATIVE
INSPIRING
FORCEFUL
CHARISMATIC
BOLD

Actions

CREATIVE

develops innovative projects and ideas

opens up new areas of experience

has natural artistic ability

uses self-expression for useful purposes

masterminds new strategies

is original and inventive

Reversed

Early Phase: You are beginning to be more original. Someone creative may play an important role. An innovative mood may be developing.

Late Phase: You are less willing to explore new possibilities. A strategic mastermind is not as available. A mood of "anything is possible" is ending.

INSPIRING

communicates enthusiasm

creates an atmosphere of excitement

sets an example that others want to follow

instills confidence

is a powerful, natural leader

Reversed

Early Phase: You are beginning to show leadership. Someone may begin to set an example. An exciting mood may be developing.

Late Phase: You are feeling less enthusiastic. There are fewer people who can rally support. An inspiring mood is not much in evidence.

FORCEFUL

seems to dominate the environment

has a commanding presence

is assertive when necessary

earns respect and willing compliance

carries authority naturally

Reversed

Early Phase: You are beginning to be more assertive. Someone may show up who can win respect and compliance. An authoritative mood may be developing.

Late Phase: You are less able to impact the environment. A forceful person with a powerful presence has moved away. A mood of command is not as accessible.

CHARISMATIC

is often showy and theatrical

enjoys making the gesture with flair

naturally becomes the focus of attention

magnetically attracts others

is watched, imitated, and talked about

Reversed

Early Phase: You are starting to become the focus of attention. A charismatic person may enter the picture. A dramatic mood may be developing.

Late Phase: You are less able to get people's attention. Someone is not as talked about as before. A showy and theatrical mood is less common now.

BOLD

is intrepid

is willing to take chances when the stakes are high

confronts opposition directly

dares to stand and be different

is unconcerned with what others think

has the courage of his/her convictions

Reversed

Early Phase: You are starting to show more courage. Someone bold who doesn't care what others think may become influential. An openness to risk may be developing.

Late Phase: You are less willing to stand out. A confrontational person has been appeased. A courageous mood is not much in evidence.

Description

The personality of the King of Wands is a combination of the positive fire energy of the Wands suit and the active, outward focus of a King. He is creative and never settles for old, tired approaches. He trusts his originality and allows his inspirations to take form. He's enthusiastic. He steps forward and takes the lead if the opportunity presents itself. Others follow when he shows them the way with confidence. He's forceful in pursuing his goals. He's not a quiet, passive observer unless that suits his purposes. He jumps in and creates results. He's dramatic and exciting.

This King is never a wallflower; more often the center of attention. He's bold and daring. He avoids the safe, easy route because he has the energy and assurance to take risks and win. The King of Wands has the courage of his convictions and always believes in himself.

In readings, the King of Wands asks you to take the kinds of *actions* he might take. For example: creating a masterpiece, leading the way, taking a risk, or making a splash. This King can also represent a man or woman who is acting as he does, or an atmosphere of excitement, daring, and drama. In a reading, he tells you that his special energy has meaning for you at this time. Let yourself be inspired by this King in whatever form he appears in your life.

Court Card Pairs

The King of Wands can form a pair with any other court card. Compare the ranks and suits of the two cards to see what such a pair might mean.

ACE OF CUPS

EMOTIONAL FORCE
INTUITION
INTIMACY
LOVE

Actions

USING EMOTIONAL FORCE

getting in touch with your feelings

letting your heart lead the way

empathizing with others

expressing deep feelings

responding viscerally

Reversed

Early Phase: You may have a chance to use emotional force. An opportunity to express your feelings may open up. Someone may respond strongly in the future. An emotional encounter is on the horizon.

Late Phase: The chance to use emotional force is fading. The chance to show your feelings is past. The time for passion is ending. You can no longer respond from the heart.

DEVELOPING INTUITION

trusting your inner voice

responding to messages from within

experiencing direct knowing

enhancing your psychic awareness

getting in tune with yourself

going with your gut reaction

Reversed

Early Phase: You may have a chance to be intuitive. Some time to go within may open up. An experience of direct knowing could occur. A psychic occasion is coming up.

Late Phase: The opportunity to be intuitive is fading. You're less able to go within now. Experiences of direct knowing are decreasing. Your gut reactions are no longer strong.

EXPERIENCING INTIMACY

feeling an attraction grow

falling in love

establishing a bond with another

developing a relationship

getting close to someone

going to a deeper level

Reversed

Early Phase: You may have a chance to be intimate. A moment of closeness is approaching. There's a potential for sharing in the situation. A new relationship is possible in the future.

Late Phase: The opportunity to be intimate is fading. You passed up a chance to get to know someone. The environment is less personal now. People are no longer willing to bond.

PROCEEDING WITH LOVE

expressing affection

opening yourself to others

responding with sympathy

letting your love light shine

giving to those in need

getting rid of negativity

forgiving and forgetting

Reversed

Early Phase: You may have a chance to be loving. Someone may be more open to your advances in the future. A caring gesture may become necessary. An opportunity to forgive may come your way.

Late Phase: The opportunity to be loving is fading. Your attentions are no longer welcome. A chance to show caring has passed. Togetherness is ending. An apology is not easy now.

Description

The Ace of Cups is a symbol of possibility in the area of deep feelings, intimacy, attunement, compassion, and love. In readings, it shows that a seed of emotional awareness has been planted in your life although you may not yet recognize it. When the seed sprouts, it could take almost any form. It might be an attraction, strong feeling, intuitive knowing, or sympathetic reaction. On the outside, it could be an offer, gift, opportunity, encounter, or synchronistic event.

When you see this Ace, examine your life to see how its loving energy could work for you. This card often means that love is the essence of the situation. It may or may not be romantic love. Look for ways in which you can begin to connect with others. Do you have someone to forgive, or do you want to ask for forgiveness? Can you set aside your anger and find peace? Would you like to drop your reserve and let your feelings show? The Ace of Cups tells you that this is the time.

This card also suggests inner attunement and spirituality. Cups are the suit of the heart, and this Ace stands for the direct knowing that comes from the heart. Trust what your feelings are telling you. Seek out ways to explore your consciousness and your connections with Spirit. Allow the power of your emotions to guide you in a new direction. Embrace the love that is the Ace of Cups.

Ace-Ace Pairs

An Ace-Ace pair shows that a new spirit is entering your life. It draws on the energy of the Ace of Cups—deep feelings, intimacy, attunement, compassion, love—plus one of these:

  Ace of Wands—creativity, excitement, adventure, courage, personal power
  Ace of Swords—intelligence, reason, justice, truth, clarity, perseverance
  Ace of Pentacles—prosperity, abundance, trust, security, groundedness

TWO OF CUPS

CONNECTION
TRUCE
ATTRACTION

Actions

MAKING A CONNECTION

joining with another

celebrating a marriage or union

cementing a friendship

establishing a partnership

working together

sharing

helping and being helped

seeing commonalities

Reversed

Early Phase: Connections may be forming. People may be coming together. Tentative links may be created. A marriage or other joining may be coming up. You may need to work with another person. Sharing may become an issue.

Late Phase: The connections are growing thin. There's less togetherness now. The links are dissolving. A marriage has taken place or is unraveling. Relationships are breaking up. You're no longer reaching out to someone.

CALLING A TRUCE

healing a severed relationship

bringing together opposites

letting bygones be bygones

coming to a satisfactory agreement

declaring peace

forgiving and forgetting

Reversed

Early Phase: Some peace overtures may be considered. A cease-fire may occur at some point. A truce may become possible. You're beginning to think about forgiveness. Warring parties may start coming together.

Late Phase: The truce is ending. Peaceful relationships are a thing of the past. The agreement is falling apart. Someone can't let bygones be bygones. Your ability to forgive is fading.

ACKNOWLEDGING AN ATTRACTION

recognizing a bond that is developing

accepting your preferences

letting yourself be drawn in

moving toward

feeling a positive response

Reversed

Early Phase: An attraction may be developing. A bond may be forming. Someone or something may pull you in. You may feel more positive in the future.

Late Phase: An attraction is ending. It's hard to imagine what you saw in someone. You no longer feel positive about the matter. The appeal is fading. People have lost interest.

Description

A man and a woman are gazing at each other, ready to share their cups (emotions). Here is the very picture of romantic and sexual attraction. The energy between these two is almost palpable. The Two of Cups shows the beauty and power created when two come together. In fact, the Two of Cups is the minor arcana equivalent of the Lovers in many ways.

The Two of Cups has a deeper meaning as well. Whenever two forces are drawn together, there is the potential for bonding. This card can stand for the union of any two entities—people, groups, ideas, or talents.

In readings, the Two of Cups tells you to look for connections, especially those that are one-on-one. Now is *not* the time to separate or stay apart; it's time to join with another and work as partners. If you are in conflict, look for a truce and the chance to forgive and be forgiven. If you are struggling with two choices or tendencies within yourself, seek to reconcile them.

Usually, the Two of Cups is welcome in a reading, but it can also sound a note of warning. The energy of two can be very compelling. If you have ever stood next to two people in love, you know what I'm talking about. They create between themselves a world of their own that can feel exclusionary to others. "Two's company, three's a crowd." Make sure that the tendency to pair off is not creating disharmony in your situation.

Some Possible Opposing Cards

Hermit—needing to be alone, solitude
Five of Wands—disagreement, staying apart, no peace
Four of Cups—self-absorbed, being alone
Five of Cups—broken relationship

Some Possible Reinforcing Cards

Lovers—union, marriage, connection
Temperance—connection, working together
Ten of Cups—kinship, family ties, connections

THREE OF CUPS

EXUBERANCE
FRIENDSHIP
COMMUNITY

Actions

FEELING EXUBERANT

bursting with energy

being in the flow

celebrating

overflowing with high spirits

feeling on top of the world

dancing and singing

putting yourself out there

Reversed

Early Phase: You may start to feel more energy. The mood may get lighter in the future. People may feel like celebrating one day. A joyous celebration may be approaching.

Late Phase: There's less excitement now. People are no longer exuberant. You're coming down from your high. The celebration is behind you. The dancing and singing are ending.

ENJOYING FRIENDSHIP

getting together with people you like

experiencing camaraderie

extending/receiving hospitality

sharing

finding companions

trusting others

relying on outside help

Reversed

Early Phase: There's a potential for friendship. You may get closer to an acquaintance. You may have to rely on a friend in the future. A chance to meet with friends may materialize.

Late Phase: A friendship is breaking up. You can no longer trust someone. There are fewer chances to meet with friends. Your buddies are less important to you now.

VALUING COMMUNITY

taking part in a support group

developing a team spirit or group bond

working together/ helping each other

uniting with others

discovering a common goal

Reversed

Early Phase: A community may come together. A team spirit could develop in the future. You're thinking of joining with like-minded people. There's a potential for neighbors to get closer. Help may become available.

Late Phase: The community is breaking up. People are losing sight of a common goal. Neighbors are less friendly. You're leaving a support group or team. Bonds are no longer holding.

Description

There are three cards in the tarot that focus on the group—each from a different point of view. For the Hierophant, it's the formal approach. For the Three of Pentacles, it's teamwork, and for the Three of Cups, it's emotions. What does it feel like to join with others? What is friendship and community? These are the questions answered by the Three of Cups.

On this card, we see three women dancing together in a circle. Their arms reach out to each other to connect their feelings (Cups). In many settings, women create and nurture the social glue that bonds people together. Of course, these feelings do not only relate to women.

In readings, the Three of Cups can signify a friend or the feelings of friendship. It can represent community—the network of support created when we interact or bond with others. When you see the Three of Cups, examine your attachments to the groups in your life from an emotional point of view. Consider reaching out to give or receive help. This card stands for all forms of support, including formal aid such as counseling and other social services.

The women on the Three of Cups also express joy and high spirits. Celebrations spontaneously arise when people feel connected, loved, and secure. The Three of Cups can stand for a mood or experience that makes you feel like dancing and singing.

Some Possible Opposing Cards

Hermit—being solitary withdrawing from the group
Nine of Wands—lack of trust, wariness
Three of Swords—lonely, isolated, hurting
Six of Swords—sad, depressed
Nine of Swords—anguished, joyless

Some Possible Reinforcing Cards

Hierophant—focusing on the group
Temperance—joining forces, working together
Four of Wands—excitement, high spirits, celebration
Three of Pentacles—working in a group

FOUR OF CUPS

SELF-ABSORPTION
APATHY
GOING WITHIN

Actions

BEING SELF-ABSORBED

concentrating on your own feelings

wanting for yourself

being unaware of others

giving out little

withholding affection

seeing only your point of view

ignoring gifts and blessings

Reversed

Early Phase: You're thinking of focusing on yourself. You may begin to ignore others at some point. Someone could withhold affection in the future. Your areas of concern may start narrowing.

Late Phase: You're becoming less self-absorbed. You're no longer wrapped up in yourself. Egotistical behavior is decreasing. Personal concerns are taking a back seat.

FEELING APATHETIC

passively accepting

losing interest

feeling disengaged

making little effort

finding life stale and flat

lacking motivation

feeling little desire

Reversed

Early Phase: You may lose interest. Desire may disappear in the future. Someday you may not care as much. People may get bored at some point.

Late Phase: The apathy is going away. You're no longer disengaged. The lack of desire is fading. People are not so passive now. Someone is less uncaring.

GOING WITHIN

being introspective

meditating/contemplating

dreaming/getting lost in reverie

pausing to reflect

withdrawing from involvement

losing outer awareness

Reversed

Early Phase: You may start focusing on your inner life. Meditation and reflection could become important. Someone is thinking of withdrawing in the future. Vivid dreams may occur at some point.

Late Phase: Introspection is decreasing. You're having fewer dreams and inner experiences. There's less focus within. Someone is no longer hard to reach.

Description

Those who enjoy kayaking and river sports know that there are areas of the river where the water flows in a dangerous circular motion. Instead of moving forward, it turns back on itself. In the same way, we can get stuck in *emotional* hydraulics.

The Four of Cups represents such periods of self-absorption. If you are self-absorbed, you tend to refer everything back to your own interests and desires. On this card, we see a man who is unaware of the cup being offered to him. He misses this gift because he's turned within. In readings, this card can indicate that you are wrapped up for the moment in your own world.

In some situations, you *must* focus on yourself. When life is too stressful, you need to devote time and energy to yourself. The Four of Cups can represent a positive period of self-reflection and renewal. By taking the time to go within to dream, muse, and reflect, you restore your emotional balance.

The Four of Cups is sometimes a sign of apathy—your life may seem stale and flat because you've lost interest in the activities that used to bring you pleasure. You lack motivation. At such times, the Four of Cups can show that you're stuck emotionally. You need something to focus on that will so engage your mind and heart that your path down river becomes clear.

Some Possible Opposing Cards

World—involvement, caring, taking part
Four of Wands—excitement, high energy, optimism
Two of Cups—connection, sharing with others
Eight of Pentacles—making an effort, working hard

Some Possible Reinforcing Cards

Hermit—withdrawing, being introverted
Four of Swords—contemplating, taking time alone
Six of Swords—listless, depressed

CUPS

FIVE OF CUPS

LOSS
BEREAVEMENT
REGRET

Actions

SUFFERING A LOSS

letting go of a hope

giving up the win

experiencing a setback

being defeated

having a possession taken away

saying goodbye

Reversed

Early Phase: You may experience a loss. Someone may leave in the future. A possession could become vulnerable. There's a potential for defeat. You may eventually lose hope.

Late Phase: The loss is behind you. You're dealing with a defeat. You experienced a setback. A theft has occurred. You've said your goodbyes. The letting go is ending.

FEELING BEREFT

breaking up a relationship

feeling deprived of love

longing to be reunited

grieving

feeling sorrow

Reversed

Early Phase: You could miss someone later. A loved one may depart in the future. A time of bereavement could occur. A mood of sadness may develop. You're thinking of a possible separation.

Late Phase: The period of bereavement is ending. You're no longer feeling sad. The loved one has departed. The loss of the relationship is behind you. You're feeling less deprived now.

FEELING REGRET

being disappointed by events

wanting to turn back the clock

wishing for what might have been

believing you made the wrong choice

acknowledging mistakes

Reversed

Early Phase: You may feel regret in the future. Someone may have second thoughts. An apology may become necessary. You may feel remorse someday. Tomorrow you may kick yourself.

Late Phase: You no longer feel regret. Remorse is decreasing. There's little point in crying over spilt milk. You have fewer reservations now.

Description

The Five of Cups is about loss. On this card, we see a figure draped in black and covered in grief. He so dominates the card that it is hard to look beyond him. The Five of Cups refers to that time when the pain of a loss is most acute. This man is looking only at the overturned cups in front of him. For now, he cannot acknowledge the two cups that are still standing.

In readings, the Five of Cups can alert you to the possibility of loss (great or small) and its associated emotions—sorrow, regret, denial. The loss can be tangible (money, relationship), or intangible (opportunity, reputation). You may feel discouraged by this card, but it does have a positive side. Every loss opens new possibilities for growth because every loss initiates change. But change is hard to accept. No matter how much we accept intellectually that we must go with the flow, if that flow separates us from what we love, our feelings say, "No!"

In a story from *Zen Flesh, Zen Bones,*[7] the master Hakuin is falsely accused of fathering a child. He's ruined, but he accepts his loss and takes tender care of the child for a year. Suddenly, the real father appears, and just as willingly, Hakuin yields the child to its parents, accepting *loss* again. We who are not Zen masters may not flow quite so lightly with events, but we can learn from this story. The more we struggle to keep what is gone, the more we suffer.

Some Possible Opposing Cards

Lovers—establishing a relationship
Judgement—absolving yourself releasing regret
Six of Wands—triumph, winning
Two of Cups—relationship
Nine of Cups—contentment, satisfaction

Some Possible Reinforcing Cards

Death—loss, goodbyes
Three of Swords—separation, loss of love, heartache
Six of Swords—sadness
Five of Pentacles—rejection, lack of support, loss of approval

SIX OF CUPS

GOODWILL
INNOCENCE
CHILDHOOD

Actions

EXPERIENCING GOODWILL

acting kindly or charitably

doing a good turn for another

sharing what you have

having a noble impulse

receiving a gift

feeling blessed

being well-intentioned

Reversed

Early Phase: You may feel goodwill eventually. Someone could be generous in the future. Good intentions may exist at some point. There's a potential for sharing. A gift may be forthcoming.

Late Phase: Goodwill is decreasing. You're no longer feeling accommodating. There's less compassion now. The time for gifts is past. Help is less available now.

ENJOYING INNOCENCE

feeling simple contentment

surrounding yourself with goodness

being blissfully unaware

having a clear conscience

shunning corruption

being acquitted

appreciating simple joys

Reversed

Early Phase: Innocence may be recognized. Your conscience may clear eventually. An acquittal may be approaching. Someone may be found blameless in the future.

Late Phase: The period of innocence is ending. You're no longer blissfully unaware. There's less resistance to corruption now. The desire to be good is fading. Someone was acquitted.

FOCUSING ON CHILDHOOD

being with a child or young person

feeling carefree

being taken care of

feeling nostalgic

indulging in play

having a baby

Reversed

Early Phase: A baby or child may become important. A pregnancy or birth could occur. You may get involved with children. There's a potential for play. Childhood memories may surface.

Late Phase: A pregnancy or birth has occurred. You're no longer focused on children. Playful moments are decreasing. Someone is acting less childish. A baby or child is becoming less central.

Description

In the film *Parenthood* there is a scene in which all the members of a large family come together to witness a birth. As the camera moves from person to person, we see as if for the first time the uniqueness of each one. There is a sweetness in the air that builds until we see its very embodiment—the new baby. This is the spirit of the Six of Cups.

It is a truism that there is violence, anger, and mean-spiritedness in the world. Certainly, there is enough of this, but there is also much goodwill and caring. A mother hands a drink to her child. A friend lends his car for the weekend. A worker fills in for a sick colleague. The Six of Cups is a card of simple goodness. It encourages you to be kind, generous, and forgiving.

The Six of Cups also represents innocence—a word with many shades of meaning. You can be innocent in the strictly legal sense of lack of guilt. You can be innocent of the truth—unaware of some secret. You can be lacking in deceit or corruption—innocent of ulterior motive. Finally, you can be virtuous or chaste. All these possibilities can apply to the Six of Cups.

Notice that the two figures on the Six of Cups appear to be children. Often this card represents a baby or young child. In a larger sense, it embraces all of childhood and the feelings we associate with youth (ideally!)—being carefree, playful, secure, and loved. Children are our treasure, and the special sweetness of the Six of Cups is a quality to be treasured as well.

Some Possible Opposing Cards

Devil—negativity, corruption, coveting
Nine of Wands—lack of innocence, believing the worst
Five of Swords—cynical, hostile, selfish
Seven of Swords—deceiving, manipulating
Nine of Swords—guilty

Some Possible Reinforcing Cards

Star—good will, sharing
Ten of Cups—feeling blessed, happy, joyful

CUPS

SEVEN OF CUPS

WISHFUL THINKING
OPTIONS
DISSIPATION

Actions

INDULGING IN WISHFUL THINKING

creating fantasies

dreaming

getting caught up in illusions

letting your imagination run wild

kidding yourself about the facts

building castles in the air

waiting for your ship to come in

lacking focus and commitment

avoiding putting ideas to the test

Reversed

Early Phase: Wishful thinking could become a problem. You may lose touch with the truth at some point. Illusions may develop a life of their own. A fantasy could get stronger in the future.

Late Phase: You no longer believe in the dream. The bubble has burst. Hope is fading. The fantasy is less appealing now. You've let go of the illusion.

HAVING MANY OPTIONS

being offered many alternatives

facing an array of choices

believing in limitless possibilities

looking at a wide, open field

getting to pick and choose

Reversed

Early Phase: Options may increase at some point. You could have more choices in the future. More possibilities may develop. Your vision could expand.

Late Phase: Your choices have narrowed. There are fewer options now. People can no longer pick and choose. Some possibilities have been removed. You eliminated some alternatives.

FALLING INTO DISSIPATION

overindulging

letting everything go

becoming disorganized

eating/drinking/partying to excess

neglecting your health

entering into addictive patterns

being inclined toward indolence

being lazy

procrastinating

Reversed

Early Phase: Laziness could become a problem. Loose living may start to be attractive. You could let everything go in the future. The environment could get disorganized. An addiction may develop.

Late Phase: The dissipation is ending. You're no longer overindulging. The addiction is coming under control. You're less disorganized now. The carousing is ending.

Description

As I gaze around the room right now, taking in the casual disarray, I know the Seven of Cups speaks to me—for better or worse. It says, 'Yes, order and hard work are nice, but... isn't it more fun to just let everything go?" Letting everything go is what the Seven of Cups is all about.

It's easy to worship the gods of efficiency and neatness. We like trim lawns, alphabetized filing systems, and time management—the world of the Emperor. We admire order in all its forms and want everything to be just right. The Seven of Cups provides the balance. This card stands for all that is sloppy impractical, and lax.

When the Seven of Cups appears in a reading, it is important to look carefully at how disordered your situation is. Is everything too controlled and regular? Perhaps you need to let things fall apart a little. When a rigid system breaks up, there can be a tremendous release of creativity. The man on the Seven of Cups is amazed by all the options he has.

On the other hand, if you are in a chaotic situation, some tightening may be necessary. No one is happy and productive in a crazy environment. Regularity gives structure to life. Taken to an extreme, the looseness of the Seven of Cups can lead to harmful patterns of decadence, addiction, and self-indulgence.

Sometimes the laziness applies to your thoughts and dreams. It is easy to wish for something, but not so easy to make that wish come true. When you see this card, make sure that you are backing up your plans with work and effort. Tighten up your life and commit to doing what it takes to reach your goals ... even if it means (sigh) cleaning house.

CUPS

Some Possible Opposing Cards

Magician—focus and commitment
Emperor—discipline, structure
Temperance—balance, moderation
Four of Pentacles—order, control
Eight of Pentacles—working hard, applying yourself
Nine of Pentacles—discipline, restraint, refinement

Some Possible Reinforcing Cards

Devil—overindulgence, dissipation
Moon—illusions, unrealistic ideas, fantasy
Nine of Cups—sensual excess

EIGHT OF CUPS

DEEPER MEANING
MOVING ON
WEARINESS

Actions

SEEKING DEEPER MEANING

focusing on personal truth

leaving the rat race

looking for answers

concentrating on what is important

starting on a journey of discovery

finding out the facts

devoting more time to the spiritual

Reversed

Early Phase: You may start seeking deeper meaning. A hunger for truth could develop. A journey of discovery may begin in the future. Spiritual matters could become important. The atmosphere may turn serious.

Late Phase: You're less concerned with meaning now. Honest answers no longer matter. The serious tone is disappearing. People are forgetting what's important. Your spiritual yearnings are fading.

MOVING ON

realizing the current cycle is over

abandoning a hopeless situation

disentangling yourself

starting on a trip of unknown length

letting go

finishing up and walking away

Reversed

Early Phase: You may need to move on in the future. The time to let go is approaching. Someone may decide to walk away. You're thinking of abandoning the situation.

Late Phase: Someone has moved on. You've removed yourself from the problem. A door has closed. You've said your goodbyes. A phase is ending. You no longer need to move on.

GROWING WEARY

feeling drained by demands

dragging through the day

feeling tired and listless

lacking energy

losing hope

getting weighed down by worries

becoming burned out

Reversed

Early Phase: You could become fatigued. Someone may grow tired of the situation. Worry could consume you in the future. Burnout may become an issue. A struggle may eventually wear you out.

Late Phase: Lack of energy is no longer a problem. The weight of the world has been lifted off your shoulders. You feel less tired now. The risk of burnout is ending. The mood of resignation is lifting.

Description

A psychologist friend once told me that when a group is ready to break up, the members give off subtle signs to that effect. They display a certain restlessness. They arrive late to meetings, communicate less, and seem distracted. At some level the participants know it is time to move on, but they need a while to work up to that final step.

This process applies in many situations where an ending is approaching. Nothing is permanent in life. Sooner or later, everything slips away ... or we slip away from it. The Eight of Cups stands for those moments when we realize, once and for all, that the past is gone. What was true is no longer true. The signs of change are in our face, and we must accept them. It is time to move on.

Moving on can mean a physical change such as leaving a job, location, or relationship. It can also mean an inner change—releasing old patterns, especially those that have dominated our thoughts and emotions. On the Eight of Cups, we see a man leaving on a journey. He has turned away from his old feelings (cups/river) to strike out on a new path. Sometimes moving on can mean searching for a deeper truth or reality. One day we wake up and realize that we have been asleep in our own lives—living a dream that no longer satisfies.

Some changes can be wearying. Endings are not always easy. One of the signs of a readiness to leave is lack of energy. When you feel tired and dispirited, you know that something is wrong, and it's time for a new direction. Reexamine your life and your priorities. You will find where in your life you need to move on.

Some Possible Opposing Cards

Strength—endurance, strength
Sun—vitality, high energy
Nine of Wands—hanging on, persevering

Some Possible Reinforcing Cards

Hermit—searching for deeper meaning
Death—moving on, leaving
Three of Wands—going on a trip, going into new territory
Eight of Wands—finishing up, ending a chapter
Six of Swords—moving on, going on a trip

CUPS

NINE OF CUPS

WISH FULFILLMENT
SATISFACTION
SENSUAL PLEASURE

Actions

. . . .

HAVING YOUR WISH FULFILLED

achieving what you desire

obtaining your goal

getting what you think you want

having your dream come true

Reversed

Early Phase: You may realize your heart's desire. A goal could get closer. Someone's wish may be granted in the future. A prayer may be answered.

Late Phase: The time for getting your wish is past. You're no longer focused on a dream. Achieving your goal is less important now. Your desire is fading.

. . . .

FEELING SATISFIED

indulging in a little smugness

enjoying the situation just as it is

feeling pleased as punch

getting the results you hoped for

feeling all's well with the world   ·

being contented

Reversed

Early Phase: You could become satisfied. The situation may get better. There's a potential for contentment. You may be pleased with your results in the future.

Late Phase: You're less satisfied now. The situation is no longer gratifying. Contentment is on the decline. Someone has upset the apple cart. People are not as smug as they were.

❈

ENJOYING SENSUAL PLEASURE

savoring a delicious meal

appreciating the arts

making love

relaxing

experiencing beauty and luxuries

enjoying physical exertion

Reversed

Early Phase: You could begin seeking pleasure. A chance to enjoy your senses may come up. A sexual encounter may occur. You may have more luxury in the future.

Late Phase: Your focus on pleasure is decreasing. Sensual experiences are less common. Sex is no longer as central. Surroundings are not as delightful. You can't afford to indulge at the same level.

Description

The man on the Nine of Cups reminds me of the cat who ate the canary. Any cat who manages to catch one is going to feel pretty smug about it. This is the feeling tone of the Nine of Cups—pure indulgence and self-satisfaction.

At the physical level, the Nine of Cups is a sign of delight in all the senses. This card encourages you to seek pleasure and enjoy your body in every way. You can commune with the natural world as well—the body of Mother Earth. She, too, delights in sharing her abundance.

At the personal level, the Nine of Cups indicates contentment with the way things are. Notice how the man is seated confidently with arms folded and a smile on his face. He has everything he wants. "See all my cups!" he seems to say. "Aren't they great?"

Sometimes it's wonderful to sit back and revel in the knowledge that all's right with the world. But a word of caution: you may be tempted to indulge yourself at the cost of someone else (like our mischievous cat!). This may feel great at the time, but sooner or later the feathers around your mouth will be discovered, and regret will set in.

In many tarot traditions, the Nine of Cups is known as the Wish Card. It shows your wish will come true. A wonderful prospect, but you must be sure you know what you really want and accept the responsibilities that go with your wish.

Some Possible Opposing Cards

Hermit—focusing less on the senses
Five of Cups—regret

Some Possible Reinforcing Cards

Empress—enjoying the senses
Lovers—sexual pleasure
World—achieving your heart's desire
Six of Wands—pride in self, achieving what you want
Seven of Cups—sensual excess

TEN OF CUPS

JOY
PEACE
FAMILY

Actions

FEELING JOY

embracing happiness

having a sense of well-being

radiating love

delighting in good fortune

counting your blessings

expressing delight

Reversed

Early Phase: You could feel joy. Moments of happiness may start to occur. There is potential for love. The future may be brighter. A more positive outlook could develop.

Late Phase: Your happiness is fading. There's less joy in the air. It's getting harder to count your blessings. The period of good fortune is past. Love is no longer strong.

ENJOYING PEACE

experiencing serenity

doing away with hostilities

restoring harmony

reducing stress and tension

feeling contented and at ease

calling a truce

relaxing

Reversed

Early Phase: A movement toward peace may start. An accord may become possible. Warring parties may begin talking. You may become calmer and more relaxed. Harmony may return in the future.

Late Phase: The peace is ending. The time for reconciliation has passed. There's less desire for agreement now. The tranquil mood is evaporating. You're no longer responding calmly.

LOOKING TO THE FAMILY

working for peace in the home

going on a family event

reaffirming a family commitment

supporting a relative in need

bonding with family members

forgiving someone in the family

Reversed

Early Phase: The family may come together. Family harmony may be possibile. A family matter may be resolved soon. A family celebration may be coming up.

Late Phase: Family togetherness is declining. Someone has shaken up the family. A family celebration has ended or was unable to occur. Family matters are becoming less important. You're no longer connected to your family.

Description

On the Ten of Cups we see a loving couple with their carefree children. A rainbow of cups is overhead blessing the scene. This is a symbol of what our emotional life could be at its best.

First, there is joy. Joy goes beyond happiness, contentment, enjoyment. It is the feeling that comes when we know at the deepest level that we are one with all that is, and it is good. Unfortunately, this is not exactly a common feeling! Too often we are blinded by the trials of life and overwhelmed by their challenges. Joy exists, though, and is our birthright.

Peace is another aspect of the Ten of Cups—the serenity that comes when all elements are in harmony. There is inner peace and outer peace, which are reflections of each other. When you are in harmony with yourself, you *experience* harmony in your environment. When you see the Ten of Cups, know that an end to hostility (both within and without) is possible.

In readings, this card often signals a time of abundant blessings. Look for ways to realize joy and create peace. You may find the key to happiness in your family. Your family is the group of people you are attached to emotionally—for better or worse! If there is trouble in your family right now, work to restore harmony. The time is right for greater closeness.

Some Possible Opposing Cards

Devil—lack of joy or peace
Tower—upheaval, chaos
Three of Swords—heartbreak, loneliness
Nine of Swords—anguish, sorrow, despair
Ten of Swords—in the pits, feeling victimized

Some Possible Reinforcing Cards

Lovers—family relationships, bonding
Star—joy, positive feelings, blessings
World—happiness, emotional fulfillment
Six of Cups—feeling blessed, happy, joyful

PAGE OF CUPS

BE EMOTIONAL
BE INTUITIVE
BE INTIMATE
BE LOVING

Actions

BE EMOTIONAL

be moved or touched

let your feelings show

respond to beauty

be sentimental or romantic

shed your detachment

let your heart lead the way

Reversed

Early Phase: An opportunity to be emotional may arise. Someone may let her feelings show. You may have a chance to be romantic. A time to appreciate beauty may come up.

Late Phase: You were moved by an occasion. An emotional period is behind you. Someone is less guided by the heart now. Feelings are less in evidence.

BE INTUITIVE

receive guidance from within

act on a hunch

remember your dreams

have a psychic experience

experience direct knowing

trust your gut reaction

Reversed

Early Phase: You may be called on to trust your gut. A chance to trust your intuition may arise. The opportunity to act on a hunch may be approaching. Direct knowing may become more available.

Late Phase: You are less open to inner guidance now. An intuitive impulse is behind you. A psychic experience occurred. A chance to act on a hunch is fading.

BE INTIMATE

start or renew a love affair

meet someone you're attracted to

get closer to someone

go beyond formalities

have a special moment of togetherness

solidify a friendship

share something personal

Reversed

Early Phase: An opportunity for intimacy may present itself. You may become closer to someone. A chance to be less formal may arise. Someone may have a chance to share something personal.

Late Phase: A love affair is ending. A chance to act on an attraction is behind you. Someone experienced a moment of togetherness. There are fewer opportunities to make friends now.

BE LOVING

make a thoughtful gesture

express sympathy and understanding

forgive yourself

forgive someone who has hurt you

apologize to someone you have hurt

mend a broken relationship

respond with caring rather than anger

refuse to judge or condemn

Reversed

Early Phase: You may be called on to forgive someone. An opportunity to avoid judging may present itself. A loving gesture may become possible. Someone may need to demonstrate caring.

Late Phase: The chance to mend a relationship has passed. You apologized and were forgiven. Someone reached out to you. Opportunities to love are less frequent now.

CUPS

Description

The Page of Cups is Cupid bringing you opportunities for love. He delivers real chances to experience romance, deep feelings, and the inner life—the wonders of the Cups suit. In readings, this Page suggests that an opening may appear that stirs your emotions, pulls at your heartstrings, or brings you great joy. When you see such a chance, act on it!

The Page of Cups can also stand for a child or young-at-heart adult whose interactions with you involve emotional needs, moodiness, love, intimacy, or spirituality. Sometimes the Page of Cups implies that your entire situation is suffused with the spirit of love and emotion. At such times, feel free to express and enjoy your feelings with lighthearted abandon.

Court Card Pairs

The Page of Cups can form a pair with any other court card. Compare the ranks and suits of the two cards to see what such a pair might mean.

KNIGHT OF CUPS

ROMANTIC/OVEREMOTIONAL
IMAGINATIVE/FANCIFUL
SENSITIVE/TEMPERAMENTAL
REFINED/OVERREFINED
INTROSPECTIVE/INTROVERTED

Actions

ROMANTIC/OVEREMOTIONAL

idealizes love/lacks self-restraint

emphasizes feelings/is often jealous

concentrates on the poetry of life/tends to be gushy and melodramatic

remembers special occasions/blows hot and cold in affections

expresses sentiments beautifully/brings flowers, but forgets to put gas in the car

Reversed

Early Phase: You may be becoming more romantic, but also overemotional. Someone who likes beauty, but not hard work may be entering the picture. A mood of expressed love, but also jealousy may be developing.

Late Phase: You are becoming less gushy, but also less feeling. Someone sentimental, but melodramatic is leaving the picture. A mood of emotions with little self-restraint is ending.

IMAGINATIVF/FANCIFUL

can tap the fertile unconscious/indulges in idle daydreams

looks beyond the obvious/has big ideas that come to nothing

never takes the mundane path/has an unrealistic approach

spins marvelous tales/has an overactive imagination

is visionary/can shade the truth

Reversed

Early Phase: You may be becoming more imaginative, but also more unrealistic. Someone who likes big ideas but not follow-through may be entering the picture. A dreamy but unproductive mood may be developing.

Late Phase: You are becoming less out-of-touch, but also less visionary. Someone who dreams, but without results is leaving the picture. A mood of looking within with little focus is ending.

THE BIG BOOK OF TAROT

SENSITIVE/TEMPERAMENTAL

is aware of moods and feelings/is prone to mood swings

helps others open up/can be petulant and sulky

responds deeply to life/gels melancholy and depressed

understands the pains of others/broods excessively

is tactful and diplomatic/takes offense easily

Reversed

Early Phase: You may be becoming more sensitive, but also more temperamental. Someone who is diplomatic, but also broody may be entering the picture. A mood of sympathy, but also melancholy may be developing.

Late Phase: You are becoming less sulky, but also less tactful. Someone who responds deeply, but also takes offense is leaving the picture. A mood of deep feelings, but with depression is ending.

INTROSPECTIVE/INTROVERTED

values the inner life/focuses inward to excess

tries to understand why/may avoid active participation

questions motivations/is driven to self-examination

seeks self-improvement/exaggerates personal failings

sees below the surface/can't relax around others

REFINED/OVERREFINED

appreciates beauty in all forms/leaves dirty work to others

seeks the finest/can't face unpleasantness

creates a pleasing environment/lacks robust good health

understands subtlety/emphasizes style over substance

is suave and gracious/gets overwhelmed by pressure

Reversed

Early Phase: You may be becoming more refined, but also more fragile. Someone who likes a pleasing environment, but not unpleasantness may be entering the picture. A gracious but superficial mood may be developing.

Late Phase: You are becoming less frail, but also less sensitive. Someone who loves style, but without substance is leaving the picture. A cultivated but shallow mood is ending.

Reversed

Early Phase: You may be becoming more introspective, but perhaps too much. Someone who works on self-improvement, but in a driven way may be entering the picture. A mood of reflection, but also withdrawal may be developing.

Late Phase: You are becoming less introverted, but also less self-aware. Someone who understands motivations, but avoids taking part is leaving the picture. A mood of inner focus, but in a vacuum is ending.

Description

On the positive side, the Knight of Cups is a sensitive soul. He is a poet—a lover of all things romantic and refined. He uses his imagination in wondrous ways and taps the deepest levels of emotion. He knows how to create beauty and share it with others.

On the negative side, this Knight is prone to flights of fancy and illusion. His melodramatic moods are legendary, and his emotions often get the better of him. He's too temperamental and takes offense easily. He can't stand unpleasantness and will always let others deal with it.

In readings, a Knight of Cups shows that his sensitive style is involved in the situation in some way—as an aspect of you, someone else, or the atmosphere in general. You need to ask yourself, "Is this Knight's energy helping or hurting?"

If his style is evident, then balance is needed. Are your feelings appropriate or excessive? Are your daydreams unrealistic? Is someone's moodiness driving you crazy? Is your home life ruled by emotion rather than common sense? It may be time for a change.

If this Knight's energy is missing, a dose of poetry may be called for. Are you too restrained? Express your feelings. Do you always make the most practical choice? Go for the extravagant one instead. Do you avoid introspection? Take some time to look within and think about your life. Let the Knight of Cups introduce you to his world of romance and beauty.

Court Card Pairs

The Knight of Cups can form a pair with any other court card. Compare the ranks and suits of the two cards to see what such a pair might mean.

QUEEN OF CUPS

LOVING
TENDERHEARTED
INTUITIVE
PSYCHIC
SPIRITUAL

Actions

LOVING

turns away wrath with caring

is unconditionally accepting

is sensitive to the feelings of others

dispels anger and hate

has infinite patience

Reversed

Early Phase: You are beginning to be more accepting. Someone patient and kind may enter the picture. A mood of sensitivity may be growing.

Late Phase: You care less than before. A loving person has been pushed aside. A mood of acceptance is ending.

TENDERHEARTED

is easily moved by another's pain

reacts with sensitivity and compassion

is kind and gentle with all creatures

can never turn away someone in need

feels what others are feeling

Reversed

Early Phase: You may become more tender hearted. Someone compassionate may play an important role. A sensitive mood may be developing.

Late Phase: You are less moved by another's pain. Someone is not as willing to help. A mood of concern for others is ending.

INTUITIVE

*is always tuned to emotional undercur-
rents*

senses the climate of a situation

is guided by the heart

trusts an inner sense of what is true

understands without having to be asked

Reversed

Early Phase: You are starting to be more intuitive. Someone who understands may enter the
picture. A mood of sensitivity to undercurrents
may be developing.

Late Phase: You are less able to trust your inner
voice. Someone is losing the ability to read the
climate. A mood of respect for hunches is ending.

PSYCHIC

is open to the unconscious

has a well-developed sixth sense

can have a telepathic bond with another

has a finely tuned sensibility

is a natural medium

Reversed

Early Phase: You are beginning to open to
the unconscious. A psychic or medium may
be consulted. A mood of attunement may be
developing.

Late Phase: You are becoming less focused on
inner work. A telepathic bond with someone is
breaking. A mood of appreciation for intuitive
work is ending.

SPIRITUAL

feels oneness with All That Is

has reverence for all life

finds joy in communion

appreciates the deeper meanings of life

sees the world as a holy place

Reversed

Early Phase: You are starting to appreciate the
spiritual side of life. Someone may open to a
feeling of communion. A mood of reverence
may be developing.

Late Phase: You feel less joy than before. A
religious figure may lose influence. A mood of
holiness is not much in evidence.

Description

The personality of the Queen of Cups combines the positive water energy of the Cups suit with the inward focus of a Queen. Because she has a sweet, loving, and sensitive nature, the Queen of Cups has a kind word for everyone and never reacts with anger or impatience. There is a gentleness about her that soothes and calms. Compassion is her watchword. Her reactions to the world are guided by her feelings.

In all matters, she lets her heart lead the way. She senses emotional currents and knows what others are experiencing without having to ask. She is never moody, but understands moods and their influence. She trusts her intuition and so is more open to knowledge that comes from within herself and beyond. She is often moved by the beauty and tragedy of life. The Queen of Cups feels deeply and has a reverence for all aspects of creation. Her love includes and embraces everyone and everything.

In readings, the Queen of Cups asks you to *think and feel* as she does. For example: Are you aware of the emotional climate? Are you feeling loving? Do you trust your heart? Have you received an intuitive message? Have you been moved by another's pain?

This Queen can also represent a man or woman who is like her or an atmosphere of gentle love, acceptance, and respect for feelings. In a reading, she tells you that her special energy has meaning for you at this time. Let yourself be inspired by this Queen in whatever form she appears in your life.

Court Card Pairs

The Queen of Cups can form a pair with any other court card. Compare the ranks and suits of the two cards to see what such a pair might mean.

KING OF CUPS

WISE
CALM
DIPLOMATIC
CARING
TOLERANT

Actions

WISE

gives good advice

has a deep grasp of human nature

teaches through loving attention

knows what others need for growth

sees right to the heart of the matter

understands many levels of experience

Reversed

Early Phase: You are beginning to understand your situation more deeply. Someone wise may step forward who can give good advice. A mood of loving attention may be developing.

Late Phase: You are experiencing less clarity of vision. Someone who knows what people need has left. A mood of understanding is ending.

CALM

maintains his/her composure

has a quieting influence on others

is emotionally stable and secure

keeps his/her head in a crisis

never seems nervous or tense

Reversed

Early Phase: You are beginning to regain your composure. Someone emotionally stable may play an important role. A peaceful mood may be developing.

Late Phase: You are less able to keep your head in a crisis. Someone calm with quiet influence is not as available. A mood of peace and quiet is ending.

THE BIG BOOK OF TAROT

DIPLOMATIC

can balance the needs of many people

keeps everyone working together happily

can diffuse a tense situation

achieves goals through subtle influence

says just the right word at the right time

Reversed

Early Phase: You are starting to appreciate the value of diplomacy. Someone may appear who can diffuse a tense situation. A mood of working together may be developing.

Late Phase: You are less willing to balance everyone's needs. There are fewer people who know how to convince quietly. A mood of diffusing conflict is ending.

CARING

responds to emotional needs

is a natural healer and therapist

takes action to help those in need

feels compassion for the less fortunate

does volunteer and charity work

Reversed

Early Phase: You are thinking of volunteering. A therapist may become involved. A caring mood may be developing.

Late Phase: You are feeling less compassionate now. The need for a healer is ending. A mood of attention to others is not much in evidence.

TOLERANT

has open and broad-minded views

accepts the limitations of others

is comfortable with all types of people

allows others their freedom

is patient in trying circumstances

Reversed

Early Phase: You are becoming more open to broad-minded views. Someone who allows more freedom may enter the picture. A mood of acceptance may be developing.

Late Phase: You are no longer as tolerant as before. Someone who is comfortable with people may be leaving. A mood of allowance is ending.

Description

The personality of the King of Cups is a combination of the positive water energy of the Cups suit and the active, outward focus of a King. He is wise and understanding with a deep knowledge of the world that comes from the heart. He is a teacher and way-shower who guides his students with loving attention. He cares about others sincerely and always responds to their needs with compassion. He heals with a gentle touch and a quiet word.

The King of Cups is calm and relaxed in all situations, seeming to know intuitively what is called for at any moment. Others turn to him for advice because they know he will listen attentively. There is always a peacefulness around him that others respond to. He is tolerant of all points of view and shows patience in the most trying circumstances. He gives others freedom to grow and develop in their own ways without asking anything in return.

In readings, the King of Cups asks you to take the kinds of *actions* he might take. For example: responding calmly in a crisis, using diplomacy rather than force, reaching out to help, or accepting a different point of view. This King can also represent a man or woman who acts as he does, or an atmosphere of caring, tolerance, and understanding. In a reading, he tells you that his special energy has meaning for you at this time. Let yourself be inspired by this King in whatever form he appears in your life.

Court Card Pairs

The King of Cups can form a pair with any other court card. Compare the ranks and suits of the two cards to see what such a pair might mean.

ACE OF SWORDS

MENTAL FORCE
FORTITUDE
JUSTICE
TRUTH

Actions

USING MENTAL FORCE

being objective

thinking your way through

finding out the facts

analyzing the situation

using your intellect

applying logic and reason

Reversed

Early Phase: You may have a chance to use mental force. You may be able to express your thoughts. Someone may become reasonable in the future. You may need to be more objective.

Late Phase: The opportunity to use mental force is fading. There are fewer intellectual challenges now. The chance to share your ideas is past. The time for thinking of a solution is ending. You no longer trust your analysis.

HAVING FORTITUDE

overcoming adversity

facing problems

resolving a situation

finding the strength to overcome

surmounting obstacles

being undaunted by setbacks

Reversed

Early Phase: You may have to show fortitude. Your resolve may be tested in the future. You may need to face your problems. An obstacle may be on the horizon. You may require inner strength.

Late Phase: The opportunity to show fortitude is fading. The test of your endurance is ending. The obstacle has been worked around. Setbacks are no longer a problem. The need for courage is no longer strong.

SEEKING JUSTICE

righting a wrong

championing a cause

doing what is right

establishing the truth

accepting responsibility

wanting what is fair

Reversed

Early Phase: You may get a chance to be just. You may need to focus on what's fair. You could be offered an equal shot. Someone may try to make up for a past wrong. A matter of principle may come up.

Late Phase: The opportunity to be just is fading. You can no longer correct a mistake. The support for fair play is ending. You're less focused on doing what's right. Someone has revealed bias or prejudice.

PROCEEDING WITH TRUTH

dispelling doubts

cutting through confusion

seeing through illusions

having clear understanding

being honest

finding out what is real

Reversed

Early Phase: You may have a chance to be truthful. You could decide to be honest. Someone may open up to the facts. Your sincerity may be acknowledged. A revealing encounter may be coming up.

Late Phase: The opportunity to be truthful is fading. It's not as easy to be honest now. A chance to put everything on the table has passed. People no longer want to face reality. Someone has refused to confess.

Description

The Ace of Swords is a symbol of possibility in the area of intelligence, reason, justice, truth, clarity, and fortitude. In readings, it shows that a seed of clear understanding has been planted in your life although you may not yet recognize it. When the seed sprouts, it could take almost any form. It might be a compelling idea, desire for the truth, call to justice, or a need to be honest. On the outside, it could be an offer, gift, opportunity, encounter, or synchronistic event.

Sometimes this Ace stands for a challenge that will test you in some way. Life never goes smoothly for long. Sooner or later a hurdle shows up, and the Ace of Swords can tell you when one is coming. This card is also a reminder to you to face your challenge, whatever it is, with courage, honesty, and a firm resolve. In every challenge, there is opportunity.

When you see the Ace of Swords, examine your life to see how its clean, sharp energy could work for you. Think about your problem objectively. Look for situations that are unjust or confusing and resolve to set them right. Above all else, commit to being honest and ethical. This card tells you that you do have the inner resources to overcome all obstacles and find the truth of your situation. That is the promise of the Ace of Swords.

Ace-Ace Pairs

An Ace-Ace pair shows that a new spirit is entering your life. It draws on the energy of the Ace of Swords—intelligence, reason, justice, truth, clarity, perseverance—plus one of these:

Ace of Wands—creativity, excitement, adventure, courage, personal power

Ace of Cups—deep feelings, intimacy, attunement, compassion, love

Ace of Pentacles—prosperity, abundance, trust, security, groundedness

SWORDS

TWO OF SWORDS

BLOCKED EMOTIONS
AVOIDANCE
STALEMATE

Actions

BLOCKING EMOTIONS

denying true feelings

stifling a natural response

keeping another at arm's length

hiding distress

turning a deaf ear

being defensive

maintaining your cool

Reversed

Early Phase: You may start shutting down emotionally. Your heart may become hardened. You're thinking of hiding your feelings. Walls may begin to form. Someone may become distant and cool.

Late Phase: You're unblocking your emotions. The ice is beginning to melt. Someone is less defensive now. You can no longer bottle up your feelings.

AVOIDING THE TRUTH

refusing to look at facts

pretending everything's fine

ignoring the warning signs

closing your eyes to what's going on

avoiding an unpleasantness

choosing not to know

Reversed

Early Phase: You may begin avoiding someone. Someone may start ignoring a problem. An unpleasantness may be swept under the rug. People may start pretending.

Late Phase: You can no longer avoid the situation. You've decided to stop pretending. People are less inclined to ignore the truth. It's no longer necessary to keep up a show.

BEING AT A STALEMATE

feeling afraid to act

reaching an impasse

staying stuck

refusing to decide

being unwilling to rock the boat

staying on the fence

Reversed

Early Phase: A stalemate may develop. Positions may become fixed in place. Options may begin disappearing. You may be heading toward an impasse. It may get harder to maneuver in the future.

Late Phase: The stalemate is dissolving. People are no longer fixed in their positions. There's less fear of making a move. You're less reluctant to rock the boat.

Description

On the Two of Swords, we see a young woman who has put a barrier of swords across her heart. Her rigid posture tells us of her struggle to keep her feelings under control. She is fending off any approach from the outside. "Nothing comes in, and nothing goes out," she seems to say.

The Two of Swords is about the barriers we put up between ourselves and others and those we create within ourselves. Internally, we block off emotions and refuse to feel them. We avoid looking at the truth and pretend that everything's OK. We think one way, but feel another. In countless ways, we divide off parts of ourselves and try to maintain them even when we know they need to be reconciled.

In readings, the Two of Swords often appears when you are not willing to accept some truth about yourself or the situation. What are you really feeling? Are you resisting tender feelings because you might be hurt? Are you furious even though you're smiling? What are you refusing to look at? Notice the blindfold on this woman. She can't look at the truth or even acknowledge that there is trouble.

The most common barrier is a closed heart. When we cut ourselves off emotionally, we *sever* the connection that allows our love to flow outward. Sometimes this action is necessary, but it always comes at a great price. Every time we close off our heart, we find it more difficult to open again.

Another barrier between people is a deadlocked situation. When two parties are set in their positions—*cut off* from each other—there is a stalemate. To break it, the "opponents" must come out from behind their swords and listen to each other. The lesson of the Two of Swords is that barriers are not the answer. We must stay open if we are to find peace and wholeness.

Some Possible Opposing Cards

Fool—opening up, uninhibited
Wheel of Fortune—moving, getting things going
Justice—accepting the truth, accepting responsibility
Star—free flow of positive feelings
Three of Wands—moving forward, looking at the facts

Some Possible Reinforcing Cards

Moon—self-deception, not seeing the truth
Nine of Wands—being defensive, closing yourself off
Seven of Swords—running away from the truth
Four of Pentacles—stalemate, blockage

THREE OF SWORDS

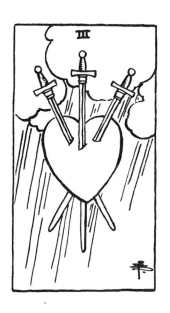

HEARTBREAK
LONELINESS
BETRAYAL

Actions

FEELING HEARTBREAK

causing heartbreak

suffering emotional pain

hurting inside

being disappointed

getting some unsettling news

having your feelings hurt

hurting someone's feelings

receiving little solace

Reversed

Early Phase: You may suffer pain in the future. You could be heading toward some heartbreak. You may begin feeling vulnerable emotionally. It's possible you could hurt someone in the future.

Late Phase: The heartbreak is behind you. The pain is dulling somewhat. You're coming to terms with your disappointment. You're no longer hurting someone.

FEELING LONELY

being separated

wandering far from home

being spurned or rejected

feeling isolated from those you love

being deserted in time of need

feeling lost

Reversed

Early Phase: You may begin feeling lonely. A time of separation may be approaching. You may decide to reject someone, or be rejected. Your friends and loved ones may start pulling away.

Late Phase: You're no longer feeling lonely. Loved ones are less distant. A separation is ending. You're putting a rejection behind you. Isolation is becoming less of a problem.

SWORDS

EXPERIENCING BETRAYAL

discovering a painful truth

finding your trust misplaced

being let down/letting someone down

getting stabbed in the back

breaking your word

turning or acting against

Reversed

Early Phase: You may begin feeling less trustful. You may be betrayed in the future. Someone may turn against you. You may start seeing signs of dishonesty. You're thinking of breaking your word or vows.

Late Phase: A betrayal has passed. The period of lying and deceit is ending. The painful revelations are behind you. You let someone down, but have resolved to mend your ways.

Description

You open the door to find your partner in the arms of someone else. You overhear your best friend laughing at you behind your back. Your business partner has been cheating you. Your world has been turned upside-down. You're stunned, disbelieving, and heartbroken.

The image on the Three of Swords clearly pictures this sudden pain. You literally feel as if someone has taken a sharp object and jabbed it through your heart. Even something as minor as a snippy remark can feel this way. Notice how this card contains just a heart and three swords. When your heart is breaking, you feel as if that is all you are—an open wound.

In readings, the Three of Swords often represents the nasty little curveballs that life can throw sometimes. Betrayal, abandonment, rejection, separation, a reversal of fortune. These hurts are painful because they hit you when you least expect them. If you have drawn this card, it is likely there is something amiss in your life that you are unaware of or unwilling to acknowledge. Curve balls hit us when we're looking the other way. Examine your situation carefully. Don't take anything for granted. Listen to your inner voice; it will help you locate the problem.

It is also possible that you are contemplating hurting someone else. With this card I think it is important to remember we're all human—we all make mistakes, sometimes serious ones. In the end, trust in the goodness of life and try to live up to that ideal. When you slip, forgive yourself, and try to forgive others in turn, but, even better, head off trouble before it arrives.

Some Possible Opposing Cards

Lovers—intimacy, feeling love

Three of Cups—companionship, trust

Ten of Cups—joy, love, peace, togetherness

Some Possible Reinforcing Cards

Five of Cups—separation, loss of love, heartache

Nine of Swords—anguish, heartbreak

Five of Pentacles—rejection, separation, lack of support

FOUR OF SWORDS

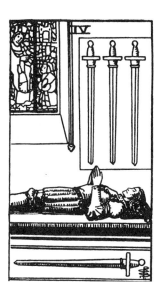

REST
CONTEMPLATION
QUIET PREPARATION

Actions

RESTING

taking a break

giving your body time to heal

avoiding overexertion

finding peace and quiet

relaxing body and soul

taking life easy

Reversed

Early Phase: The pace may start to slow. You may need to take a break soon. A rest period may be approaching. You may have an opportunity to relax.

Late Phase: Your break period is ending. Your recovery is almost complete. The pace is no longer slow. Moments of peace and quiet are less frequent now.

CONTEMPLATING

gaining a better perspective

listening for your inner voice

taking time alone to think

standing back from the situation

examining your motivations

reviewing where you are

Reversed

Early Phase: A time for reflection may be approaching. You may need to stop and think things over. You could withdraw from the action for a time.

Late Phase: A period of contemplation is ending. You no longer need time alone to think. Your meditation is coming to an end. The thoughtful moments are decreasing.

SWORDS

··

QUIETLY PREPARING

consolidating inner resources

making sure your base is secure

getting ready for the future

coming to terms with what is

tying up loose ends

stabilizing

Reversed

Early Phase: You may begin preparations. Someone may be getting ready behind the scenes. You may need to secure your base in the future. Planning may become vital.

Late Phase: The preparation phase is over. You no longer need to secure the situation. You did what you needed to do. There's less focus on planning now.

Description

The Swords cards all stand for trials of some kind, but the Four suggests feelings of peace and stillness. Why is this card different? Because it represents the challenge to be quiet! Sometimes resting and doing nothing are the ultimate challenge. Activity can be a habit that is very difficult to break. There is always so much to do, and modem society beguiles us with its attractions and distractions. The result is that we forget to stop and be still.

In readings, the Four of Swords is often a sign that you need to slow down and get some rest. If you are recovering from an illness, allow yourself quiet time to heal. Even if you feel healthy, you are risking getting sick if you don't take a break.

The Four of Swords also represents taking time to think things over without hurry. It is important to step back and gain perspective. This is especially true when you are facing an ordeal or big event. You need quiet preparation time to gather your strength and center your energy. Picture an Olympic diver on the high board. She doesn't climb the ladder and then dash out. She stops, motionless as she readies herself for the burst of activity to come. This is the only way to bring the best to our endeavors.

Sometimes the Four of Swords implies that you are or could be shifting focus from the external to the internal. When we are silent, we can more easily go within. The knight in the picture appears to be praying or meditating deeply. Actually, he appears to be dead! For those who are addicted to activity, rest and quiet can seem like death, but that is certainly not the case. Stillness has its own rewards, but they must be recognized and sought.

Some Possible Opposing Cards

Magician—being active, focusing outward
Wheel of Fortune—rapid pace, lots of movement
Eight of Wands—making your move, rushing
Ten of Wands—overexerting, taking on too much
Two of Pentacles—having fun, balancing many activities

Some Possible Reinforcing Cards

High Priestess — resting quietly, contemplating
Hermit — contemplating, being quiet
Hanged Man — rest, suspended activity
Four of Cups — contemplating, taking time alone
Six of Swords — rest, recovery
Seven of Pentacles — pausing to reflect, assess

FIVE OF SWORDS

SELF-INTEREST
DISCORD
OPEN DISHONOR

Actions

ACTING IN YOUR OWN SELF-INTEREST

setting aside the concerns of others

looking out for number one

thinking of your own needs

knowing you must concentrate on yourself

encountering selfishness

indulging in power plays

gloating

going for the win-lose result

Reversed

Early Phase: You may need to put yourself first. Selfishness may become more obvious. Someone may initiate a power play. A dog-eat-dog environment may develop.

Late Phase: There's less selfishness now. People are no longer self-absorbed. The blatant power plays are ending. The "me-first" mood is decreasing.

EXPERIENCING DISCORD

being in a hostile environment

feeling people are set against each other

choosing to battle

having an "us-against-them" mentality

recognizing ill will

experiencing conflict

Reversed

Early Phase: The fighting may resume. A mood of ill will may develop. The environment could get nasty. A battle may be brewing. You could become angry and out of sorts. People may start to take sides.

Late Phase: The conflict is ending. The environment is no longer openly hostile. The ill will is fading. There's less anger and shouting. The biggest battle is behind you.

THE BIG BOOK OF TAROT

WITNESSING OPEN DISHONOR

losing your moral compass

letting ends justify means

sacrificing integrity

losing sight of what is right

achieving a dubious victory

knowing of criminal activity

Reversed

Early Phase: You may begin losing your moral compass. You're thinking of an illegal or unsavory act. Criminal activity may be exposed in the future. A test of integrity may be approaching. You could be tempted to take the low road.

Late Phase: A test of your integrity is behind you. Obvious dishonors are decreasing. You're no longer tempted to cheat. Criminal activity is in the past. The unsavory atmosphere is fading.

Description

The Five of Swords is about self-interest. Society tells us to think of others, yet we resist. How can we ignore our own concerns and still survive? This dilemma comes from our definition of self. If we view our self as our personality/body, our interests become those that relate to that self. Do I have enough to eat? Am I happy? Do I have all I want?

We are connected to everyone in the long run. In truth, our self *is* the world. What we do to that world, we do to ourselves. This is so basic, but so easy to forget day to day.

In readings, the Five of Swords can mean that you or someone else is forgetting this larger view of self. You are defining your interests too narrowly. Sometimes this card implies a *need* to put your own interests first. If you are being abused or taken advantage of, you must get free. If you are worn out by demands, take care of yourself. If it is your turn, step forward. Just be aware that if you hurt others in the process, your victory will not feel complete.

The Five of Swords also represents hostility—from a cross word to warfare. When the cords that bind us are broken, we experience dis-cord. This card can signify dishonors that are fairly open. Cheats, lies, tricks, even crimes. You may be on the receiving end or the perpetrator. Either way, hold to a larger view of who you are. Find the solution that is best for everyone.

Some Possible Opposing Cards

Emperor—following the rules, obeying the law
Justice—having integrity, doing what is right
Temperance—working with others, harmony, cooperation
Six of Cups—innocent, well-intentioned, kind

Some Possible Reinforcing Cards

Five of Wands—discord, people set against each other
Seven of Wands—"me-against-them" mentality conflict
Seven of Swords—dishonor, separation from others

SWORDS

SIX OF SWORDS

THE BLUES
RECOVERY
TRAVEL

Actions

FEELING THE BLUES

experiencing a low-level sadness

just keeping your head above water

working to get through the day

feeling somewhat depressed

avoiding the lows, but also the highs

feeling listless

functioning, but not much more

Reversed

Early Phase: You may become depressed. You may be heading toward a low period. Life may begin losing its sparkle. You may need to face your sadness.

Late Phase: You're no longer sad. The mood of depression is lifting. You're putting the blues behind you. Your energy is returning. You're no longer discouraged.

RECOVERING

dealing with the effects of trauma

getting over a tough time

picking up the pieces

starting to cope

beginning to get your health back

heading toward a more positive place

feeling hope again

Reversed

Early Phase: A time of healing may be approaching. You may have to focus on recovery. The after effects may become noticeable. You may begin mending.

Late Phase: The recovery period is ending. The healing process is behind you. The shock of the trauma is no longer as severe. Your convalescence is coming to an end.

TRAVELING

changing location

moving from one place to another

taking a trip

experiencing a change of scene

being uprooted

going on a journey

entering into a new frame of mind

Reversed

Early Phase: You may have to leave on a trip. Someone may be planning a move. A change of scene may be coming up. An opportunity to travel may materialize. An inner journey may start.

Late Phase: You're returning from a trip. A move is behind you. You've taken an inner journey. A change of scene has been nearly completed. Travel is less likely now.

Description

At one point in *The Pilgrim's Progress,* the hero Christian (who is also on a Fool's Journey) becomes mired in the Slough of Despond. He struggles for a time until drawn out by Help. Help tells him that . . . "many fears, and doubts, and discouraging apprehensions . . . settle in this place."[8]

The Slough of Despond is a good name for the Six of Swords. Sometimes this card represents a dull, listless state. Nothing is seriously wrong, but nothing is really right either. You're getting by, but not thriving. In the picture, the figures in the boat seem sad and disengaged. Life is indeed uninteresting when we feel the blues.

In a more positive vein, the Six of Swords can indicate recovery. This is especially true when you have just experienced a tough time or psychological blow. During the crisis, you felt numb and disconnected; nothing mattered at all. Now you are beginning to heal and pick up the pieces of your life. The travelers in our boat are at least moving forward. They are headed toward a new place, even if they are not yet ready to eagerly embrace those shores.

In fact, the Six of Swords can indicate travel and moves of all kinds. This could mean an actual change of scene, relocation, or trip, but not necessarily. A journey can also take place on the inner planes as we move from one frame of mind to another.

Although the Six of Swords does not promise great joy, it also avoids the depths of despair. A slough is not a bottomless pit, but simply a hollow or depression. When you see this card, know that even though the situation is not ideal, you are moving toward a more positive place. Change is in the air, and new, more hopeful conditions lie ahead.

Some Possible Opposing Cards

Strength—having heart, unshakable resolve
Sun—vitality, enthusiasm
Four of Wands—excitement, celebration
Three of Cups—high spirits, exuberance
Two of Pentacles—fun

Some Possible Reinforcing Cards

Ten of Wands—getting by, struggling along
Four of Cups—feeling listless, depressed, uncaring
Five of Cups—sadness
Eight of Cups—moving on, going on a trip
Four of Swords—rest, recovery
Nine of Swords—depression, sadness

SEVEN OF SWORDS

RUNNING AWAY
LONE-WOLF STYLE
HIDDEN DISHONOR

Actions

RUNNING AWAY

shirking responsibility

sneaking off

leaving

avoiding obligations

being afraid to face the music

taking the easy way out

hiding from the truth

procrastinating

Reversed

Early Phase: You're thinking about leaving. You may shirk a responsibility. Someone may try to sneak off. You may want to run away at some point.

Late Phase: You're no longer running away. The desire to escape is not so strong. There's less procrastination. Avoidance is decreasing.

BEING A LONE WOLF

feeling you don't need anyone else

wanting independence

deciding not to help

keeping something to yourself

preferring solitude

staying aloof

wanting to go it alone

holding people at arm's length

Reversed

Early Phase: You may need to be alone in the future. You're thinking of going solo. People may drift apart. A mood of alienation may develop. Independence may become attractive.

Late Phase: The lone wolf is rejoining the pack. People are no longer acting in isolation. Your desire for independence is fading. The need to stay apart is ending. Independent action is less acceptable now.

CHOOSING HIDDEN DISHONOR

deceiving or being deceived

covering your tracks

maneuvering behind the scenes

being two-faced

seeing others take the rap

avoiding a shameful secret

lying or stealing

Reversed

Early Phase: You're thinking of doing something unworthy. You may head down a slippery slope. Someone may lie or cheat in the future. A crime or unpleasantness may be covered up.

Late Phase: Dishonorable acts are decreasing. You're extricating yourself from a dubious situation. You no longer want to live without integrity. You're putting the lies and cheating behind you. A shady past is less important now.

Description

The Seven of Swords is tied to the Five of Swords because both involve separation from others. On the Seven we see a man tiptoeing away from society (the colorful pavilions). He's taken some swords and seems rather pleased with his successful heist. He gives the impression of having secret, solitary plans.

This card sometimes represents the "lone-wolf" style—the desire to run lone and free. In films, the lone-wolf hero always acts totally on his own. He discovers, investigates, and solves every problem using only his own wits and resources. He believes he's successful because he ignores the fumbling efforts of ordinary people.

In readings, the Seven of Swords can be a sign that you or someone else wants to be a lone wolf. You feel that you will be more effective and comfortable on your own. This approach is useful when you need to bypass an ineffectual group or assert your independence, but it can also be troubling. We can't be happy and productive for long without some commitment to others. If you feel inclined to act alone, make sure this isolation is really working for you.

Sometimes the Seven of Swords means that you are running from something—commitment, responsibility, hard work, love. You may be procrastinating, letting problems slip because you don't want to deal with them. Sometimes we just have to face what has to be faced. The Seven of Swords lets you know when you are making things worse for yourself and others by running away.

The Seven of Swords can also indicate a hidden dishonor—a choice you or another has made that does not do justice to the highest. We all make wrong choices that we want to hide. Some of these are minor, some serious. Your inner voice will tell you when this is happening. When you see the Seven of Swords, take a good look at what you're doing because hidden dishonors will eat away at your happiness and self-respect.

Some Possible Opposing Cards

Hierophant—working within the group
Justice—accepting responsibility, being above board
Ten of Wands—meeting obligations, being responsible
Six of Cups—innocent, kind, open, noble

Some Possible Reinforcing Cards

Hermit—being alone, staying away from others
Two of Swords—avoiding the truth
Five of Swords—dishonor, separation from others
Nine of Pentacles—relying on yourself, acting on your own

EIGHT OF SWORDS

RESTRICTION
CONFUSION
POWERLESSNESS

Actions

FEELING RESTRICTED

being fenced in by obstacles

staying in a limited situation

feeling trapped by circumstances

experiencing few options

being blind to freedom

feeling persecuted

Reversed

Early Phase: You may start feeling hemmed in. Restrictions may be put in place. There may be fewer choices in the future. Oppression may become a problem. The walls may begin closing in.

Late Phase: Restrictions are decreasing. You're feeling less confined. There are fewer obstacles in your way now. Oppression is ending. Freedom no longer seems impossible.

FEELING CONFUSED

being unsure which way to turn

feeling at a loss

lacking direction

feeling overwhelmed

floundering around

needing guidance and clarity

not understanding what is happening

Reversed

Early Phase: You may become uncertain. Confusion may increase. People could start floundering and lose purpose. Mixed messages may be sent at some point.

Late Phase: There's less uncertainty now. You no longer feel so overwhelmed. The period of confusion is behind you. Lack of direction is ceasing to be a problem.

FEELING POWERLESS

waiting for outside rescue

doubting anything you do will help

avoiding responsibility

feeling victimized

accepting inaction

Reversed

Early Phase: You may lose power. Weakness could become a problem. People may start feeling vulnerable. Someone may become feeble or incapacitated.

Late Phase: You're no longer feeling like a victim. Doubts about your power are almost gone. Feelings of helplessness are fading. People are no longer immobilized.

Description

The woman on the Eight of Swords is lost and alone. She can't see because she is blindfolded. She can't reach out because she is bound. She can't move freely because she is caught in a prison of swords. It seems she has wandered far from home—her place of security is away on the hill. How can she get back? The Eight of Swords stands for those times when we feel lost, confused, and powerless. Help and relief seem very far away.

Sometimes we feel restricted by circumstances. We wake up one day in an impossible situation. A dead end job. A troubled relationship. Mountains of debt. How did this happen? We have no idea. Even little problems can make us feel trapped. There just doesn't seem to be a way out. Other times life seems fine—on the surface. "I have everything I want. I should be happy, so what's the problem?" We just don't know. We're confused and unsure.

In readings, the Eight of Swords is often a sign that you are heading toward (or already in) a situation in which you will feel a lack of freedom and choice. Such situations are tricky because the more you get into them, the more restricted you feel.

When you see this card, remember that you do have choices, and you do have power. No matter how trapped you feel, you can find a way out if you believe it is possible. Wriggle free, tear off the blindfold, and kick down those swords. Solutions are not always easy, but they exist.

Some Possible Opposing Cards

Magician—feeling powerful, knowing what's going on
Chariot—self-confidence, focus
Two of Wands—power, boldness
Four of Wands—freedom, lack of restriction
Three of Pentacles—competence, know-how, planning

Some Possible Reinforcing Cards

Devil—confusion, restriction
Moon—confusion, lack of clarity
Ten of Swords—victim mentality, powerlessness

NINE OF SWORDS

WORRY
GUILT
ANGUISH

Actions

WORRYING

doubting all will go well

brooding

making yourself sick over your troubles

going over and over an issue

feeling anxious and tense

getting all worked up

Reversed

Early Phase: You may begin worrying. Some problems may preoccupy you in the future. You may have trouble sleeping. People could become apprehensive. Some anxious moments may be coming up.

Late Phase: You're worrying less now. The situation no longer seems troubling. Anxious moments are decreasing. Everyone seems less upset.

FEELING GUILTY

regretting some offense

refusing to forgive yourself

wanting to turn back the clock

focusing on your "sins"

being hard on yourself

denying that you did your best

getting overwhelmed by remorse

Reversed

Early Phase: You may feel guilty. You may have trouble forgiving yourself. Feelings of remorse may develop. You could experience regret in the future. Someone may be found guilty.

Late Phase: The guilt is decreasing. You're no longer being hard on yourself. There's less cause for regret now. The time for remorse is ending. A guilty verdict has been declared.

. . . .

SUFFERING ANGUISH

despairing/feeling depressed

feeling you've reached your limits

having sleepless nights

going through a dark night of the soul

forgetting joy/wanting to cry

Reversed

Early Phase: You may begin to despair. You may start crying more often. Painful memories could begin to surface. Someone may become depressed. The mood may get darker.

Late Phase: The anguish is fading. The dark times are behind you. The depression is lifting. You've been through a dark night of the soul.

Description

It makes sense that the figure on the Nine of Swords is in bed—it is during the night that our griefs and regrets come to mind most intensely. Who has not lain awake at 4 a.m. filled with worries that refuse to go away?

Unlike the pain of the Three of Swords, which *seems* to come from without, the Nine of Swords represents the pain we generate from within when our fears and doubts overwhelm us. Worry is probably the most common. Will everything work out OK? What am I going to do? The thoughts go around and around—impossible to turn off.

Guilt is another source of pain. Whether guilt comes from something we've done or not done, the distress can be very real. Finally, there is just pure anguish. Sometimes the pain of life is so total that we just feel like crying into our hands.

Needless to say, the Nine of Swords is not the most pleasant of cards, but it doesn't always indicate major distress. Often it is just a sign of some element of unhappiness or trouble—a vulnerable spot in your life. This card is often a warning from your Inner Guide that the path you are going down may be a difficult one. If you approach the Nine of Swords in this spirit—as a caution sign—you will be able to use it constructively. Examine your situation carefully—even a small change can make all the difference.

Some Possible Opposing Cards

Star—serenity, peace of mind
Judgement—lack of guilt, absolution
Three of Cups—being on top of the world, in the flow
Six of Cups—innocence
Ten of Cups—joy, peace, delight

Some Possible Reinforcing Cards

Devil—despair, lack of joy
Ten of Wands—worrying
Three of Swords—anguish, heartbreak
Six of Swords—depression, sadness

SWORDS

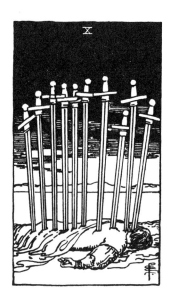

TEN OF SWORDS

BOTTOMING OUT
VICTIM MENTALITY
MARTYRDOM

Actions

BOTTOMING OUT

having nowhere to go but up

knowing it's darkest before the dawn

being at the lowest point

feeling things can't possibly get worse

preparing for an upturn

reaching the pits

Reversed

Early Phase: A low period may be developing. Events may start going from bad to worse. You may enter a downward spiral. There may be some backsliding in the future.

Late Phase: The lowest point is behind you. You weathered the storm, and now the skies are clearing. You hit rock bottom, but managed to pull through. The discouraging signs are fading.

FEELING LIKE A VICTIM

bemoaning your fate

feeling powerless

seeing life as hostile

suffering from an attack

wondering "Why me?"

feeling self-pity

being on the receiving end

Reversed

Early Phase: You may begin feeling like a victim. Someone may start indulging in self-pity. Attacks may become more frequent. You may suspect someone is targeting you. The victim role may become more central.

Late Phase: The situation seems less threatening. The attacks are decreasing. You're no longer on the receiving end. The period of powerlessness is ending.

BEING A MARTYR

putting your own interests last

being self-deprecating

feeling like a doormat

taking a back seat

letting others go first

sacrificing

Reversed

Early Phase: You may start feeling like a door-mat. Others could begin taking advantage. You may need to sacrifice in the future. Someone may be martyred for a principle. A mood of resignation may set in.

Late Phase: The martyr role is fading. You no longer need to put others first. The time of sacrifice is ending. There's less need to take a back seat now. The ordeal of suffering is behind you.

Description

The Ten of Swords appears to be a card of terrible misfortune, but surprisingly, it often represents troubles that are more melodramatic than real. The man on this card has quite a few swords in his back. Wouldn't one be enough? Isn't ten a little excessive? Perhaps this gentleman's suffering—though sincere—is exaggerated as well.

One meaning of the Ten of Swords is hitting rock bottom. When one disaster follows another, we feel devastated at first, but eventually we throw our hands up and laugh. It's so bad, it's funny! In films, the hero says, "What else could possibly go wrong?" and we know that's a signal for the bucket of water to fall on his head. When you see the Ten of Swords, know that the last bucket has fallen, and you can expect a turn for the better.

This card can also show when you're in victim mentality. You're certain that the whole world is picking on you just to make your life difficult. I picture the man lifting his head and saying, "You think you've got it bad . . . a cut on the finger. I've got ten swords in my back . . . count 'em—ten! Then he drops his head back down with a sigh. When we're in victim mentality, we think everything is horrible, hopeless, and impossibly unfair.

Being a martyr is also a favorite Ten of Swords activity. In this case, the man would say with a weak wave of his hand, "No ... you go on. Have fun. Don't think about me. I'll just stay here with these swords in my back ... but I want you to enjoy yourself." Being a martyr in this sense is not the same as making a sacrifice for another with no strings attached. With the Ten of Swords, either is possible, but doing a good turn for someone else is more satisfying without the strings.

I don't mean to make light of misfortunes because, of course, there are many real tragedies in the world. Sometimes the Ten of Swords indicates a sad event, but you know when this is the case. There is not even a hint of laughter in your heart. Most of the time the Ten of Swords has a lighter side. It is as if your Inner Guide is gently kidding you about how you are handling your own personal tale of woe. When you see the Ten of Swords, check your attitude and know you've reached the point where things will definitely begin to look up.

SWORDS

Some Possible Opposing Cards

Chariot—self-assertion, power, victory
Two of Wands—power, self-confidence
Six of Wands—self-promotion, being on top of the world
Nine of Cups—satisfaction, happy with conditions

Some Possible Reinforcing Cards

Hanged Man—sacrifice, martyrdom
Eight of Swords—victim mentality, powerlessness

PAGE OF SWORDS

USE YOUR MIND
BE TRUTHFUL
BE JUST
HAVE FORTITUDE

Actions

USE YOUR MIND

analyze the problem

use logic and reason

reexamine beliefs

develop an idea or plan

study or research the facts

learn or teach

think everything through

Reversed

Early Phase: An analytic approach may become necessary. An opportunity to learn or teach may develop. Someone may need to reexamine beliefs. A period of reflection may be approaching.

Late Phase: People are no longer being reasonable. A chance to develop a plan has passed. You are less likely to think things through now. A period of study and research is fading.

BE TRUTHFUL

act honestly

face the facts

stop deceiving

clear up any confusion

expose what is hidden

speak directly

Reversed

Early Phase: Something hidden may be exposed. The need to speak clearly may be called for. You may have a chance to be truthful. The time to face facts is approaching.

Late Phase: The confusion is less now. A chance to be honest is behind you. The need for deception is ending. A secret was revealed.

BE JUST

right a wrong

act ethically

treat others equally

champion a cause

try to be fair

accept responsibility

acknowledge the other point of view

Reversed

Early Phase: An opportunity to right a wrong may present itself. A chance to be fair is possible. You may be called on to do what is right. Someone may face justice.

Late Phase: An equitable solution is behind you. Ethical behavior is fading. A worthy cause has been addressed. The chance for a just resolution is ending.

HAVE FORTITUDE

face problems squarely

refuse to be discouraged

meet setbacks with renewed energy

keep a firm resolve

move out of depression

keep your chin up and head high

keep trying

Reversed

Early Phase: You may be called on to show resolve. Someone may become more encouraged. A time of facing setbacks is approaching. A chance to show fortitude may develop.

Late Phase: Resolve is fading. The ability to keep trying is ending. You faced a problem squarely. There are fewer setbacks now.

Description

The Page of Swords is a messenger bringing you challenges. He suggests that an opportunity for growth may come your way in the guise of a problem or dilemma. These challenges may not be your favorites. In fact, you probably will want to say "Thanks ... but no thanks."

The Page of Swords asks you to embrace these difficult situations. Think of them as trials designed to test your mettle. If you accept and prevail, you will become stronger and more resilient. In meeting these challenges, you are encouraged to use the tools of the Swords suit—honesty, reason, integrity, and fortitude.

The Page of Swords can also stand for a child or young-at-heart adult whose interactions with you involve truthfulness, ethical behavior, discouragement, or matters of the mind. This relationship is likely to be troubled or difficult in keeping with the challenges of the Swords suit.

Sometimes the Page of Swords implies that your entire situation is one suffused with the spirit of learning, discovery, and mental activities of all kinds. At such times, use your mind and enjoy the delights of the intellect.

Court Card Pairs

The Page of Swords can form a pair with any other court card. Compare the ranks and suits of the two cards to see what such a pair might mean.

KNIGHT OF SWORDS

KNIGHT of SWORDS.

DIRECT/BLUNT
AUTHORITATIVE/OVERBEARING
INCISIVE/CUTTING
KNOWLEDGEABLE/OPINIONATED
LOGICAL/UNFEELING

Actions

DIRECT/BLUNT

frank and outspoken/tactless and rude

gets straight to the point/may have a brusque manner

does not mince words/does not spare the feelings of others

tells others where they stand/can't hold his or her tongue

gives an honest answer/shows little discretion

Reversed

Early Phase: You may be becoming more direct, but also more indiscreet. Someone who is outspoken, but without subtlety may be entering the picture. A frank but tactless mood may be developing.

Late Phase: You are becoming less unfeeling, but also less honest. Someone candid, but rude is leaving the picture. A mood of telling it like it is, but without sensitivity is ending.

AUTHORITATIVE/OVERBEARING

speaks with assurance/tends to be domineering

commands attention/forces a position on others

acts with total certainty/expects immediate compliance

gives orders naturally/does not welcome dissent

has great influence/acts high-handedly

Reversed

Early Phase: You may be becoming more authoritative, but also more domineering. Someone who likes to give orders, but without dissent may be entering the picture. A mood of certainty, but without questioning may be developing.

Late Phase: You are becoming less overbearing, but also less influential. Someone clearly in charge, but also bossy is leaving the picture. A forceful but imperious mood is ending.

INCISIVE/CUTTING

has a keen, forceful intellect/is prone to biting sarcasm

penetrates to the core/lacks sensitivity

expresses ideas succinctly/can be critical

is sharp and alert/has a barbed wit

debates well/derides stupidity

Reversed

Early Phase: You may be becoming more incisive, but also more critical. Someone who wins arguments, but not kindly may be entering the picture. A sharp but unforgiving mood may be developing.

Late Phase: You are becoming less insensitive, but also less forceful. Someone witty, but sarcastic is leaving the picture. A penetrating but also cutting mood is ending.

LOGICAL/UNFEELING

reasons clearly/undervalues intuition

analyzes information well/treats people like numbers

concentrates on what is correct/doesn't temper justice with mercy

can set aside emotional factors/is cut off from emotions

makes sense out of confusion/is cold and aloof

KNOWLEDGEABLE/OPINIONATED

knows what he or she is talking about/ believes he or she is always right

can expound on any topic/intolerant of other viewpoints

sought as an expert/must have last word

has well-reasoned positions/is arrogant

is highly intelligent/can be dogmatic and close-minded

Reversed

Early Phase: You may be becoming more knowledgeable, but also more opinionated. Someone who is highly intelligent, but arrogant may be entering the picture. An informed but close-minded mood may be developing.

Late Phase: You are becoming less dogmatic, but also less well-reasoned. An educated know-it-all is leaving the picture. A mood of expertise without tolerance is ending.

Reversed

Early Phase: You may be becoming more logical, but also more unfeeling. Someone who likes working with facts, but not with people may be entering the picture. A mood of reason, but without intuition may be developing.

Late Phase: You are becoming less aloof, but also less objective. Someone analytical, but cold is leaving the picture. A clear-thinking, but hardhearted mood is ending.

Description

On the positive side, the Knight of Swords is a master of logic and reason. He has a keen intellect that grasps the fine points of any subject. He speaks clearly, directly, and always with authority. His judgments are sure and free of emotion. Others rely on his lucid analyses of problems and solutions.

On the negative side, this Knight is not a master of diplomacy. He can be downright tactless and rude. When he thinks you are wrong, you'll know it. He's convinced of his own superiority and has little tolerance for stupidity. He expects others to comply with his views. To him, feelings are irrelevant and illogical.

In readings, a Knight of Swords shows that his penetrating style is involved in the situation as an aspect of you, someone else, or the atmosphere in general. You need to ask yourself, 'Is this Knight's energy helping or hurting?"

If his style is evident, then balance is needed. Are you always forcing your position on others? Do you get in trouble for saying what you think? Is your partner too cold and aloof? Do your colleagues tend to be critical rather than supportive? It may be time for a change.

If this Knight's energy is missing, a dose of clear-sightedness may be called for. Are you too emotional? Let your head rule your heart next time. Do you overvalue the opinions of others? Trust your own authority. Are you afraid to offend? Speak your mind. Let the Knight of Swords introduce you to his world of reason and self-assurance.

Court Card Pairs

The Knight of Swords can form a pair with any other court card. Compare the ranks and suits of the two cards to see what such a pair might mean.

QUEEN OF SWORDS

HONEST
ASTUTE
FORTHRIGHT
WITTY
EXPERIENCED

Actions

HONEST

faces the truth, even if unpleasant

is upfront with everyone

likes everything on the table

plays by the rules

avoids lies and deception

Reversed

Early Phase: You are thinking about being more honest. Someone who plays by the rules may become involved. A truthful mood may be developing.

Late Phase: You are less willing to face the truth. Someone who is a straight-shooter may become important. A mood of openness is ending.

ASTUTE

sizes up a situation quickly

understands hidden motives and desires

is difficult to fool, trick, or con

figures out the unspoken rules and agendas

is quick on the uptake

Reversed

Early Phase: You are becoming more astute. Someone quick on the uptake may be called in. A savvy mood may be developing.

Late Phase: You are losing touch with the hidden agendas. A shrewd person has been removed. A mood of dirty tricks is ending.

FORTHRIGHT

is direct and open in all dealings

gets to the heart of the matter

acts without pretense or guile

is straightforward and no-nonsense

can be candid when necessary

Reversed

Early Phase: You are becoming more candid and open. A no-nonsense individual may play a role. A straightforward mood may be developing.

Late Phase: You are less willing to be forthright. A guileless person has been removed. A mood of transparency is ending.

WITTY

has a delightful sense of humor

diffuses awkward situations with a funny remark

never takes anything too seriously

laughs at everything, including him- or herself

Reversed

Early Phase: You are beginning to display your sense of humor. Someone witty who likes to joke may enter the picture. A mood of fun may be developing.

Late Phase: You are less willing to joke around. A fun-loving companion is no longer close. A mood of lightheartedness is ending.

EXPERIENCED

has seen and done it all

has strength due to life's hard knocks

is free of self-righteous judgments

has realistic expectations

Reversed

Early Phase: You are becoming more experienced. Someone who knows the ropes is in the wings. A mood of realistic expectations is developing.

Late Phase: You are losing faith in your skills. An old hand has been shown the door. A tough-minded mood is ending.

Description

The personality of the Queen of Swords combines the positive air energy of the Swords suit with the inward focus of a Queen. You can always count on her to tell you exactly how it is. Above all else she admires honesty, and she lives by her commitment to being truthful. Lies, tricks, and games are of no interest to her, but she's not easy to fool. She is experienced in the ways of the world, good and bad.

The Queen of Swords can size up a situation quickly. She understands human folly, but doesn't condemn it. She knows when cow manure is being thrown around and simply finds clever ways around it. She prefers being straightforward and direct. Her observations are candid, but never hurtful. In fact, this Queen has a delightful sense of humor. She likes a good laugh and always has a witty comeback ready-to-hand. She knows that life isn't meant to be taken too seriously. The Queen of Swords is refreshing in her candor and lack of pretense.

In readings, the Queen of Swords asks you to *think and feel* as she does. For example: Are you being completely honest? (Check this one first!) Do you see the humor in the situation? Are you getting right to the point? Have you figured out what's really going on? Are you letting yourself be fooled?

This Queen can also represent a man or woman in your life who is like her, or an atmosphere of honest, direct communication. In a reading, she tells you that her special energy has meaning for you at this time. Let yourself be inspired by this Queen in whatever form she appears in your life.

Court Card Pairs

The Queen of Swords can form a pair with any other court card. Compare the ranks and suits of the two cards to see what such a pair might mean.

KING OF SWORDS

INTELLECTUAL
ANALYTICAL
ARTICULATE
JUST
ETHICAL

Actions

INTELLECTUAL

is comfortable in the world of the mind

uses thought creatively

grasps information quickly and completely

inspires and challenges through ideas

ably carries out research

is knowledgeable

Reversed

Early Phase: You are becoming more knowledgeable. An intellectual person may play an important role. A mood of creative thinking may be developing.

Late Phase: You are having trouble grasping all the information. Someone who trusts the data may be removed. A mood of mental challenges is ending.

ANALYTICAL

cuts through confusion and mental fog

applies reason and logic

is talented with games and other mental challenges

easily breaks up complicated subjects

is adept at argument and debate

understands a problem quickly

Reversed

Early Phase: You are beginning to think more logically. Someone argumentative may cause trouble. A mood of mental clarity may be developing.

Late Phase: You are losing the ability to be analytical. A person who understood the problem has left. A mood of respect for reason is ending.

ARTICULATE

is adept at language and verbal skills

communicates ideas successfully

is a stimulating conversationalist

often serves as a group spokesperson

is a lucid writer and speaker

Reversed

Early Phase: You are becoming more skilled at writing and speaking. Someone who can speak for the group may step forward. A mood of articulate communication may be developing.

Late Phase: You are less able to speak up for yourself. An effective speaker is leaving. A mood of productive talk is ending.

ETHICAL

is a moral/ethical leader

encourages high standards

works against corruption and dishonesty

takes the high road in all dealings

lives by his/her highest principles

JUST

renders honest, insightful judgments

understands and honors all sides of an issue

is concerned about truth and fairness

views situations with a dispassionate eye

is impartial and objective

Reversed

Early Phase: You are becoming more objective. Someone who respects truth may enter the picture. A mood of impartiality may be developing.

Late Phase: You are less willing to respect all sides of the issue. An honest judge has been removed. A mood of justice and fairness is ending.

Reversed

Early Phase: You are starting to work against corruption. A moral leader may provide inspiration. A mood of respect for high standards may be developing.

Late Phase: You are not as ethical as before. Someone who takes the high road may lose influence. A mood of truthfulness is ending.

Description

The personality of the King of Swords is a combination of the positive air energy of the Swords suit and the active, outward focus of a King. He is a man of intellect who can absorb and work with information of all kinds. As a master of reason and logic, he analyzes any problem with ease. He can work out solutions quickly and explain them lucidly to others. In a chaotic situation, he cuts through the confusion and provides the clarity needed to move forward. Others seek him out to present their case as he speaks with eloquence and insight. He is always truthful and can be relied on to handle any situation fairly and honorably.

When a judgment is called for, the King of Swords can render an impartial but just decision. He is incorruptible and lives by the highest ethical standards. He encourages those around him to do the same, and they often live up to his expectations.

In readings, the King of Swords asks you to take the kinds of *actions* he might take. For example: telling the truth, thinking up a solution, communicating well, or judging fairly. This King can also represent a man or woman who is acting as he does, or an atmosphere of reason, honesty, and high standards. In a reading, he tells you that his special energy has meaning for you at this time. Let yourself be inspired by this King in whatever form he appears in your life.

Court Card Pairs

The King of Swords can form a pair with any other court card. Compare the ranks and suits of the two cards to see what such a pair might mean.

ACE OF PENTACLES

MATERIAL FORCE
PROSPERITY
PRACTICALITY
TRUST

Actions

USING MATERIAL FORCE

focusing on concrete results

having a real-world impact

working with the physical

achieving tangible results

improving the body/health

becoming involved with nature

Reversed

Early Phase: You may have a chance to use material force. Physical strength may become necessary. Ideas could become more tangible. You may need to be more concrete. The natural world may become important.

Late Phase: The opportunity to use material force is fading. There are fewer physical challenges now. The chance to build something real is past. People are less interested in results. The environment is no longer being protected.

PROSPERING

having the means to reach a goal

enjoying abundance

drawing to you what you need

flourishing

seeing efforts rewarded

increasing assets

experiencing growth

Reversed

Early Phase: You may have a chance for prosperity. A chance to invest may come up. The financial environment could improve in the future. Your assets may start to increase. You may get the support you need.

Late Phase: The opportunity to be prosperous is fading. An investment offer has been withdrawn. Chances to make money are no longer common. The climate of abundance is ending. Spending can't be as free now.

BEING PRACTICAL

using common sense

getting down-to-earth

taking advantage of what works

being realistic

grounding yourself in the real world

accepting the tools at hand

Reversed

Early Phase: You may have a chance to be practical. A realistic solution could materialize. You may need to focus on the tools at hand. Someone may become more down-to-earth. A real-world concern may come up.

Late Phase: The opportunity to be practical is fading. There's less support for the reasonable choice. Being sensible is no longer valued. The commonsense approach is being discarded.

PROCEEDING WITH TRUST

believing in the good faith of others

feeling safe and protected

knowing you have total security

operating from a known position

having a support system

knowing the situation is stable

consolidating a firm base

Reversed

Early Phase: You may have a chance to trust or be trusted. Someone may ask you to believe. Your reliability may be tested at some point. Someone may depend on you in the future.

Late Phase: The opportunity to trust or be trusted is fading. Someone no longer has faith in you. Your word is not good enough anymore. Your desire to believe is nearly gone. You're not as gullible as you were.

Description

The Ace of Pentacles is a symbol of possibility in the area of prosperity, abundance, trust, security, and groundedness. In readings, it shows that a seed of productivity has been planted in your life although you may not yet recognize it. When the seed sprouts, it could take almost any form. It might be a feeling of centeredness, desire for results, or need to focus on practical matters. On the outside, it could be an offer, gift, opportunity, encounter, or synchronistic event.

When you see this Ace, examine your life to see how its solid energy could work for you. Now is not the time for fantasy, drama, or daring. It is a time to be real and centered. Seek out comfortable, reliable experiences that make you feel secure. Build a foundation of trust in your life both within and without. Your common sense will tell you what to do. Focus on the natural world to help you stay grounded. Enjoy your body and the joys of material existence.

The Ace of Pentacles can be a sign that you will be able to make your dreams real. Your ideas are ready to be turned into something tangible. Figure out what will work and make it a reality. You can now attract all the wealth you need to get your projects going. Tap into the material force of the Ace of Pentacles, and all your enterprises will flourish.

Ace-Ace Pairs

An Ace-Ace pair shows that a new spirit is entering your life. It draws on the energy of the Ace of Pentacles—prosperity, abundance, trust, security, groundedness—plus one of these:

Ace of Wands—creativity, excitement, adventure, courage, personal power

Ace of Cups—deep feelings, intimacy, attunement, compassion, love

Ace of Swords—intelligence, reason, justice, truth, clarity, perseverance

TWO OF PENTACLES

JUGGLING
FLEXIBILITY
FUN

Actions

. . . .

JUGGLING

keeping everything in balance

coping with demands

getting people to work together

making sure all areas are covered

having a lot of irons in the fire

moving forward smoothly

emphasizing all aspects equally

Reversed

Early Phase: There may be more demands in the future. A busy period may lie ahead. You may need to cover all the bases. Balance may become important.

Late Phase: The busy time is ending. You no longer have to struggle for balance. Demands were handled; now the pace is slowing. There's less need to juggle now.

BEING FLEXIBLE

adapting quickly

feeling free to try new approaches

going with the flow

refusing to let change throw you

opening to developments

seeing the possibilities

handling challenges

changing directions easily

Reversed

Early Phase: There may be more flexibility in the future. You may be able to adapt. Someone may open to change. New options could develop at some point.

Late Phase: There's less flexibility now. You're no longer open to change. Your options are narrowing. The alternatives are disappearing.

HAVING FUN

doing something you enjoy

taking time to play

feeling in high spirits

whistling while you work

seeing the humor in the situation

kicking back

Reversed

Early Phase: A party or celebration may be coming up. You may have more fun in the future. There could be more opportunities for play. Good times may be on the way.

Late Phase: The fun is ending. People are no longer enjoying themselves. You have less time for play. A party or celebration has passed. The laughter is fading.

Description

There is nothing quite like the feeling of being graceful and effective at the same time, especially in the face of danger or a challenge. On the Two of Pentacles we see a young man dancing as he juggles his worldly concerns. The infinity sign loops around the two pentacles to suggest that he could handle unlimited problems. In the background we see two ships riding the waves easily—cruising the ups and downs of life.

In readings, the Two of Pentacles lets you know that you can juggle all demands made upon you. In fact, you will relish the excitement of every hurdle. If you do not feel this level of confidence right now, this card asks you to believe in yourself. You have all you need to meet your every goal and more. Embrace the challenge.

The Two of Pentacles also reminds you to be flexible. You need to move freely and lightly in all directions as needed. You must be supple if you want to prevail. Don't force your way through. Now is not the time to be rigid. Know that sometimes a side step, or even a back step is the surest way forward.

The Two of Pentacles is also a symbol of fun, laughter, and good times. It is definitely a high-energy card. If you are feeling tired or depressed, this card may be a sign that greater vitality will be yours. If you are feeling revved already, the Two of Pentacles could be a warning against overstimulation. .

Some Possible Opposing Cards

Hierophant—following the program, being conventional
Five of Wands—being at cross-purposes, not working out
Four of Swords—rest, quiet, low activity
Six of Swords—the blues, feeling listless

Some Possible Reinforcing Cards

Temperance—balance, finding the right mix
Four of Wands—fun, excitement, parties

THREE OF PENTACLES

TEAMWORK
PLANNING
COMPETENCE

Actions

WORKING AS A TEAM

coordinating with others

finding all the needed elements

functioning as a unit

getting the job done together

contributing to the group

cooperating

combining efforts

Reversed

Early Phase: You may become part of a team. There's potential for cooperation. The group could come together in the future. A spirit of camaraderie may develop.

Late Phase: A team is breaking up. People are no longer functioning as a unit. Everyone is starting to go separate ways. There's less coordination and cooperation.

PLANNING

organizing resources

following a schedule

operating in the know

nailing down the details

being an ant, not a grasshopper

reviewing beforehand

going over possible problems

being prepared

Reversed

Early Phase: You're thinking of making a plan. You may get organized at some point. The preparation stage may begin. A schedule could be implemented in the future.

Late Phase: There's less planning now. The schedule is slipping. The details are no longer being worked out. The preparation stage is ending. Your orderly projections are less reliable.

· ·

BEING COMPETENT

getting the job done

meeting your goals

proving your ability

achieving more than what's expected

knowing what to do and how to do it

being up to the job

Reversed

Early Phase: Someone may be more competent in the future. The system may start to work. People may begin handling their assignments better. You may find the skills you need.

Late Phase: The job is no longer getting done properly. Tasks are being neglected. You're losing confidence in your abilities. You have less faith in the system.

Description

In the *Mission Impossible* series, a crack team of specialists is given a dangerous assignment. They have to strategize, coordinate resources, and draw on skill and ingenuity to complete the mission. This is the Three of Pentacles in action: teamwork, planning, and competence. The Three of Pentacles is one of the cards in the tarot that focuses on the group. (The Three of Cups and the Hierophant are the others.)

Pentacles are grounded and practical; this card represents a task-oriented team—people who are working cooperatively toward a common goal. There are few jobs that can be accomplished alone. Sometimes the Three of Pentacles is a sign that you will be more productive if you work with others. You don't have to do it all by yourself.

This card can also show a need for planning and preparation. Now is not the time to rush into something or begin a project with only a vague idea of what it's about. You need to think everything through, go over all the possibilities, and make sure you work out the details.

The Three of Pentacles also represents competence—the ability to get the job done. This card tells you that you have the skills and knowledge you need. You can attract capable people and create a successful environment. Know that the situation is (or will be) in good hands, but be sure to concentrate on excellence in your work.

Some Possible Opposing Cards

Five of Wands—lack of teamwork, no cooperation
Seven of Wands—opposition, dissension
Eight of Swords—not feeling up to the job, lacking direction
Nine of Pentacles—doing it yourself, not focusing on teamwork

Some Possible Reinforcing Cards

Hierophant—working in a team or group
Temperance—combining forces
Three of Wands—planning, preparing for the future
Three of Cups—working in a group

FOUR OF PENTACLES

POSSESSIVENESS
CONTROL
BLOCKED CHANGE

Actions

WANTING TO POSSESS

keeping what you have

getting your share

acquiring material goods

hanging on to someone

being greedy

penny-pinching

declaring ownership

saving

Reversed

Early Phase: You may become possessive. Jealousy or greed may develop. You may need to protect what you have. Someone may try to stake a claim.

Late Phase: You're less concerned with holding on. A focus on ownership is decreasing. There's no longer reason to be possessive. Jealousy is diminishing. People are less tied down.

MAINTAINING CONTROL

wanting to be in charge

denying weakness

directing

demanding compliance

insisting on your own way

imposing structure

setting limits and rules

creating order

Reversed

Early Phase: A need for order may develop. Limits and rules may become necessary. You could be asked to step in and take charge. There may be more structure in the future.

Late Phase: The structure in place is breaking up. Rules are no longer being followed. There is less control now. The level of organization is decreasing. You're losing your handle on the situation.

. . . .

BLOCKING CHANGE

maintaining the status quo

refusing to look at new approaches

stagnating

obstructing new developments

wanting things to stay the same

resisting the flow

Reversed

Early Phase: A period of stagnation may be coming. Obstructions may occur. Resistance could become a problem. You may encounter roadblocks.

Late Phase: Blocks to change are decreasing. Resistance is fading. You're less opposed to new ideas and approaches. People are no longer committed to the status quo.

Description

Spend time with a two-year-old, and you will soon hear the sounds of the Four of Pentacles: "No!" and "Mine!" These are the cries of the ego, just developing in the young child. The desire for control is the hallmark of the Four of Pentacles.

Some control *is* valuable. In chaotic situations, a firm hand is needed to provide structure and organization. But too often the urge for control can stifle creativity and individual expression. In readings, this card asks you to weigh carefully the level of control in your situation.

The Four of Pentacles can stand for issues of ownership. You may be involved in getting and keeping money; you may be having problems with possessiveness or jealousy. Use the energy of this card to preserve and defend, but not to lay claim.

The Four of Pentacles also implies blocked change. It's as if the stubborn little man on the card is thwarting your every move. Opposition may come from those who want to maintain the status quo. It may also come from within yourself. Are you resisting change that is truly needed? We often cling to the familiar even when we know it's not for the best.

The lesson of the Four of Pentacles is that control is impossible. We stand in the world as in a great ocean. Who could manage or possess such power? The only way to keep from drowning is to ride the currents. The ocean will support us as long as we swim with the flow.

Some Possible Opposing Cards

Fool—being spontaneous, impulsive
Empress—openhearted, lavish
Wheel of Fortune—movement, rapid changes
Hanged Man—letting go, not trying to control

Some Possible Reinforcing Cards

Emperor—control, structure, order
Chariot—control
Two of Swords—stalemate, blockage
Ten of Pentacles—liking the status quo, conserving

FIVE OF PENTACLES

HARD TIMES
ILL HEALTH
REJECTION

Actions

EXPERIENCING HARD TIMES

running into material troubles

losing a job or income

feeling insecure

going through a period of hardship

lacking what you need

struggling to make ends meet

Reversed

Early Phase: Signs of financial trouble may develop. Hard times may be approaching. A period of lack could be on the horizon. You may feel insecure in the future.

Late Phase: The worse times are behind you. You no longer have to struggle so hard. There are fewer financial concerns. Practical problems are decreasing.

SUFFERING ILL HEALTH

feeling run-down and tired

refusing to take care of yourself

neglecting your body and its needs

feeling ragged around the edges

seeking medical attention

abusing your body

Reversed

Early Phase: A health concern may develop in the future. A physical problem could show up. Your body may send you warning signs. You may start feeling weak. Stress and tension may become a problem.

Late Phase: The health crisis is behind you. A medical problem is less serious. You no longer feel run-down and weak. Stress levels are decreasing. The symptoms are disappearing.

PENTACLES

BEING REJECTED

lacking support

having the door slammed in your face

taking an unpopular position

being ostracized

feeling excluded

standing alone

receiving disapproval

Reversed

Early Phase: You may start seeing signs of disapproval. A rejection could occur in the future. Someone may refuse to go along. The door could be slammed in your face. Your proposal may be rebuffed.

Late Phase: Rejection is no longer an issue. You're feeling less excluded. The period of disapproval is behind you. You're no longer concerned with dismissal.

Description

The two figures on the Five of Pentacles are cold, hungry, tired, sick, and poor. They show us what it feels like to be without—to lack the basic ingredients of life. This is the specter that haunts so many in our world—a reality that is all too immediate. Those of us who are more fortunate may not have experienced this extreme, but we still recognize suffering. When we do not have what we want and need, it hurts.

In readings, the Five of Pentacles can represent several kinds of lack. First, there is poor health. It is hard to tackle life's challenges when we do not have our vitality and strength. This card can be a signal that you are neglecting the needs of your body. You are moving away from complete physical well-being, so you must take steps to discover and correct the problem.

This card can also be a sign of material and economic setbacks. There is no doubt that life is harder when we lack money or a decent job. When we are struggling to make ends meet, all other problems are magnified. Even if we are comfortable, we can still feel insecure, afraid that misfortune will take away all that we have worked for.

The Five of Pentacles can also represent rejection or lack of acceptance. We are social animals and feel pain when excluded from our group. We want to be included, not only for our emotional well-being, but also for mutual support. Being rejected can mean physical hardship as well.

The Five of Pentacles relates to material lack, but it also has a spiritual component. From the stained-glass window, we can guess that these two figures are outside of a church. Comfort is so close at hand, but they fail to see it. The church symbolizes our spirits which are perfect and whole in every way. We are meant to enjoy abundance in all areas of life, but sometimes we forget that this is our birthright. Whenever you experience hardship, know that it is only temporary. Look for the spiritual center that will take you in and give you shelter.

Some Possible Opposing Cards

Strength—strength, stamina
Temperance—good health
Sun—vitality, strong constitution
Six of Wands—acclaim, recognition
Seven of Pentacles—material reward

Some Possible Reinforcing Cards

Tower—hard times
Ten of Wands—struggling to make ends meet, hard times
Five of Cups—rejection, lack of support, loss of approval
Three of Swords—rejection, separation, lack of support

SIX OF PENTACLES

HAVING/NOT HAVING:
  RESOURCES
  KNOWLEDGE
  POWER

Actions

HAVING/NOT HAVING:
RESOURCES

giving/receiving

taking care of/being taken care of

sponsoring/being sponsored

supporting/being supported

offering/receiving a gift or reward

acquiring/not acquiring what you need

Reversed

Early Phase: You may have to think about resources in the future. You may need to take care of someone or be taken care of. A gift or reward may be offered. Issues of support may materialize.

Late Phase: There's less focus on resources. You no longer need to take care of someone or be taken care of. The time for a gift or reward is past. Support issues are decreasing.

HAVING/NOT HAVING:
KNOWLEDGE

teaching/learning

imparting/receiving information

becoming/finding a mentor

offering/taking advice

showing/being shown the ropes

knowing/not knowing a secret

Reversed

Early Phase: You may have to think about information in the future. You may start to teach or study. You may seek advice or be sought for your knowledge and opinion.

Late Phase: There's less focus on knowledge. The need to seek or offer advice is fading. You no longer want to teach or study. What people know is less important.

HAVING/NOT HAVING: POWER

leading/following

dominating/submitting

acting with authority/deference

asserting/denying your wishes

coercing/being coerced

doing all the talking/listening

Reversed

Early Phase: You may have to think about power in the future. You may need to follow or lead. Issues of dominance and submission may become important.

Late Phase: There's less focus on power. The need to assert your authority or submit to someone is fading. Leadership issues are decreasing.

Description

The Six of Pentacles is a difficult card to describe because it falls in the shadowy area between the lack of the Five of Pentacles and the affluence of the Ten of Pentacles. These two cards represent the extremes of not having and having. The Six of Pentacles covers the huge middle ground where it is not exactly clear who has what.

On this card, a well-to-do gentleman is tossing a few coins to a beggar while another supplicant waits to the side. The giver holds the scales of justice as if claiming the right to decide who deserves blessings and who does not. In this picture we see both sides: what it means to give *and* to receive, to dominate *and* to submit, to be on top *and* to be on the bottom. It seems clear who has and who hasn't, but is it? Life is not that simple, and how quickly fortunes change.

In readings, the Six of Pentacles asks you to look very deeply into the whole issue of what *having* really means both materially (resources) and immaterially (knowledge, power, love). You may see yourself on one side or the other, but this card asks you to reconsider. Think of the successful executive who suddenly declares bankruptcy. The tyrannical invalid who dominates through weakness. The teacher who learns from her students. The parent who controls by giving away money.

The keywords for the Six of Pentacles include both the have and have-not sides of each meaning. Sometimes this card is a clear sign one way or the other. You *will* get the gift, give advice, or defer to another. In all cases, though, you should question the obvious and go deeper. Why are you in the situation you're in, and where is it leading? Who is really in charge? What's really going on?

Some Possible Opposing and Reinforcing Cards

Opposing and reinforcing cards do not work in the usual way with the Six of Pentacles because this card can mean either (or both) sides of the same issue—having or not having. The other cards in a reading can help you figure out which side applies in your case. The following cards also deal with this issue:

Empress—abundance, physical comfort
World—affluence, material fulfillment
Ten of Wands—struggling to make ends meet, hard times
Five of Pentacles—lack, not having
Seven of Pentacles—material reward, having
Ten of Pentacles—affluence, having

SEVEN OF PENTACLES

ASSESSMENT
REWARD
DIRECTION CHANGE

Actions

ASSESSING

evaluating the status

reflecting on progress to date

reviewing what's been done

pausing to check results

making sure you're on course

finding out where you stand

taking stock

Reversed

Early Phase: You may need to evaluate. A status check may be coming up in the future. You may want to reassess where you're headed. A break may become necessary.

Late Phase: The assessment is ending. The time for evaluation is behind you. There's less need for thinking and planning. You no longer need to take stock of the situation.

REAPING A REWARD

finally seeing some results

enjoying the first fruits

getting returns on investments

receiving payoffs

being able to let up a bit

reaching a milestone

Reversed

Early Phase: A reward may be offered in the future. You may see some returns on your investment. A milestone may be coming up. A token of esteem may be presented.

Late Phase: The time for a reward has passed. Compensation is no longer available. The milestone is behind you. You've already received whatever was coming.

PENTACLES

CONSIDERING A DIRECTION CHANGE

pondering alternatives

thinking about change

opening to a new strategy

questioning your choices

standing at a crossroads

Reversed

Early Phase: You may need a direction change in the future. Change may become more acceptable. A crossroads may be reached at some point. Someone may alter course.

Late Phase: The time for change is fading. The window of opportunity is closing. You're no longer weighing alternatives. A course adjustment is behind you.

Description

On the Seven of Pentacles we see a man who has labored long and hard in his garden. The foliage is full, the blossoms are out—it seems that his work has paid off. Now he's taking a break to admire his handiwork. How satisfying it is to see such results!

The Seven of Pentacles is a time-out card. It represents those moments after a rush of activity when we stop to catch our breath and look around. The man in the picture has paused · to contemplate the fruits of his own labors. In readings, the Seven of Pentacles can indicate a reward that will come your way, particularly as a result of your own efforts. Take it and enjoy.

This card is also a call for assessment—take the time to be sure you're meeting your goals. Pause to take time to reflect on the what and why of your actions. Are you still on course? Getting the results you want? Serious problems can develop if you don't take stock.

The Seven of Pentacles can also indicate a crossroads. In life, there's a tendency to continue with familiar routines. To go in a new direction isn't easy. The Seven of Pentacles may be telling you to figure out if you need a course correction, or even a complete about-face. You're not yet committed to a certain path, but you could be soon. Change is still possible.

The Seven of Pentacles is not a card of endings or final decisions. The game is not over, but only on hold for a moment. Once you've gotten your breath and checked your strategy, be ready to jump back in and work even harder than before.

Some Possible Opposing Cards

Wheel of Fortune—movement, action, direction change

Eight of Wands—rapid action

Five of Pentacles—lack of reward, hardship

Some Possible Reinforcing Cards

Empress—material reward

Justice—assessing where you are, deciding a future course

Judgement—decision point

Four of Swords—rest, thinking things over

EIGHT OF PENTACLES

DILIGENCE
KNOWLEDGE
DETAIL

Actions

SHOWING DILIGENCE

making an effort

working hard

applying yourself

totally being absorbed in a project

dedicating yourself to a task

plugging away

producing steady results

INCREASING KNOWLEDGE

taking a course

learning a new craft or skill

receiving training

pursuing greater understanding

researching

finding out the facts

increasing expertise

Reversed

Early Phase: You may need to work harder in the future. A demanding project may be coming up. You may get involved in a new task. People may start gearing up for a big effort.

Late Phase: The hard work is behind you. You no longer need to work up a sweat. A project is winding down. Overtime is less available. You can slow down a bit.

Reversed

Early Phase: You may begin a course of study. You may need to increase your knowledge. School may become an option. An area of research may open up.

Late Phase: The time for study and learning is ending. A course is finishing up. Your knowledge is decreasing. The research is nearing completion. You found out what you needed to know.

PENTACLES

PAYING ATTENTION TO DETAIL

being painstaking/extra careful

approaching a task methodically

getting down to the nitty-gritty

handling all the loose ends

checking and rechecking

noticing the fine points

Reversed

Early Phase: Details may become important. People could start being more methodical. The need for monitoring may become clear. Care may be required in the future.

Late Phase: Extra care is no longer required. The need to check and double-check is past. You're less painstaking now. The detail work is ending.

Description

On the Eight of Pentacles we see a young man who is hammering away at a coin. He has finished six and has another coin to go. It is clear this project absorbs all his attention. He's isolated himself from others (the town in the background) in order to concentrate. Here we see the essential elements of the Eight of Pentacles: hard work and attention to detail.

This card often implies a time of great diligence and focus. It advises you to *hammer away* at the business of the moment, whether a project, family difficulty, or unpleasant duty. Sometimes blessings fall into our laps; other times we must put out great effort to obtain them. The Eight of Pentacles tells you to give 100 percent. Just buckle down and do it. Fortunately, this kind of work is invigorating and leads to superb results.

The Eight of Pentacles can also symbolize the impulse to learn—to broaden horizons (to use an old-fashioned term). Sometimes we need to develop new skills. We do research, dig out facts, or search for greater expertise. The Hermit is looking for inner knowledge. The man on the Eight of Pentacles seeks external knowledge—the how and why of the material world.

This card can also show the need for meticulous attention. People who are painstaking are often dismissed as nitpickers, but their extra effort ensures everything is as it should be. It's a matter of caring—taking the time to check the little details. Now is not the time to be slipshod or casual. Look for errors, and tie up loose ends. The key to success is an extraordinary effort. Whatever your task, the Eight of Pentacles tells you to give it your all in every way.

Some Possible Opposing Cards

Four of Cups—lacking interest, not caring, apathetic
Seven of Cups—lazy, lacking drive

Some Possible Reinforcing Cards

Magician—focus and concentration
Hierophant—learning, studying
Nine of Wands—keeping at it, persistence

NINE OF PENTACLES

DISCIPLINE
SELF-RELIANCE
REFINEMENT

Actions

BEING DISCIPLINED

exercising self-control

showing restraint

reining in impulses

sacrificing to reach a goal

sticking to a program

taking a step-by-step approach

Reversed

Early Phase: You may need more discipline in the future. Self-control may become important. Someone may have to be restrained. A firm hand may be necessary.

Late Phase: Discipline is breaking down. Control measures are no longer in place. You're abandoning the program. People are less rigorous now. The regimen is no longer being followed.

RELYING ON YOURSELF

handling the situation alone

acting on your own

falling back on your own resources

doing it all by yourself

wanting to be alone

feeling sure your way is best

Reversed

Early Phase: You're thinking of becoming more independent. You may be on your own in the future. Someone may become more self-reliant. You may need to break away at some point.

Late Phase: It's no longer possible to do everything yourself. A period of independence is ending. Being on your own is less satisfying now. The need for self-reliance is no longer strong.

・・・・・・・・・・・・・・・・・・・・・・・・・・・・

PURSUING REFINEMENT

achieving/enjoying a comfortable lifestyle

avoiding the coarse and unsavory

being tactful and diplomatic

seeking high-minded activities

enjoying the finer things of life

remembering to be gracious

Reversed

Early Phase: People may become more courteous. You may seek more refined activities in the future. The environment may become more pleasant. There's potential for gracious living.

Late Phase: People are no longer cordial. The gracious environment is disappearing. You're less interested in refined activities now. The gloves are coming off.

Description

The woman on the Nine of Pentacles is taking a leisurely stroll through the gardens of her estate. She is clearly a lady of refinement and grace, so it is incongruous to see on her left hand a bird trained to hunt and kill on command. Falconry is an unusual hobby for a gentlewoman, but it is the key to the special nature of this card.

On one hand, the Nine of Pentacles represents all that is gracious, high-minded, and civilized. Art, music, and other forms of beauty are very much part of our physical world (Pentacles). Coins are present in this scene, but they are toward the ground. The business of life is important, but we don't have to focus on practical matters all the time. We can enjoy the finer things of life. In readings, the Nine of Pentacles can imply an interest in these areas. It is also a sign that you may need to reject the coarse or offensive and seek the highest.

The Nine of Pentacles can also be a sign of discipline and self-control. This woman enjoys her cultured life because she has mastered her baser instincts—her impulses do not rule her. This falcon symbolizes all that is dark and unruly in human nature. Our shadow side can serve us well, but only when it is directed. Sometimes the Nine of Pentacles suggests that you must show restraint and self-control if you are to achieve your best efforts. You may have to "sacrifice" for the moment, but the results will be worth it.

This card is also a sign of self-reliance. Sometimes you must trust your own abilities and resist the temptation to let others do for you. Take matters into your own hands. Our elegant lady has done just that. She showed grit and determination, and now enjoys all the best life has to offer.

Some Possible Opposing Cards

Empress—earthy sensuality
Seven of Cups—being undisciplined, self-indulgent
Three of Pentacles—working in a team, doing with others

Some Possible Reinforcing Cards

Chariot—self-control, discipline
Seven of Swords—relying on yourself, acting on your own

TEN OF PENTACLES

AFFLUENCE
PERMANENCE
CONVENTION

Actions

ENJOYING AFFLUENCE

having material abundance

being free from money problems

enjoying business success

feeling financially secure

seeing your ventures flourish

having a run of good fortune

Reversed

Early Phase: Your fortunes may improve in the future. Your financial situation could get better. Business may pick up. Some prospects may develop.

Late Phase: Your run of good fortune is ending. The prosperous times have passed. You're no longer feeling financially secure. Business has taken a turn for the worse.

SEEKING PERMANENCE

looking for a solution that will last

creating a lasting foundation

feeling secure as things are

being concerned with the long term

having an orderly family life

moving beyond makeshift arrangements

nailing down the plan

Reversed

Early Phase: You may seek a long-term solution. A more permanent foundation may materialize. You may be able to settle down. A secure relationship may become more appealing.

Late Phase: Your fixed arrangement is falling apart. You're no longer focused on making the situation last. The mood of security is disappearing. A long-lasting relationship is ending.

FOLLOWING CONVENTION

staying within established guidelines

proceeding according to the rules

taking part in traditions

becoming part of the Establishment

being conservative

trusting in the tried-and-true

continuing in known patterns

Reversed

Early Phase: You may become more conservative. Rules may need to be followed. Someone may decide to go along with convention. A tradition may be honored.

Late Phase: You're no longer following a tradition. The mood is becoming less conventional. Known patterns are less effective. People are growing disenchanted with the old ways.

Description

On many cards, we see a cluster of buildings off in the distance. In the Ten of Pentacles, we finally arrive in that village—in the middle of the marketplace. The family we see is carrying on the affairs of everyday life. A patriarch, dressed in a luxurious robe, pats his hounds as he watches over the younger generations. A man and woman converse in passing as their child plays at their feet. Coins (money) are in the air.

The Ten of Pentacles stands for the ultimate in worldly and material success. Sometimes I jokingly call it the "fat cat card" because it reminds me of the aura of prosperity that surrounds wealthy men and women of business. This is the card you want to see if you are wondering how your latest enterprise will turn out. Wealth and affluence are yours.

When we achieve material success, we naturally want it to last. This is the conservative, Establishment side of the Ten of Pentacles. Why rock the boat when life is fine just the way it is? In readings, this card often stands for convention—following established guidelines and maintaining the status quo. Fat cats are rarely radicals; they love tradition and the tried-and-true. Sometimes it is important to trust the known ways, but only when change is inadvisable.

The Ten of Pentacles is also concerned with permanence. Change is an unavoidable part of life, but constant change is uncomfortable. We need stability and the chance to work for a secure foundation in life. In readings, this card may be telling you to concentrate on the long-term. Work toward a lasting solution. Now may be the time to settle down and make the arrangements that will work for you far into the future.

Some Possible Opposing Cards

Two of Wands—being original, avoiding convention
Three of Wands—exploring, going into untested areas
Five of Pentacles—hard times, material lack

Some Possible Reinforcing Cards

Empress—affluence, luxury, physical comfort
Hierophant—conforming, following rules, conservative
Lovers—permanent unions, family ties
World—affluence, material fulfillment
Four of Pentacles—enjoying the status quo, conserving

PENTACLES

PAGE OF PENTACLES

HAVE AN EFFECT
BE PRACTICAL
BE PROSPEROUS
BE TRUSTING/TRUSTWORTHY

Actions

HAVE AN EFFECT

make your plans real

mold the physical world

use your body

experience nature

achieve tangible results

act on your dreams

set events in motion

Reversed

Early Phase: You may have a chance to achieve results. An opportunity to make plans may arise. The time to act is approaching. Someone may make an impact.

Late Phase: An opportunity to make dreams real has passed. The time to carry out plans is ending. Someone has already set events in motion. It's harder to work for results now.

BE PRACTICAL

take a realistic approach

apply the tools at hand

find a solution that works

use common sense

stop daydreaming

work with what you have

concentrate on what's effective

Reversed

Early Phase: You may be called on to make something work. Someone may need to become more practical. A time to be realistic is approaching. An opportunity to use common sense may come up.

Late Phase: An opportunity to find a workable solution has passed. People are ignoring realistic approaches. Chances to be practical are fading. The time for effective action is behind you.

BE PROSPEROUS

draw to you what you need

increase your means

grow and expand

enrich yourself

go out to meet success

seek abundance

become secure

Reversed

Early Phase: You may have a chance to get what you need. An opportunity to be prosperous may arise. A time to grow and expand may come up. Someone may see an opening for greater security.

Late Phase: An opportunity for enrichment is behind you. The time for expansion is ending. Someone has already been rewarded. You have fewer chances for security now.

BE TRUSTING/TRUSTWORTHY

accept that the solution is well in hand

have faith in others

accommodate uncertainty

accept others at their word

keep your word

prove yourself dependable

stick by your commitments

establish credibility

Reversed

Early Phase: An opportunity to be dependable may arise. Someone may show himself as trustworthy. You may have a chance to keep your word. A time for commitments may present itself.

Late Phase: An opportunity to show credibility has passed. The time to be trusting is ending. Someone has already proven reliable. Chances to show faith are fewer now.

Description

The Page of Pentacles is a messenger bringing you opportunities for prosperity. He delivers real chances to experience wealth, abundance, security, and solid achievement—the wonders of the Pentacles suit. In your readings, this Page suggests that an opening may appear that promises enrichment, comfort, trust, or the chance to make your dreams real. When you see such a chance, act on it!

   The Page of Pentacles can also stand for a child or young-at-heart adult whose interactions with you involve stability, trust, commitment, safety and material needs. Sometimes the Page of Pentacles implies that your entire situation is suffused with the spirit of physical enjoyment. At such times, feel free to have fun with your body, skills, and possessions in a lighthearted way. Revel in the delights of being alive on the Earth at this time.

Court Card Pairs

The Page of Pentacles can form a pair with any other court card. Compare the ranks and suits of the two cards to see what such a pair might mean

PENTACLES

KNIGHT OF PENTACLES

KNIGHT OF PENTACLES

UNWAVERING/STUBBORN
CAUTIOUS/UNADVENTUROUS
THOROUGH/OBSESSIVE
REALISTIC/PESSIMISTIC
HARDWORKING/GRINDING

Actions

UNWAVERING/STUBBORN

is dogged in pursuit of a goal/is hard-headed and obstinate

will not quit/digs into a position

stands firm against opposition/must have his or her own way

stays fixed to a chosen course/refuses to listen to reason

keeps true to personal convictions/ resists compromise

Reversed

Early Phase: You may be becoming more persistent, but also more stubborn. Someone who likes hard work, but not play may be entering the picture. A dogged but uncompromising mood may be developing.

Late Phase: You are becoming less obstinate, but also less unwavering. Someone who sticks to his guns, but without listening to reason is leaving the picture. A mood of determination, but without compromise is ending.

CAUTIOUS/UNADVENTUROUS

checks and double-checks/is too conservative

examines all angles beforehand/misses chances by waiting

proceeds slowly and carefully/is reluctant to try something new

prefers the safe, known path/settles for safe, small gains

is prudent and careful/is afraid of risking

Reversed

Early Phase: You may be becoming more cautious, but also more unadventurous. Someone who takes great care, but obsessively may be entering the picture. A prudent but overly conservative mood may be developing.

Late Phase: You are becoming less risk-averse, but also less careful. Someone who checks everything, but to excess is leaving the picture. A safe but predictable mood is ending.

THOROUGH/OBSESSIVE

*takes care of every detail/doesn't know
when to quit*

is meticulous/is too picky

*wraps up all loose ends/must have
everything just so*

*never leaves a job half done/is inflexible
and compulsive*

is painstaking/insists on perfection

*completes anything started/can't leave
well enough alone*

Reversed

Early Phase: You may be becoming more thorough, but also more obsessive. Someone who takes care of the details, but compulsively may be entering the picture. A painstaking but inflexible mood may be developing.

Late Phase: You are becoming less picky, but also less methodical. A perfectionist who doesn't know when to quit is leaving the picture. A meticulous but all-consuming mood is ending.

HARDWORKING/GRINDING

*becomes dedicated to a task/focuses too
narrowly on work*

*is diligent and industrious/can be
humorless and grim*

*produces as much as two people/sees
playtime as wasteful*

*tackles any chore vigorously/drives
everyone too hard*

*is tireless and unflagging/forgets life
should be fun*

REALISTIC/PESSIMISTIC

*is willing to look at the facts/
concentrates on what's wrong*

*faces the truth/thinks others are
dreamers*

*is not lured by false hopes/sees a glass
as half empty, not half full*

*assesses circumstances candidly/takes
the gloomy view*

*predicts problems in advance/dooms a
project from the start*

Reversed

Early Phase: You may be becoming more realistic, but also more pessimistic. Someone who can face hard truths, but without seeing past them may be entering the picture. A fact-based but gloomy mood may be developing.

Late Phase: You are becoming less pie-in-the-sky, but also less hopeful. Someone who sees problems, but only problems is leaving the picture. A tough-minded, but downbeat mood is ending.

Reversed

Early Phase: You may be becoming more dedicated, but also more driven. Someone who likes to work hard, but without taking a break may be entering the picture. A productive but humorless mood may be developing.

Late Phase: You are becoming less grim, but also less diligent. Someone tireless, but to a fault is leaving the picture. A mood of industry without fun is ending.

PENTACLES

Description

On the positive side, the Knight of Pentacles is like a bulldog. Once he bites down, you can be sure he won't let go. He's dogged in pursuit of his goals. A hard worker, he has tremendous stamina and dedication. Every job is always completed down to the last detail. He's careful and prudent, never wasteful. He knows the facts and is immune to false promises.

On the negative side, this Knight is a bit stodgy and dull. He's not known for his playful sense of humor. Work always comes first. He tends to be inflexible and obsessive about little details. Stubborn to a fault, he refuses to give in even when wrong—something he'll never admit. He doesn't like change or risk and will always take the gloomiest view.

In readings, a Knight of Pentacles shows that his cautious style is involved in the situation as an aspect of you, someone else, or the atmosphere in general. You need to ask yourself, "Is this Knight's energy helping or hurting?"

If his style is evident, then balance is needed. Are you working too hard? Do you refuse to listen to reason? Do you have a perfectionist in your life? Is the atmosphere around you one of gloom and doom? It may be time for a change.

If this Knight's energy is missing, a dose of prudence may be called for. Are you spending too much? Maybe it's time to slow down. Do you give up too soon? Dig in and refuse to quit. Is your work often careless, late, or incomplete? Next time resolve to work up a sweat and get the job done. Let the Knight of Pentacles introduce you to his world of care and persistence.

Court Card Pairs

The Knight of Pentacles can form a pair with any other court card. Compare the ranks and suits of the two cards to see what such a pair might mean.

QUEEN OF PENTACLES

NURTURING
BIGHEARTED
DOWN-TO-EARTH
RESOURCEFUL
TRUSTWORTHY

QUEEN of PENTACLES

Actions

NURTURING

gives love and support

creates a warm, secure environment

makes people feel better

responds to the natural world

has a green thumb

has a way with children and animals

Early Phase: You are beginning to create a nuturing environment. A caregiver may play an important role. A mood of love and support may be developing.

Late Phase: You are less involved with the natural world. Someone who works with children is leaving. A mood of caring is ending.

BIGHEARTED

will do any service for others

is a soft touch

always has an open door and welcoming smile

gives freely and abundantly

is warm, generous, and unselfish

Reversed

Early Phase: You are beginning to feel more generous. Someone service-oriented may enter the picture. A mood of selflessness may be developing.

Late Phase: You are less willing to be a soft touch now. A bighearted provider is less available. A mood of welcome is ending.

PENTACLES

DOWN-TO-EARTH

handles problems matter-of-factly

allows others to be themselves

has no pretensions or affectations

takes a simple, sensible approach

appreciates all the senses

Reversed

Early Phase: You are starting to adopt a sensible approach. A matter-of-fact person may become important. A mood of appreciation for the senses may be developing.

Late Phase: You are less down-to-earth than before. Someone guileless has been overlooked. A mood of prudence is ending.

RESOURCEFUL

finds a use for whatever's at hand

is handy and versatile

makes a little go a long way

gets around every obstacle

comes up with what's needed

Reversed

Early Phase: You are starting to be more resourceful. Someone who can overcome difficulties may be called in. A practical mood may be developing.

Late Phase: You are less able to come up with what's needed. A problem-solver is no longer available. A mood of making do is ending.

TRUSTWORTHY

keeps confidences and secrets

is loyal and steadfast

comes through in a pinch

keeps faith with others

is true to his/her word

Reversed

Early Phase: You are beginning to be more trusting. Someone loyal may be counted on. A mood of keeping faith may be developing.

Late Phase: You are less likely to stay steadfast. Someone who keeps secrets is no longer in the picture. A mood of honesty is ending.

Description

The personality of the Queen of Pentacles combines the positive earth energy of the Pentacles suit with the inward focus of a Queen. If you were to visit the Queen of Pentacles, the first thing she would say is "Come in, come in. It's great to see you. Have a bowl of soup!" No one is more welcoming and nurturing than she. Her greatest pleasure is to care for others—making sure they are happy and secure. Her home is always overflowing with children, pets, plants, and footloose friends. She is warm and generous to all.

In day-to-day matters, she is sensible and practical. She doesn't have a lot of time for elaborate plans and other craziness. If something needs doing, she just takes care of it without a lot of fuss and bother. If necessary, she makes do with little and always comes through in a pinch. There is a down-to-earth, matter-of-factness about her. She is always loyal and steadfast. Because she is trusting by nature, others trust her completely. When you are hurting or in need, the Queen of Pentacles will calm your fears and share your troubles.

In readings, the Queen of Pentacles asks you to *think and feel* as she does. For example: Are you feeling warm and caring toward others? Are you being sensible? Have you been true to your word? Do you feel generous? Can you be counted on when times are tough?

This Queen can also represent a man or woman who is like her, or an atmosphere of warmth, trust, and security. In a reading, she tells you that her special energy has meaning for you at this time. Let yourself be inspired by this Queen in whatever form she appears in your life.

Court Card Pairs

The Queen of Pentacles can form a pair with any other court card. Compare the ranks and suits of the two cards to see what such a pair might mean.

KING OF PENTACLES.

KING OF PENTACLES

ENTERPRISING
ADEPT
RELIABLE
SUPPORTING
STEADY

Actions

ENTERPRISING

makes any venture successful

finds opportunity everywhere

attracts wealth

takes an idea and makes it work

*is a natural manager and
    businessperson*

has the Midas touch

Reversed

Early Phase: You are beginning to be more enterprising. A competent manager may become involved. A mood of financial success may be developing.

Late Phase: You are having trouble maintaining a venture. A businessperson is pulling out. A mood of success in work is ending.

ADEPT

is informed about practical matters

has a wide range of natural abilities

has quick reflexes

is skillful with his/her hands

handles any situation competently

Reversed

Early Phase: You are becoming more skillful and adept. A competent doer may join the team. A mood of respect for ability may be developing.

Late Phase: Your reflexes are not what they were. Someone with know-how may become involved. A mood of proficiency is ending.

RELIABLE

meets all commitments and promises

assumes responsibility

is dependable and unfailing

can be counted on in a crisis

serves as a rock for others to lean on

Reversed

Early Phase: You are starting to keep your commitments. Someone dependable may play an important role. A mood of responsibility may be developing.

Late Phase: You are less reliable than before. The one you could count on is gone. A mood of keeping promises is ending.

SUPPORTING

encourages the accomplishments of others

readily jumps in to help

is a philanthropist

gives generously of time and attention

sponsors worthwhile projects

Reversed

Early Phase: You are starting to give more generously. A supportive person may enter the picture. A mood of encouragement may be developing.

Late Phase: You are less willing to be a sponsor. A reliable assistant has decided to leave. A mood of helpfulness is ending.

STEADY

works toward a goal with firm resolve

avoids mood and behavior swings

has regular habits and activities

maintains a calm, even approach

is a stabilizing influence

Reversed

Early Phase: You are becoming more regular in your habits. Someone who provides stability may have an influence. A mood of steady calm may be developing.

Late Phase: You are less able to avoid mood swings. Someone with an evenhanded approach is out of the picture. A mood of firm resolve is ending.

Description

The personality of the King of Pentacles is a combination of the positive earth energy of the Pentacles suit and the active, outward focus of a King. He might as well be called King Midas as he turns everything he touches to gold (riches of all kinds). He finds opportunity everywhere and succeeds at whatever he sets his mind to. He is enterprising and adept. Whatever the task, he handles it competently, drawing on his wide range of skills and practical knowledge. He's a jack-of-all-trades—and master of all as well.

The King of Pentacles is always dependable and responsible. Others rely on him completely because he never fails them. He gives generously of his time and resources because he knows that by giving more, you receive more. He encourages others in their accomplishments and lends his support whenever it is needed. He has a steady, even temperament that adds an element of stability to any situation. When he has set a goal for himself, he pursues it with firm resolve until he's successful.

In readings, the King of Pentacles asks you to take the kinds of actions he might take. For example: keeping a commitment, fixing something that's broken, making money, or sponsoring a new enterprise. This King can also represent a man or woman who is acting as he does, or an atmosphere of steady, reliable competence. In a reading, he tells you that his special energy has meaning for you at this time. Let yourself be inspired by this King in whatever form he appears in your life.

Court Card Pairs

The King of Pentacles can form a pair with any other court card. Compare the ranks and suits of the two cards to see what such a pair might mean.

Part Four

TAROT SPREADS

Chapter Six

ELEMENTS OF SPREADS

A spread is a predefined template or pattern that defines how to distribute and interpret the cards in a reading. A spread gives you a predictable way to enhance your intuition without stifling it. It adds structure to the otherwise free flow of a reading. Most tarot readers like having a spread to follow, but not one that's too restrictive. They want to be free to improvise, but not in a vacuum. This is the purpose of the tarot spread.

The basic unit of a spread is the position—a placeholder for one card. Figure 8 shows a simple spread with three positions in a row. A different card has been placed in each position. This shows what a sample reading might look like using this spread.

Figure 8. A 3-card spread with cards drawn

A spread is defined in four ways by its positions: total number, placement order, shape, and meanings.

Number of Positions

A spread can have from one to seventy-eight positions—the number of cards in a standard deck. Spreads can be divided roughly into three groups by size:

Small spreads—1-4 positions

Small spreads are easy to learn and use. They convey concise information directly. They're useful when you need a few basic insights quickly. Chapter Eight covers small spreads.

Medium spreads—5-19 positions

Most spreads fall in this category. This range is small enough to be manageable, but large enough to cover a topic in some depth. Medium spreads are quite varied. They take longer to learn and interpret, but they offer more detail. The Celtic Cross is a medium-sized spread (See Chapter Nine).

Large spreads—20+ positions

Large spreads are not as useful as you might think. They can be unwieldy and difficult to grasp as a whole. Also, having so many cards tends to water down the value of each one. Still, large spreads can be revealing if carefully structured. They offer grand vistas you can study over time. Rahdue's Wheel includes all 78 cards and creates a vast tableau of one person's life.

Placement Order

It's clearly impossible to place every card in a spread at the same time, so an order of placement is necessary. Every position in a spread has a number to show its turn as the cards are laid out. In figure 9, the first card off the deck would be placed to the left in position 1. The second card would go in the middle, and the third card, to the right.

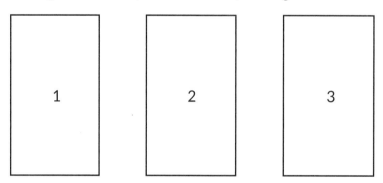

Figure 9. Numbers show placement order

Placement order is important because the meaning of a card is influenced by its position. Also, your impression of the reading as a whole develops as each new card is revealed. In many spreads, the first position is key. It sets the tone, especially when it's isolated or in the center. The positions that follow build up the meaning. The last card often shows an outcome or result, summing up the earlier cards.

Spread Shape

The shape of a spread is determined by the relationship of its positions. In theory, a spread can take any shape, but most have a recognizable design such as a line, triangle, or circle. Such shapes also show up as subgroups within a spread. The pattern of a spread often reflects its theme. The Horoscope spread is in the shape of the traditional circle that forms a person's birth chart. The twelve cards correspond to the twelve houses of astrology.[9]

Position Meanings

Imagine showing a picture of yourself to a friend. You're smiling in the picture, but there's no clue as to why. Now, imagine showing your friend the same picture, but this time in a frame labeled "My first day at work." Suddenly, the picture takes on new meaning. The label tells your friend how to interpret your smile.

In a spread, positions act as labeled frames. A frame is a holder with an empty place for a picture. A position is a holder with an empty place for a card. The meaning of each position comes from its assigned "label." This meaning affects whatever card falls in that position during a reading. It provides a context for the card—a frame of reference.

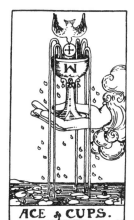

The Ace of Cups can symbolize love. In a position labeled "What I desire," the Ace of Cups implies a desire for love. In a position labeled "What I fear," this same card implies a fear of love. In both cases, the traditional card meaning is the same, but the implication is different. In a frame labeled "My last day at work," your smile takes on a whole new meaning!

Positions are the building blocks of a spread. Each position/card combination creates a unique message that blends their meanings. The messages for all the cards combine to form the meaning of the spread as a whole.

The positions in a spread are defined by its creator. I have explored hundreds of spreads created by many card readers. Sometimes there are unique and unusual positions, but more often the same positions show up over and over. I have come to think of positions as having an energy of their own, just as cards do.

You can study and work with positions independently of any spread. The Flex Spread Position reference section is a collection of useful positions (page 310). Each one has a name, keywords, description, and examples. You'll learn more about these positions in Chapters Ten and Eleven.

VALUE OF STRUCTURE
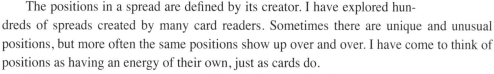

Take your deck in your hand, and turn over the top card. Place it face up anywhere in front of you. Decide on a quick keyword interpretation for the card. Now, turn over the next card, and place it somewhere haphazardly. Assign a keyword to it as well. Continue on in this way, trying to keep all the cards vividly present in your mind.

Be aware of your comfort level as you go. It's easy to keep track of a few cards, but it gets harder as the number grows. At some point, do you start losing your "grasp" of all the cards?

Now, repeat the exercise, but this time, put the cards into some kind of order as you go. Use any guiding principle such as number or suit to group cards together. Notice how this aids understanding. How many cards can you remember when there is structure?

Chapter Seven

SPREAD SHAPES

A tarot spread has two levels of meaning. The first comes from the individual positions. The second comes from the overall design or shape of the spread—how the positions are arranged. If a spread's shape is familiar, it's easy to learn and remember. If the positions are random, the spread makes less sense. Structure conveys order and meaning.

Design Principles

Most spread patterns follow four design principles:

Symmetry

Symmetry is balance among parts. Most spreads use symmetry for beauty and harmony. Positions often mirror each other. Even-numbered spreads tend to be solid and regular—every position has its counterpart. Odd-numbered spreads are more dynamic—lone positions create tension.

Spacing

The space between positions is usually uniform. The exception is the use of a wider margin to define a lone position or group of positions. In Figure 10, the single position in the center is set off by the extra space around it. Most positions in a spread are separate from each other; they do not overlap. One exception is position 2 of the Celtic Cross spread. It is on top of position 1 turned 90 degrees.

Repetition

Positions are often repeated for balance and uniformity. A spread about two people may have two duplicate sets of cards—one for each person. In Figure 10, the 3-card groups to each side are duplicates.

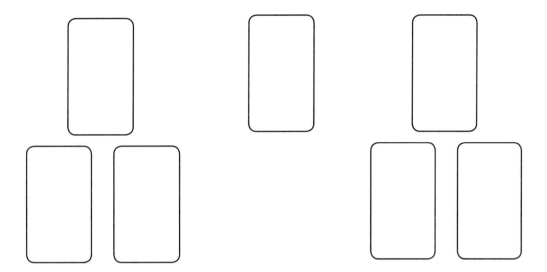

Figure 10. Spacing helps define position groups

Orientation

Most positions are oriented so they are straight up-and-down. They echo the card images when viewed normally. Occasionally positions are angled or horizontal to highlight a certain relationship to the other cards. An arrow spread may have two angled positions to create the impression of the arrowhead.

Spread Patterns

Certain shapes have archetypal meanings. A spread with such a shape resonates with the universal meaning of that form. It has the ability to open us to deeper levels. A spread can also have these shapes as subgroups.

Single

A solitary position announces "I'm special." In the center of a spread, it shows central importance—a hub of interest. On the side, it shows a unique stance. A single can be at the end of a line to show where all the other positions are leading. Figure 10 shows a single in the center.

Pair

A pair consists of two positions that belong together. A pair creates a two-sided dynamic. It shows two similar or opposing qualities. Position pairs are interpreted in relation to each other.

Line

A line is three or more cards in a row—horizontal, vertical, or diagonal. A line can mean "interpret us as a group"—all the positions in the line refer to the same subject. Sometimes,

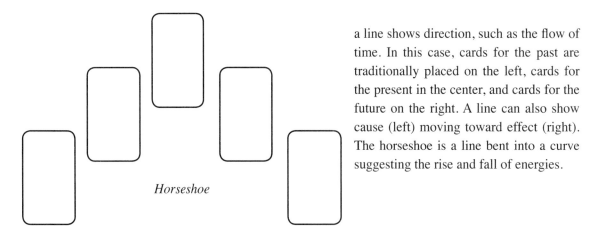

Horseshoe

a line shows direction, such as the flow of time. In this case, cards for the past are traditionally placed on the left, cards for the present in the center, and cards for the future on the right. A line can also show cause (left) moving toward effect (right). The horseshoe is a line bent into a curve suggesting the rise and fall of energies.

Triangle

A triangle is a set of three positions in a cluster. One kind has two cards on the bottom and one on top. The two "combine" to point to the third—their sum or integration. Another kind has one position on the bottom and two on top showing two developments arising from the same root. You can add more positions to create a "V" shape. The pyramid shape adds horizontal lines with each line containing one additional position.

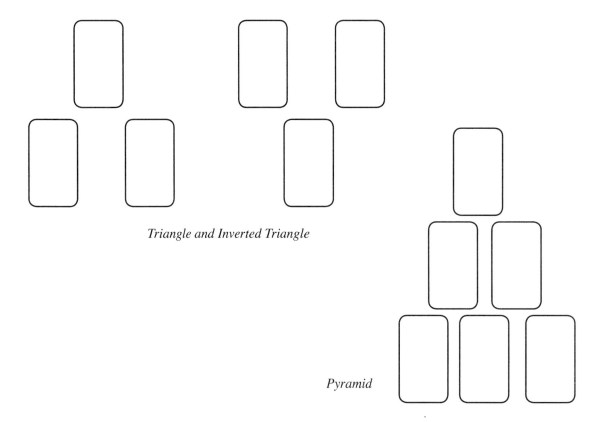

Triangle and Inverted Triangle

Pyramid

THE BIG BOOK OF TAROT

Cross

A cross is made up of two perpendicular lines. The simplest form has positions in the four directions: north, south, east, and west. Usually there is a fifth position in the center as a point of integration. A cross can be extended in any direction with extra positions. The arms of a cross can be the same length or different. The "T" and "L" shapes are variations of the cross.

Greek Cross

Bridge

A bridge is a single position or line connecting two other lines or groups. Some examples are the "H" and "A" shapes. A bridge literally bridges two entities. It shows what joins them or brings them together. Figure 10 shows a single, central position as a bridge.

Circle

A circle suggests unity. In a circle spread, all the positions belong together. They are elements of one whole. The months of the year are often placed in a circle spread. Sometimes, positions in a circle show the many qualities of a subject whose essence is given by a single position in the center.

Grid

A grid is a set of lines grouped together in a square or rectangle. Often, each line is defined as a unit with the meaning of each position fixed by its row and column. Figure 11 shows a grid spread that compares three people over time. The middle position shows "mom" in the "present." The lower right position shows "dad" in the "future." Grid spreads are quite versatile. You can create many variations by changing the line definitions.

Figure 11. A three-by-three grid spread

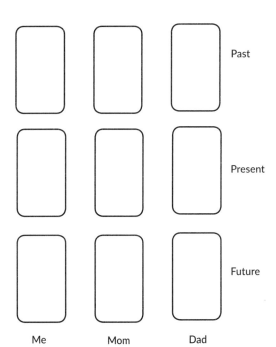

SHAPE AWARENESS

Look for geometric shapes in your environment. Pay attention to the patterns in objects, but also to their influence in the abstract. How does it feel when people are in pairs, lines, circles, or triangles? When are bridges in effect? Try to get in touch with the archetypal energies of different shapes in different circumstances.

SPREAD SHAPE EXPLORATION

Try using some of these spread designs for your readings. Look for situations where the unique design of a spread suits your circumstances. A cross spread might clarify the clash of two opposing factions. A circle spread might help you see how family members perceive a subject of common interest (card in the center). There are many possibilities.

Chapter Eight

SMALL SPREADS

The simplest spread of all is the one-card spread. You choose a subject and turn over one card to gain insight into that subject. You might think there is not much useful information to be gained from one card, but that is not the case! What a one-card spread lacks in diversity, it gains in simplicity and directness. The guidance you receive from one card is succinct and easy to remember.

Daily Reading

The daily reading is a one-card spread with a time period subject—one day. The purpose of the daily reading is to heighten your awareness of one approach to life for a single twenty-four-hour period.

To establish a daily reading practice, follow the guidelines found here and in the Learning Procedure section in Chapter One (page 9). Keep a journal, if you can. After a while, you will find it interesting to go back and trace the pattern of your choices.

I started studying the tarot in earnest when I was spending my days caring for my two boys, both under five. One day I calculated the distribution of my daily cards to that point and found the following:

* *Wands—24*

* *Cups—44*

* *Swords—41*

* *Pentacles—57*

* *Major Arcana—56*

How clearly this described my life at that time—heavy on the real world (Pentacles) and basic forces (major arcana) and not so heavy on individual creativity (Wands).

You will probably be surprised to find that you draw certain cards over and over. Of the fifty-seven Pentacles I recorded, I drew the Ace and Queen eleven times each! At home with my children, so many of my days reflected the themes of these two cards. The Queen of Pentacles is the ultimate nurturing mother. The Ace of Pentacles offers opportunities to enjoy the material side of life, and it doesn't get more material than changing dirty diapers!

I picked these two cards so often that I became suspicious about them. I examined them closely one day to see if I had damaged them in such a way that I would be more likely to select them. They appeared no different from the others. I was simply drawn to them because they expressed my situation at that time. The cards you select frequently will tell you about your concerns.

Three-Card Spreads

Three-card spreads are also simple, but provide a little more detail about a subject. The number three is a powerful, archetypal number. It communicates the idea of two factors combining or developing into a third. It also implies one factor branching into two different paths or choices.

Many traditional spreads have three cards, such as Past/Present/Future or Romance/Career/Health. You can create a variety of three-card spreads using the Flex spread which will be discussed in Chapters Ten and Eleven.

Quick Insight Spread

The Quick Insight spread uses three positions from the Celtic Cross (page 283): position 1—the heart of a matter, position 2—some related factor, and position 9—guidance. The first two positions capture the core dynamic of a subject –its essential energy (1) and some other factor (2). The guidance card (3) to the right provides perspective on that combination.

Figure 12 shows a sample Quick Insight spread. The main subject is a situation—"my dispute with a contractor." A quick interpretation might be:

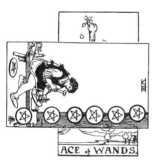

Figure 12

This situation is an opportunity to be confident and sure of success (Ace of Wands in position 1). A factor for change (position 2) is that I need more detail and knowledge before I can take advantage of that opportunity (Eight of Pentacles). The guidance card reinforces this idea, but with stronger energy (Hierophant—major arcana). Since the Hierophant and Eight of Pentacles are reinforcing cards, the guidance is a strong push toward learning and studying. The message of this reading is, "I should become more informed and educated to encourage the potential for success in this contract dispute."

Small spreads are easy to use on a regular basis. They give you the opportunity to connect with your Inner Guide frequently. Small spreads are meant to be quick, so the reading procedure for them is simplified (see the Simplified Reading Procedure page 330). If you never go beyond small spreads, you will still gain tremendous value from your tarot cards.

Chapter Nine

THE CELTIC CROSS SPREAD

T he Celtic Cross is probably the oldest and most popular spread. It has survived so long because the layout of the cards is simple, but powerful. A strong energy has built up around this spread due to its use by so many people over the years.

The Celtic Cross is divided into two sections: the cross on the left and the staff on the right. The circle/cross positions give you a snapshot of certain key aspects of a subject at the time of a reading. The staff positions comment on what is pictured in the cross.

The Circle/Cross

This section simulates the Celtic cross found throughout Ireland. This type of cross has a circle linking the four perpendicular spokes—a symbol of the joining of spirit and matter and the unity of all events in time.

The two central positions are a mini-cross (shown in gray). Position 1 represents the heart of the matter—the hub around which everything else is turning. Position 2 literally crosses position 1 to show some factor impacting the first.

The mini-cross is nested within a larger cross of two lines. The horizontal line shows time moving from the past on the left (4) into the near future on the right (6). The vertical line is awareness moving from what is unconscious or unknown on the bottom (3) to what is conscious or known on the top (5).

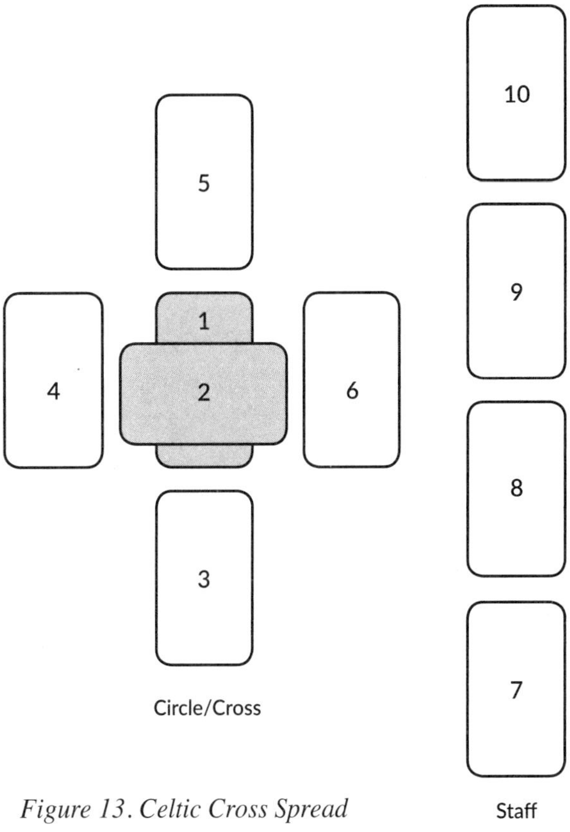

Figure 13. Celtic Cross Spread

Circle/Cross

Staff

The Staff

In the four positions of the Staff section, you receive insight about yourself (7) and others (8), guidance (9), and a probable outcome (10). Detailed descriptions of the Celtic Cross positions are given at the end of this chapter.

Positions Pairs in the Celtic Cross

One reason the Celtic Cross is so powerful is that it contains so many built-in position pairs.

Position 1—Position 2

The first two positions form an obvious pair because position 2 sits right on top of position 1. Traditionally position 2 is said to be"that which is crossing you." The 1–2 pair can show two

factors coming together either on a collision course or for mutual support. Sometimes the central issue (1) is affected by a factor for change (2).

Sharon asked for a reading shortly after she reunited with her boyfriend. They had broken up a few weeks before because she wanted marriage and children, and he was reluctant. Now, they were engaged. She drew the Ten of Cups (1) and the Six of Pentacles (2).

The Ten of Cups shows the joy of romance and family that is the promise of this couple's future. The Six of Pentacles suggests that there are still issues of give-and-take to work out. This card symbolizes the subtle (or not so subtle!) dance of dominance/submission that is a factor here.

Position 3—Position 5

The 3-5 pair represents different levels of awareness. You can learn about real feelings (3) vs expected feelings (5), or deeper truths (3) vs surface appearances (5). Sometimes these positions reveal the wisdom of your Higher Self (3) vs the beliefs of your ego-self (5).

Nicole did a reading to find out what to do about her friend Ann. Ann had asked Nicole to lie to her (Ann's) ex-husband about where she and their children were. Nicole drew the Ten of Wands (3) and the Ten of Cups (5).

Nicole *thought* she should provide love and support to Ann and try to help keep peace in their family (Ten of Cups). At a deeper level, though, she was having trouble saying no. She felt burdened by the responsibility of the request and resented being dragged into this messy situation (Ten of Wands).

THE BIG BOOK OF TAROT

Position 4—Position 6

Positions 4 and 6 are mirror images. Position 4 is the past, and position 6, the near future. Together they form the two halves of the circle of time that surrounds the present (position 1). These cards can show something moving away (4) vs approaching (6), or something to be released (4) vs something to be embraced (6). Sometimes position 4 shows what has already been experienced vs what is yet to be experienced (6).

In a reading about a possible career change, I drew the Seven of Pentacles (4) and the Eight of Wands (6). The Seven of Pentacles is a card of assessment—the need to take stock before a decision. Here it suggests that such questioning needs to end. The time for quick action and conclusion is at hand as shown by the Eight of Wands. This pair seems to be saying, "OK, you've thought long enough. Now, go ahead and make your move, whatever it is."

Position 7—Position 8

We experience ourselves as separate from an outside world, but in fact we are tied to our environment by countless threads of cause and effect, emotion and thought. The 7–8 pair shows connections between you and your environment. The environment can be a person, group, or the atmosphere in general.

Cynthia didn't share what was on her mind during a reading until she saw Justice (7). When I told her this card can mean having to accept the results of a past action, she volunteered that she was worried about being pregnant. The timing was just not right for her and her boyfriend; however, she was comforted to see the Lovers (8) as her environment. This card suggests that the environment is loving and supportive. Her boyfriend—lover—is standing by. This card also reinforces the sexual context.

Position 9

Traditionally, position 9 represents your "hopes and fears," but I often use it as a guidance card. When you read the cards for yourself, you need a card to help you pull everything together. Position 9 can pair with any of the other positions to elucidate the reading. It can show an approach to take, a way to proceed, a key person or obstacle, or a perspective on the whole situation. It can also reveal a surprise or "wild card" in the situation.

One day I received a letter from my son's teacher. She wanted to talk to me about an incident in class. I drew the Five of Wands (9). I assumed this card meant my son was working at cross-purposes with those around him.

Later, I learned more details: my son had poked another child repeatedly with a pencil. This came as a surprise as he had never done such a thing before. In fact, the image on the

Five of Pentacles was showing me the exact problem—a young person holding a long piece of wood (a pencil) and using it repeatedly as a weapon (five figures)!

Position 5 and Position 10

Position 10 is a projected outcome. It represents the most likely development if all the factors in a situation continue unimpeded on their current trajectory. This outcome is not a given. You can alter or reinforce this course by changing the conditions that exist in the moment.

Sometimes you can pair position 10 with position 5 to compare what you think (5) with what is projected (10). When position 5 reinforces position 10, your beliefs are flowing with the thrust of events. If they are at odds, then some introspection is in order.

You're working on your Ph.D. and have set the date for your oral presentation. You do a reading to see how well you are progressing and draw the Six of Wands (5) and the Nine of Swords (10). This pair is giving you a loud wake-up call. You are picturing a triumphant victory parade for yourself, but the projected outcome is the opposite—an anxious experience. You might want to take steps to make sure your projected future is more in keeping with your goal.

As you can see, there are many insights to be gained from the Celtic Cross. This spread will serve you well whenever you're seeking a more in-depth picture of a certain subject. See Appendix C for a series of three readings that used the Celtic Cross.

CELTIC CROSS SPREAD STUDY

Shuffle the deck and lay out ten cards in the Celtic Cross spread. Now, read the description for each position as given below. Become familiar with the positions and how they work together. Explore the spread in more depth by interpreting the cards you have drawn in position pairs as described in this section. Imagine any meaningful relationship that comes to mind spontaneously. Let a story of whatever kind develop as you play with the connections. The goal is to get to know the positions and to appreciate the wealth of insights this spread has to offer.

Celtic Cross Spread Position Meanings

Celtic Cross Spread Keyword Chart

POSITION 1	POSITION 2	POSITION 3
Heart of the Matter	Opposing Factor	Root Cause
Present Environment (Outer)	Factor for Change	Unconscious Influence
Present Environment (Inner)	Secondary Factor	Deeper Meaning
Primary Factor	Reinforcing Factor	Unknown Factor
POSITION 4	**POSITION 5**	**POSITION 6**
Past	Attitudes and Beliefs	Future
Receding Influence	Conscious Influence	Approaching Influence
Resolved Factor	Goal or Purpose	Unresolved Factor
Quality to Let Go	Alternate Future	Quality to Embrace
POSITION 7	**POSITION 8**	**POSITION 9**
You as You Are	Outside Environment	Guidance
You as You Could Be	Another's Point of View	Key Factor
You as You Present Yourself	Another's Expectations	Hopes and Fears
You as You See Yourself	You as Others See You	Overlooked Factor
	POSITION 10	
	Outcome (Overall)	
	Outcome (Inner State) Outcome (Actions)	
	Outcome (Effects)	

CELTIC CROSS POSITION 1

HEART OF THE MATTER

central issue

major concern

basic worry or upset

primary focus

focal point

fundamental problem

PRESENT ENVIRONMENT (OUTER)

"that which covers you"

　—traditional

surrounding circumstances

immediate problem at hand

what's going on around you

what you're dealing with

external factors

PRESENT ENVIRONMENT (INNER)

internal factors

how you feel about the situation

key personal quality

basic state of mind

emotional state

what's going on inside of you

PRIMARY FACTOR

major influence

dominant characteristic

outstanding feature

most important element

most striking quality

CELTIC CROSS POSITION 2

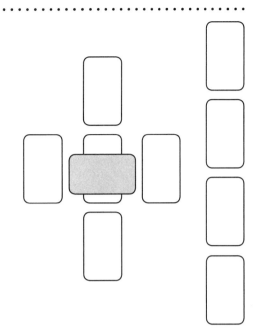

OPPOSING FACTOR

"that which is crossing you"
  —traditional

contrary element

source of resistance

balancing tendency

moderating influence

rival or subversive agent

FACTOR FOR CHANGE

something out of left field

unpredictable element

new consideration

unbalancing force

surprise

what's rocking the boat

SECONDARY FACTOR

tangential concern

another source of information

side issue

subordinate problem

minor factor

REINFORCING FACTOR

supporting feature

additional emphasis

cooperating person

extra attraction

magnifying force

related issue

Placement: To place the card in position 2 correctly, rotate the card 90° clockwise and lay it on top of card 1. Card 2 is reversed if the top of the card's image is on the left after placement.

CELTIC CROSS POSITION 3

ROOT CAUSE

source of the problem

basis of the situation

why things are as they are

childhood or past life (karmic) influence

reason behind events

starting point

UNCONSCIOUS INFLUENCE

"that which is beneath you"

—traditional

unrecognized motivations

unacknowledged goals

most basic impulses

driving needs or desires

denied or rejected aspects of self

DEEPER MEANING

larger picture

fundamental pattern

all-embracing point of view

soul purpose

underlying context

what's really going on

UNKNOWN FACTOR

hidden influence

unrecognized contribution

undiscovered participant

concealed agenda

behind-the-scenes machinations

CELTIC CROSS POSITION 4

SOMETHING RELATED TO THE PAST

quality

person

belief

event

opportunity

orientation

concern

hope

fear

RECEDING INFLUENCE

feature that is losing importance

fading concern

former focus

someone/something going away

falling star

RESOLVED FACTOR

fully realized quality

completed task

what's been wrapped up

what can be set aside

what's been taken care of

QUALITY TO LET GO

outmoded approach

what's no longer useful

unnecessary baggage

someone/something no longer needed

factor to be discarded

CELTIC CROSS POSITION 5

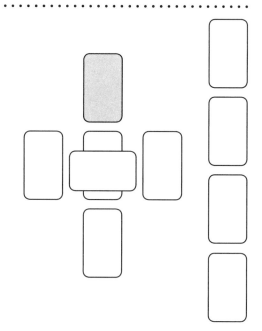

ATTITUDES AND BELIEFS

what you accept as true

assumptions

convictions

how you view what is happening

delusions or illusions

where you are placing your trust

CONSCIOUS INFLUENCE

what's on your mind

what you're focusing on

what you're worried about

what you're obsessed about

what you acknowledge

what is known

GOAL OR PURPOSE

aspirations

what you intend to achieve

expectations for the future

what you've set your heart on

preferences

desired result

ALTERNATE FUTURE

"what could come into being"
—traditional

potential development

different possibility

another option

what you think will happen

future you are consciously projecting

THE BIG BOOK OF TAROT

CELTIC CROSS POSITION 6

SOMETHING RELATED
TO THE FUTURE

quality

person

belief

event

opportunity

orientation

concern

hope

fear

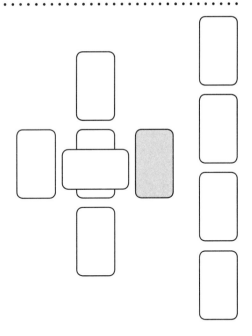

APPROACHING INFLUENCE

feature that is gaining importance

developing concern

coming focus

someone/something coming nearer

rising star

UNRESOLVED FACTOR

unrealized quality

incomplete task

what is still pending

what must be considered

what needs to be taken care of

QUALITY TO EMBRACE

valid approach

what will be useful

desirable attribute

someone/something that is needed

factor to be welcomed

CELTIC CROSS POSITION 7

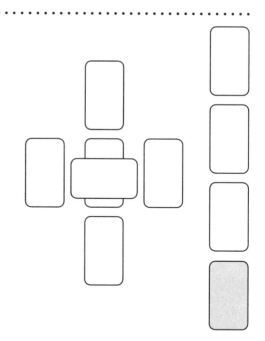

YOU AS YOU ARE

personal style

your temperament or disposition

your approach to the problem

your unique orientation

your point of view

your way of being

your position or stance

YOU AS YOU COULD BE

inner resource to tap

talent or ability you can use

what you are capable of

an ideal to live up to

a possible approach

what you want to be

your goal for yourself

YOU AS YOU PRESENT YOURSELF

your public face

how you think you should be

mask you show the world

what you do for appearances' sake

role you accept

self-imposed duty

your false self

YOU AS YOU SEE YOURSELF (TRADITIONAL)

your self-image

your beliefs about yourself

your sense of where you are

your fears about yourself

your assumptions about yourself

how you limit yourself

how you magnify yourself

CELTIC CROSS POSITION 8

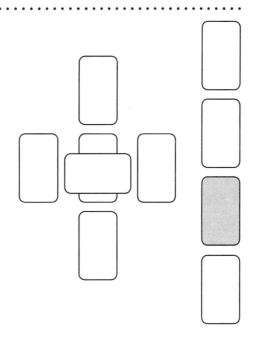

OUTSIDE ENVIRONMENT

"that which surrounds you"
  —traditional

atmosphere

emotional climate

physical and social milieu

setting for the situation

playing field

context in which you must operate

ANOTHER'S POINT OF VIEW

how another sees the situation

the other person's side

another slant on the problem

different outlook

an objective opinion

ANOTHER'S EXPECTATIONS

what others want from you

demands placed on you

what another thinks you should be or do

claims of others on you

outside restrictions imposed on you

your assigned role

YOU AS OTHERS SEE YOU

"how others see you"—traditional

how you are coming across

how you're being assessed

public opinion about you

impression you create

effect you have on others

CELTIC CROSS POSITION 9

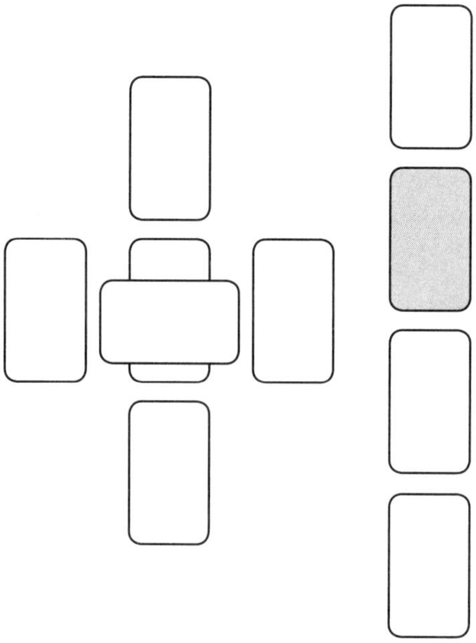

GUIDANCE

what you might do

how best to proceed

how you can make a change

word of warning

truth of the matter

different approach

helpful suggestion

honest assessment

KEY FACTOR

fundamental aspect

lesson to be learned

what explains everything

clue to what is happening

what you need to know

connecting link

HOPES AND FEARS (TRADITIONAL)

what you're afraid of

what you suspect is true

what you're avoiding

personal demon

what you long for

your dream

your ideal

your secret desire

OVERLOOKED FACTOR

something you haven't considered

missing piece of the puzzle

someone else who has a role to play

something else to consider

element of surprise

underestimated influence

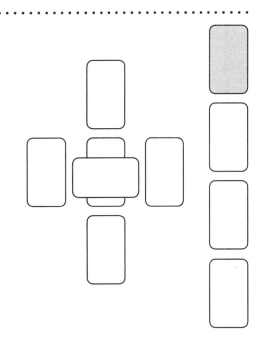

OUTCOME (OVERALL)

the most likely result

what may come to pass

how the situation may be resolved

where everything is leading

probable resolution

OUTCOME (INNER STATE)

how you will end up feeling

what your mood will be

understanding you will gain

lesson you will absorb

attitude you will assume

quality or ability you will realize

OUTCOME (ACTIONS)

what you may have to do

how you may succeed or fail

conduct you will have to adopt

required behavior

what you may accomplish

approach you may have to take

OUTCOME (EFFECTS)

how someone else will be affected

how the environment will change

what others will do

possible countermeasure or backlash

possible benefit or reward

improvement that will occur

change in status

Chapter Ten

THE FLEX SPREAD

When I was learning the tarot, I tried new spreads from time to time, but somehow, I always returned to my old reliables—the few spreads I knew and trusted.
They worked for me because they were comfortable and familiar. Eventually, I
decided there had to be a better way to make it easier to learn and use new spreads. The result
is the flex spread.

The flex spread is a framework for creating different layouts. It's similar to a regular
spread, but, instead of having fixed positions, it has areas that "hold" positions of different
types. Before you do a reading, you choose the positions for each area based on what you
want to explore. In this way, you create a customized spread as simple or elaborate as you
wish for any reading situation.

Flex spreads are designed for subject readings because they revolve around a main subject you select beforehand. Open readings do not work well with the flex spread because you
do not want to consciously choose positions for these readings.

Figure 14 shows the five areas of the flex spread. The numbers show the card placement
order. You number all the positions in an area before moving on to the next. If you don't use
an area at all, you simply skip over it and continue on with your position numbering.

The Main Subject Area

A mandala is a geometric design that symbolizes the cosmos. Most mandalas are circular,
suggesting wholeness and unity. A circle also has a center around which everything turns.

The flex spread is like a mandala in that it, too, has a center—the main subject position
(1). Each flex spread is oriented around a main subject you designate and name before beginning. The main subject can be of any type. It shows a central or key feature of the subject—its
essence at the time of the reading. A subject's essence is its heart, so this position goes in the
heart of the spread.

The main subject is the only required position in the flex spread. All other positions are
optional. In fact, the most basic flex layout consists of just this one position. What could be
simpler?

The main subject is the only position that can be of any subject type. For example, you
can focus on your health, a problem, or you yourself.

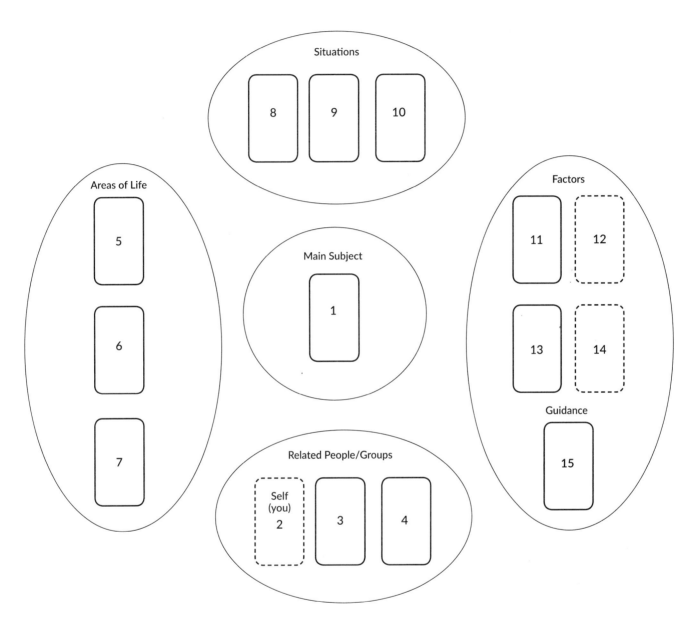

Figure 14. The five areas of a sample flex spread. Numbers show the placement order if all areas are used.

Related Subject Areas

The flex spread has three related subject areas of three different types. These are listed below with their placement order:

related people and groups—below, left to right

related areas of life—left, top to bottom

related situations—above, left to right

A related subject is always interpreted in relation to the main subject and draws its meaning from that association. You can have any number of related subjects, or none at all. You can have several in one area, but just one in another—whatever combination works best. Chapter Eleven gives some examples of flex spreads with various related subject configurations.

If you're not the main subject, I highly recommend designating the leftmost position in the related people/groups area to be a position representing you. This self position will highlight your relationship to the main subject directly.

The Factors and Guidance Area

The Factors and Guidance area is to the right of the main subject. Factors are different from related subjects because factors describe certain qualities of the main subject. They highlight different aspects that may be of interest in a given reading. For example, you can explore such questions as:

What is the main subject avoiding?

What is enduring about the main subject?

What has contributed to the current status of the main subject?

What is stabilizing about the main subject?

The answers to these questions would be suggested by the cards that fall in the appropriate factor positions.

Factor positions are interpreted according to the main subject type. For example, if you are the main subject, the Inside factor shows your inner thoughts and emotions. If an event is the main subject, the Inside factor shows the event's internal dynamics—what's going on inside, or behind the scenes.

In Chapter Eleven, I describe twenty different factor positions. Each is paired with another position that is its opposite. An example is Known and Unknown. A card in the Known position might show what the main subject knows, while the Unknown factor shows what he does not know. It's often interesting to include both factors in a pair so you can compare opposite influences. The placement order for factors is top to bottom, with opposing pairs, if any, placed side by side.

Guidance

Guidance is a unique position. Every other position shows a neutral, energetic picture of something to do with the main subject. A card in Guidance gives you a point of view coming from the wisdom of your Inner Guide. It's always desirable to include the guidance position, so you can receive this personal assistance. The guidance position is centered below the factors, if any, with some space surrounding it.

MAKE A SUBJECT LIST

Create a list of subjects from your life in each of these categories: other people, groups, areas of life, and situations. See Part Five for sample areas of life. For situations, consider the problems, choices, tasks, and events you are currently involved in. You'll find this list helpful when you go to do a flex spread reading.

Chapter Eleven

CREATING AND USING FLEX SPREADS

N ow that you are familiar with the flex spread, let's look at how to create and use one for a reading. Have a paper and pencil handy because you will want to draw the layout as you go.

Choosing the Main Subject

First, choose the main subject of your reading. You may know right away what you want the subject to be, but if you're not sure, read the section about subjects in Chapter Two. Consider the subject type as well. Here are some points to keep in mind:

Self

Choose yourself as the main subject if you're mainly interested in your own experience and various aspects of your life from your perspective.

Other Person

Focus on someone else if you're concerned or curious about that person. Remember, you'll receive the information and guidance important for you to absorb, not absolute truths about the other person independent of you.

Group

A group main subject is best if you want to understand from the perspective of some group as a whole, such as a family or work unit.

Area of Life

Choose an area of life if it is of special interest to you in general, not because of a particular person or situation within that area. See Part Five for a list of possible areas of life.

Time Period

A time-period main subject is best if you're interested in all the people, issues, and events within a certain expanse of time.

Situation

Choose a situation for a main subject if you have a choice to make, or you're involved in a specific problem or event that concerns you at the moment.

Now, begin drawing your new flex spread by putting the main subject position in the center and labeling it. Assign number 1 to the position to show it's the first card to be placed. Figure 15 (page 305) shows the sample flex spread I describe throughout the flex spread creation process.

Let's say you decide to do a reading about your basketball team. You make "my basketball team" your main subject and note that this is a group type subject.

Choosing Related Subjects

Now, choose the related subject positions you want to include in three areas: people/groups, areas of life, and situations. Remember you can skip any related area if you want.

Related People/Groups

First, consider all the people and groups involved with your main subject at the moment. From these, choose only the most relevant. It would be too cumbersome, even counterproductive to include everyone.

If you are not the main subject, include a self position as #2 on the left. After that, you can assign your people/groups to positions in any order you wish. Enter the positions with their order on your flex spread drawing. Be sure to note who goes where.

For our example, you might decide to include three people/groups involved in your basketball team: you (2), your coach (3), and your main rival team, the Rockets (4).

Areas of Life

Now, add any area of life positions you're curious about in relation to the main subject. Add these positions with labels to your drawing, and number them from top to bottom.

In our example, you might decide on just one area of life—Team Health (5). You want to know more about any health issues involving the team.

Situations

Consider the situations area. You can include problems, choices, tasks, or events. Mark these positions on your layout and number them from left to right.

Create a short, descriptive label for each position. This is especially important for situations because their exact meanings are easy to forget once the reading has begun. In our example, you might include two situations: a problem labeled "Lack of Team Motivation" (6) and an event labeled "Next Game against the Rockets" (7).

Choosing Factors and Guidance

Finally, choose the factors and guidance you want to include (see pages 313–328 for descriptions). It will take a while for you to become familiar with these positions. You will have to build up some experience with them over time to be able to select the most relevant ones for a reading quickly.

In general, it's best to avoid having too many factors as your spread can become unwieldy. (On the other hand, an elaborate flex reading can be fun to explore in depth.) While you're learning, you should go slowly and limit the factors to just a few. Consider including two opposing pair factors to help you learn how they interact.

Add the factor positions to your drawing with numbers. Use the factor name as the label. Place your first factor at the top, and its opposite to the right, if included. Place the next factor below the first, with its opposite to its right. Continue in this way until you've placed all the factors you've selected. The guidance position is centered below the factors, set off by extra space.

In our example, you decide to include three factors and guidance. The factors are Inactive (8) and an opposing pair—Stabilizing (9)/Disrupting (10). You're curious about what might be inactive in the team as this could shed light on the lack of motivation problem. You also want to learn what might be influencing the team toward or away from stability. You include the guidance position (11) because it's always welcome.

Learning Your Layout

You now have a complete flex spread layout to use for your reading. Try to memorize your layout as much as possible. Visualize the positions, and see yourself placing cards in order. Once you begin a reading, it's important to follow the layout as designed. Don't change labels, switch positions, or leave any out. This helps keep your intention clear and focused, so there is no confusion.

Clarity is so important in the tarot. I can't emphasize this enough! Your reading will flow better if you know your layout well. This familiarity allows you to pay attention to your intuition rather than procedural details. But, don't be concerned if you do need to refer to your drawing during a reading.

At first, choosing and learning a layout takes a little time, but the process gets easier. Soon, the best layout for an occasion will occur to you naturally, perhaps even while you're preparing for a reading. Gradually, you will collect a set of favorite layouts for different occasions that you know work well for you.

Using our example, let's see how a flex spread reading about the basketball team might work. You decide to do a reading about the team because it is on a losing streak, and you sense a lack of motivation in the team and yourself. You want to see what's going on, especially as a very important game against the Rockets is coming up.

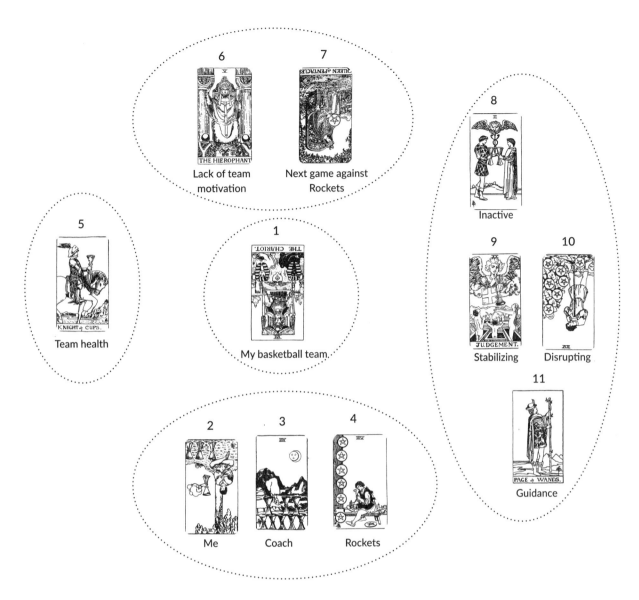

Figure 15. Sample Flex Spread Reading

You draw the cards in Figure 15. You are immediately struck by the main subject card—the reversed Chariot. Victory is indeed at a low level, but there is hope! The potential for victory is present, if not fully developed.

The reversed Four of Cups represents you. You have indeed been feeling apathetic, but the reversal suggests that feeling is fading. It seems, though, that your coach is weary and "losing hope" (Eight of Cups). The losses have been disheartening.

The team health is not great either. The Knight of Cups suggests the players may "lack robust good health" and be "prone to mood swings."

To make matters worse, the Rockets seem to be "working hard" and "producing steady results"—Eight of Pentacles.

The picture doesn't seem particularly hopeful. How can the seed of victory be developed? A possibility is suggested by the Hierophant which addresses the lack of motivation problem directly. There is a strong need for a solid group identity. The players need to "work as part of a team." However, this aspect is inactive right now (Two of Cups). The energy of "working together" and "sharing" is on hold.

The team has not been very open to a direction change—reversed Seven of Pentacles—and this is disrupting. Yet, the team can "make an honest appraisal" and be "drawn in a new direction"—Judgement. This would ground the team and provide a stable foundation.

It would be wonderful if the situation could miraculously change, but the reversed Queen of Pentacles suggests that as things stand now, the game with the Rockets may only be a start toward the goal. These opponents will be able to "get around every obstacle" and "be resourceful," even if not to a great extent (reversed).

The key to victory lies with the Page of Wands as guidance. This lack of motivation problem can be solved by seeing the moment as an opportunity to "be confident" and "enthusiastic." To "move beyond doubts" and "focus on success."

FACTOR PRACTICE

Pick a factor position to focus on each day so you can become familiar with them. The factor descriptions begin on page 313. As you read your factor's description, think about how its qualities express in you, other people, events, and situations. Try to recognize the presence of the factor as you go about your daily affairs. For example, for Blocking you would pay attention to anything that is frustrating or limiting. For Ending, you would watch for anything that seems to be fading or moving away.

CREATE AND USE A FLEX SPREAD

Design a flex spread layout for yourself using the guidelines in this section, and do a reading. After the reading, reflect on how well your layout worked. Consider these questions:

Did I receive the insights I was looking for?

Were there too many positions, or too few?

Was it easy to create the story from the positions I chose?

How useful were the factors I selected?

Keep your flex spread with any notes for future reference.

Serial Flex Spread Readings

Serial readings offer you a way to explore a train of subjects in great depth. The premise is simple. After completing a reading, you decide if you'd like to continue the session. If so, you choose a related subject card from those in your first reading and make that card the main subject of a new reading.

A serial reading is always based on a related subject card from a prior reading. You should maintain the label and type of the card. A situation card continues to represent the same situation. A related person stays as that person. For example, a card for Jeff in an original reading could become the main subject of a new, second reading centered on Jeff.

Let's say you've done a reading to look at three areas of life—work, romance and health. You are the main subject. You draw the Tower in the work position. You wonder what this is all about. You decide to explore it by doing a serial reading focused on the Tower as your new main subject.

Here's the procedure for a serial reading:

Choose the new main subject

First, make a note of the cards in your first reading so you don't forget them. Then, choose and set aside the card you want to be your new main subject. Gather up the rest of the cards and add them to the balance of the deck.

Design the new spread

Decide what your serial spread will look like. It can take any form. It can be smaller or larger than the first. You can keep some of the old positions, or add new ones. The only requirement is that you hold over one card as your new main subject. Write down the positions, their labels and placement order for your new spread.

Conduct the serial reading

Place the retained card in front of you as the new main subject. You don't need to draw a main position card as you already have one. Now, continue as you would for a regular flex spread reading. You don't have to follow all the procedural steps unless you want to, but it's important to at least reshuffle and recut the deck. Lay the cards out in the new placement order.

You can continue doing serial readings as long as you have the time and inclination. You can explore a variety of related subjects from your original reading, or you can take a subject from the second reading and continue on in a third one. Either way, you create a series of readings that are interconnected through their subjects.

Serial Readings for Extra Guidance

One particularly useful approach is doing a serial reading for extra guidance. In many readings, a certain card is especially puzzling. You know it's important, but its meaning is hazy.

Figure 16. A Serial Reading for Extra Guidance

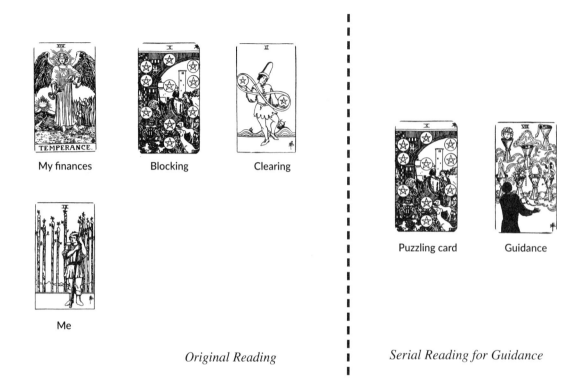

You can't quite make it fit with the others. In this case, you can do a serial reading for guidance. The puzzling card becomes the new main subject, and you add just one other position—guidance.

Let's say you've done a reading with your finances as the main subject. Your original layout included one related person (you) and two factors (blocking and clearing). The cards you've drawn are shown in the Original Reading in Figure 16.

Most of this reading makes sense to you. Your spending has been moderate overall (Temperance). You've been persevering in trying to improve your finances (Nine of Wands). You've been clearing your debt by juggling all your bills (Two of Pentacles). The only card you don't understand is the Ten of Pentacles. How can wealth be blocking? You decide to seek guidance about this card.

For guidance purposes, any card can be taken from the first reading. You are not restricted to related subjects. So, you set aside the Ten of Pentacles, then shuffle and cut all the rest of the cards. You place the Ten of Pentacles in the center, then lay out one new card in the guidance position to the right of the Ten. This is the Serial Reading for Guidance in Figure 16.

You draw the Seven of Cups. Now, you understand that wishful thinking about affluence is blocking you. The desire to be free of money problems is making you nervous. You can now interpret the Ten of Pentacles with more clarity.

A reading is an energetic event that reflects a certain moment in time. Ideally, that "moment" should be one unbroken experience. Try to complete all your serial readings in one sitting, if possible. Be sure to write down each reading before you move on to the next, so you can look for patterns and connections. The same cards often repeat in revealing ways.

You may be tempted to do many serial readings in a row. It's fascinating to watch the cards unfold in various guises, but you do want to commit to devoting time to every reading you do. You honor the tarot process in this way. Serial readings give you a chance to go deeper into the subjects that concern you. They let you look at all the relationships from different perspectives.

A SERIAL READING

Look for a chance to do a serial reading after doing a flex spread reading. Don't force one artificially, but do give one a try if the opportunity arises. Later, take time to study the two readings and all the cards. Look for patterns and connections. A serial reading can offer a new dimension of insight in your tarot practice.

Flex Spread Position Meanings

This section contains information for all the positions in the flex spread.

Main Subject

Related Person

Related Group

Related Area of Life

Related Situation

Factors and Guidance

For each position, there are keywords, a description, a reversed meaning, some interpretation examples, and the location in the spread. To refresh, Figure 17 below shows the five areas of the Flex Spread.

Here's a sample interpretation taken from the Embracing factor description: A political party is welcoming the lone-wolf style (Seven of Swords).

The type formatting shows how the interpretation was created:

lone-wolf style [bold] = one meaning of the (Seven of Swords)—sample card

welcoming [italic] = one possible meaning for the Embracing Factor

political party [underline] = sample Main Subject

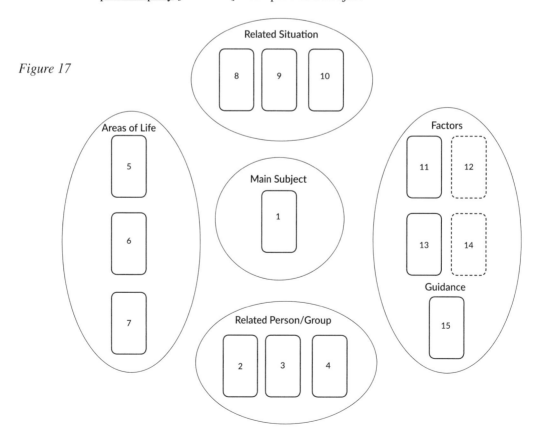

Figure 17

MAIN SUBJECT

Keywords: central issue • core • crux • essence • focus • heart of the matter • key • main idea • nature• spirit • substance • theme

Description: This position has two purposes. First, it symbolizes the main subject of a reading and serves as a visual reminder of that subject within a spread. Second, it shows some key feature of the main subject at the time of the reading.

This position captures the heart of the matter—a subject's central issue or theme. That theme may not be central for all time. It's just central at the moment. Sometimes a main subject card describes the subject as a whole. Other times, it refers to some feature playing an important role.

Reversed: Some central or key feature of the main subject is at a low level. It's not fully developed at the moment.

Examples: Main subject meaning in *italics*

> **Abundance** (Empress) is *central* to <u>you</u> at the moment.
>
> The *essence* of <u>a family problem</u> is **self-assertion** (Chariot).
>
> A **passionate charmer** *(*Knight of Wands) is a *key player* in the <u>area of romance</u>.
>
> The *essence* of <u>my dorm wing group</u> is a **low level of friendship** (reversed Three of Cups).
>
> The *spirit* of <u>the decade</u> is having **little conformity** (reversed Hierophant).

Flex-spread location: Exact center

RELATED PERSON

Keywords: approach • contribution • essence • key feature • point of view • quality • spirit • substance

Description: A related person position shows a central or key feature of someone from the point of view of the main subject. This position doesn't necessarily describe how the person views himself, or how a third party might view him. It shows what the main subject feels, believes, or expects from the person.

A related person can be labeled with a name such as Mark or a phrase such as "my son" or the "Manager of the Research." If the main subject is not you, you can include a self position to represent you as a related person.

Reversed: A person has a low level of some factor as far as the main subject is concerned. The nature of the factor is shown by the card.

Examples: (related person in *italics*)

> <u>You</u> see *a member of your support group as* **self-absorbed** (Four of Cups).

Arnold considers *his friend Eileen* to be a **wise counselor** (King of Cups).

Your neighbor is a source of **worry** (Nine of Swords) during the week.

Leona considers *your nephew* to be **reluctant to act** (reversed Magician).

The president thinks *a staff member* has **stopped working hard** (reversed Knight of Pentacles).

Flex-spread location: below the main subject

. . . .

RELATED GROUP

Keywords: approach • contribution • essence • key feature • point of view • quality • spirit • substance

Description: A related group position shows a central or key feature of some collection of people in relation to the main subject. This position doesn't necessarily describe how the group views itself, or how a third party might view the group. It shows what the main subject feels, believes, or expects from the group.

A related group can be labeled with a name such as "Sterling Construction Company" or a phrase such as "my family" or "Larry's team."

Reversed: A group has a low level of some factor as far as the main subject is concerned. The nature of the factor is shown by the card.

Examples: (related group in *italics*)

You may see *your office mates* as a lot of **fun** (Two of Pentacles).

Your grandson is a **leader** (Three of Wands) in *his scout troop*.

Your department sees *the company* as going through **movement and change** (Wheel of Fortune).

You see *your nephew* as **reluctant to act** (reversed Magician).

A choice may mean *the family* has **less prosperity** (reversed Ace of Pentacles).

Flex-spread location: below the main subject

. . . .

RELATED AREA OF LIFE

Keywords: approach • contribution • essence • key feature • point of view • quality • spirit • substance

Description: The related area of life position shows a central or key feature of an area of life from the point of view of the main subject. An area of life is defined as some consistent area in which different people, groups, and situations come and go over time. An area of life does not have to be one that the main subject is directly involved in, but often it is.

Reversed: An area of life has a low level of some factor as far as the main subject is concerned. The nature of the factor is shown by the card.

Examples: (area of life in *italics*)

> You are encouraged to **be creative** (Page of Wands) in *your career*.

> Your son feels *his health* has been **reborn** (Judgement) after successful surgery.

> There is a need for **deeper meaning** (Eight of Cups) in the *spiritual area* at a retreat.

> You **feel little attraction** (reversed Two of Cups) in a *new relationship*.

> A friend is putting **little thought** (reversed Four of Swords) into *his finances*.

Flex-spread location: left of the main subject

- -

RELATED SITUATION

Keywords: approach • contribution • essence • key feature • point of view • quality • spirit • substance

Description: A related situation shows the central or key feature of some situation of interest to the main subject. It can be a problem, choice, project, or event. A card in this position can refer to the situation as a whole or to some element within it. The situation does not have to be one the main subject is directly included in, but often it is. A related situation has a label that captures its essence, such as "my disagreement with Joe."

Reversed: A related situation has a low level of some factor as far as the main subject is concerned. The nature of the factor is shown by the card.

Examples: (related situation in *italics*):

> **Calm diplomacy** (King of Cups) is evident in *the lack of money problem* concerning your spouse.

> To your neighbor, a *book-writing project* is proving **lucrative** (Ten of Pentacles).

> *Your sister's anger* is proving to be a test of **personal beliefs** (Lovers) for you.

> For the company, **little competence** (reversed Three of Pentacles) is evident at *the trade show event*.

> *A career choice* represents **less control** (reversed Four of Pentacles) to your grandson.

Flex-spread location: above the main subject

• • •

Factors and Guidance Positions:

The following pages (314–328) provide keywords, a description, a reversed meaning, interpretation examples, and the location in the spread for a wide range of possible factors and guidance.

ACTIVE

Keywords: alive • animated • energized • engaged • enterprising • functioning • industrious • lively • occupied • spirited • vigorous • working

Description: One meaning of active is to be energetic and lively. Someone is active when busy going and doing. Another meaning is functioning. Something is active when it's in operation. Either of these meanings can apply to the active factor in relation to the main subject.

Sometimes a quality has been dormant, but is now activated. It is clearly evident in some fashion—alive and well.

Reversed: Some feature of the main subject is active, but at a low level.

Examples: (active factor in *italics*)

I am *actively* making **decisions** (Justice) in dealing with some duty.

A **pessimistic mood** (Knight of Pentacles) is *alive and well* on a project.

A **betrayal** (Three of Swords) is being *activated* on a certain day.

My partner is *actively* showing **a little defiance** (reversed Seven of Wands).

A group has settled down. It is **less** *actively* **restless** (reversed Knight of Wands) now.

Opposite Position: inactive

Flex-spread location: right of the main subject

AVOIDING

Keywords: avoiding • denying • distancing from • dodging • evading • fearing • pushing away • refraining from • resisting • retreating from • shunning • steering clear of

Description: To avoid means to deny or push away. If we fear or dislike something, we keep our distance. We try to pretend it's not true or doesn't exist. A card in the avoiding position shows something the main subject is resisting or denying.

Avoiding can be conscious or unconscious. You may realize you're avoiding—deliberately dodging—or be unaware of it. Sometimes, we avoid out of disapproval. We feel negative, even antagonistic. At other times, we simply prefer not to face something that's difficult.

Reversed: The main subject is avoiding or denying the fact that something is at a low level.

Examples: (avoiding factor in *italics*)

I am *avoiding* my **power** (Magician).

My spouse is *resisting* being a **martyr** (Ten of Swords).

Family life is changing because someone is *denying* **rejection** (Five of Pentacles).

In a situation, people are *resisting* **the restrictions on travel** (reversed Six of Swords).

The <u>high school baseball team</u> is *afraid to acknowledge* **the low level of honesty** (reversed Queen of Swords).

Opposite Position: embracing

Flex-spread location: right of the main subject

· ·

BEGINNING

Keywords: breaking ground • commencing • embarking on • entering • germinating • giving birth to • inaugurating • initiating • kicking off • launching • setting out • springing up • starting

Description: Beginning is the action of starting or commencing. A card in beginning shows a factor just becoming available to the main subject. A beginning quality can be brand new, or something reappearing. A beginning may be obvious or hidden. Sometimes a new seed has been planted, but the signs are not yet visible. When you're aware of beginnings, you have a chance to assist or reverse them.

Reversed: The main subject is beginning to experience a low level of something.

Examples: (beginning factor in *italics*)

<u>I</u> am *beginning* to feel **goodwill** (Six of Cups) toward someone.

A <u>relative</u> is *starting* to **regret** (Five of Cups) some action.

A <u>day</u> contains the *first indication* of someone's **downfall** (Tower).

<u>I</u> feel my opportunities to **mother** (reversed Empress) are *beginning* to **diminish** now that my child has left for college.

My <u>book club</u> is *starting* to be **less fun** (reversed Two of Pentacles).

Opposite Position: ending

Flex-spread location: right of the main subject

· ·

BLOCKING

Keywords: discouraging • frustrating • hindering • holding back • impeding • limiting • obstructing • opposing • preventing • restraining • retarding • slowing • thwarting

Description: Blocking energy slows and impedes. It keeps everything from moving forward. A card in blocking shows some factor obstructing progress for the main subject.

Usually blocking energy seems negative. Our impulse is to remove or neutralize whatever is standing in our way, but sometimes restraint is welcome. If events are moving forward too quickly, some limits can be helpful. Before you remove the blocks in your life, be sure they are truly hindering you.

Reversed: The main subject is feeling a low level of some block, obstruction or limitation. Sometimes, the fact that something is at a low level is blocking the main subject.

Examples: (blocking factor in *italics*)

I am feeling *blocked* in <u>my writing project</u> by a **fear** (Moon) of failure.

<u>My partner</u> is being *held back* by her tendency to **lash out** (Knight of Wands) at work.

My desire to **trust** (Page of Pentacles) is *preventing* me from recognizing the danger in <u>a situation</u>.

Now that I have my degree, **a low level of education** (reversed Hierophant) is no longer *holding me back* in <u>my career</u>.

My poor <u>health</u> is *thwarting a bit* my desire be **self-reliant** (reversed Nine of Pentacles).

Opposite Position: clearing

Flex-spread location: right of main subject

. . . .

CLEARING

Keywords: accelerating • aiding • assisting • expediting • fostering • freeing • furthering • getting rid of • hastening • helping • lending a hand to • opening • promoting • removing • unblocking

Description: Clearing means removing obstacles. When you clear something away, you get rid of it so you're free to move forward. A card in clearing shows a factor helping the main subject to advance. It aids and assists.

Clearing can create a new path or expedite an existing one. It can be recognized as helpful or destructive, depending on the circumstances.

Reversed: The main subject is receiving a low level of assistance. Sometimes, the fact that some factor is low may be clearing the way for the main subject.

Examples: (clearing factor in *italics*)

A **new burst of enthusiasm** (Ace of Wands) *is helping* me succeed in a <u>task</u>.

A **wise and caring friend** (King of Cups) *is lending* <u>me</u> a hand.

My sudden **acclaim** (Six of Wands) *is clearing the way* in <u>my work</u>.

I feel **less hopeless** (reversed Devil) <u>today</u> which *is freeing* me to get more accomplished.

Feeling **less like a victim** (reversed Ten of Swords) *is helping* me get rid of many problems in <u>my relationship</u>.

Opposite Position: blocking

Flex-spread location: right of main subject

CONTRIBUTING TO

Keywords: bringing about • causing • creating • generating • impacting • inciting • inducing • influencing • inspiring • leading to • precipitating • producing

Description: Contributing to identifies a factor that has helped bring about the current state of the main subject. It shows something influencing present conditions. Contributing to shows an important influence, but perhaps just one among many.

Contributing to is related to the past. We think of the past as causing the present, but that's not exactly true. It's the energies you carry from the past into the present that make the difference.

Reversed: The low level of some factor is contributing to the current state of the main subject. Contributing to implies something from the past affecting the present.

Examples: (contributing to factor in *italics*)

My **enterprising spirit** (King of Pentacles) *contributed to* the current abundance in my finances.

A situation has been made worse by the *impact* of everyone's **defensiveness** (Nine of Wands).

Memories of past **hard times** (Five of Pentacles) have *caused* me to be overly cautious.

Leonard was **less wholehearted** (reversed Queen of Wands) which *caused* the project to flounder.

I had **little chance for solitude** (reversed Hermit) which *contributed to* a frantic week.

Opposite Position: resulting from

Flex-spread location: right of the main subject

DISRUPTING

Keywords: changing • destabilizing • disconcerting • disordering • disturbing • overturning • shaking • shifting • shuffling • unbalancing • upsetting • unsettling

Description: A disrupting force causes change. It shakes up the status quo. A card in disrupting shows some factor that is upsetting the existing order for the main subject. The disturbance could be a quality of the main subject or an outside factor having an impact. The disturbance may be strong or mild.

Sometimes a disrupting force is destructive. At other times, it brings welcome change. It may be unsettling, but it creates an opportunity for growth. Whether or not an upsetting factor is helpful depends on all the conditions of the moment.

Reversed: A low level of some factor is disrupting or shaking up the main subject.

Examples: (disrupting factor in *italics*)

I am feeling *disrupted* by the need to **let go** (Hanged Man).

Someone **obsessive about detail** (Knight of Pentacles) is *shaking up* routines in a company.

Some **news** (Eight of Wands) is *upsetting the apple cart* at an event.

Whispers of an open dishonor (reversed Five of Swords) are *shifting* alliances at a convention.

A nation is *destabilized* when a **charismatic leader** (reversed King of Wands) **steps down**.

Opposite Position: stabilizing

Flex-spread location: right of main subject

· ·

EMBRACING

Keywords: admiring • approving • believing in • desiring • endorsing • hoping for • honoring • liking • praising • supporting • valuing • wanting • welcoming • wishing for

Description: Embracing means to enfold within or to wrap your arms around. When we embrace something, we have warm, positive feelings toward it. We want to make it part of ourselves. A card in embracing shows some quality valued by the main subject.

The positive regard can range from simple acceptance to eager support. The quality may be possessed by the main subject or just desired. You can even embrace undesirable qualities—those you know are not worthwhile or helpful.

Reversed: The main subject is embracing or desiring a low level of some factor.

Examples: (embracing factor in *italics*)

I am *embracing* my **psychic ability** (Queen of Cups).

A political party is *welcoming* the **lone-wolf style** (Seven of Swords).

A choice requires *endorsing* the need to **act** (Magician).

Matthew feels his **addiction** (reversed Devil) has **less** *value* for him now.

The school is *supporting* some **limits on freedom** (reversed Four of Wands).

Opposite Position: avoiding

Flex-spread location: right of main subject

· ·

ENDING

Keywords: ceasing • closing • concluding • expiring • fading • finishing • leaving • moving away • passing on • stopping • terminating • winding up

Description: Our lives are filled with energies that rise and fall in strength and importance. Ending represents the falling side. Something is moving away or drawing to a close. A card in ending shows a factor that has been active, but is now fading.

An ending may be just starting or quite advanced. You can welcome a downward trend or resist it. Sometimes knowing an ending is in progress can help you decide how to deal with it.

Reversed: The main subject's experience of a low level of something is ending.

Examples: (ending factor in *italics*)

<u>I</u> am *leaving* my **family** (Ten of Cups).

A <u>situation</u> may involve *stopping* a focus on **self-interest** (Five of Swords).

<u>My father</u> may be *letting go* of a need to **control** (Four of Pentacles).

The <u>project</u> is heating up, so the **low need for hard work** (reversed Knight of Pentacles) is *ending*.

<u>Today</u> donations picked up a bit. The **low level of generosity** (reversed Star) appears to be *ceasing*.

Opposite Position: beginning

Flex-spread location: right of main subject

. . . .

ENDURING

Keywords: continuing • chronic • durable • lasting • long-lived • long-term • perma-nent • persistent • prolonged • protracted • surviving • unfading

Description: Enduring means lasting over time. Something is enduring if it has the deep roots and strength to persist. A card in enduring shows a factor that has staying power.

Sometimes an enduring quality has existed for a long time and is going to continue. Other times a quality is new, but still will prove durable. Although nothing lasts forever, an enduring quality is tough enough to survive.

Reversed: Some factor involving the main subject has a low level of endurance. It lacks a certain staying power.

Examples: (enduring factor in *italics*)

<u>I</u> am glad to see that a **relationship** (Lovers) is *lasting*.

<u>My illness</u> requires hiring a good **caregiver** (Queen of Pentacles) to stay with me *long term*.

The **truce** (Two of Cups) between <u>my country</u> and another may prove to be *permanent*.

The **low level of leadership** (reversed Three of Wands) in <u>the organization</u> is likely to *endure*.

<u>Greta</u> has had **few chances to be intimate** (reversed Page of Cups) for *quite a while*.

Opposite Position: temporary

Flex-spread location: right of main subject

. . . .

ENVIRONMENT

Keywords: environment • atmosphere • surroundings • milieu • climate • ambience • setting • outer conditions

Description: Environment describes the atmosphere or conditions surrounding the main subject of a reading. It shows what is "outside" the subject, yet still impacting it. Often a card in this position conveys the general mood or climate.

Sometimes environment shows an event or activity going on around the main subject. It can point out some feature of the environment that's not yet obvious. This factor helps you stay aware of your surroundings.

Reversed: The environment around the main subject has a low level of some factor. There is little of something in the atmosphere.

Examples: (environment factor in *italics*)

There are abundant **resources** (Six of Pentacles) *all around* <u>me</u>.

The *climate* of <u>an event</u> is one of **celebration** (Four of Wands).

<u>My daughter</u> is in a place where the *atmosphere* is **restful** (Four of Swords).

There is **little patience** (reversed Strength) *surrounding* <u>the team</u> after it lost its match.

The *climate* of the <u>meeting</u> was practical; there were **few emotional outbursts** (reversed Knight of Cups).

Opposite Position: none

Flex-spread location: right of main subject

. . . .

GUIDANCE

Keywords: advice • assistance • counsel • direction • enlightenment • help • opinion • point of view • recommendation • suggestion • wisdom

Description: The guidance position helps you understand the message of a reading in relation to the main subject. It offers insight that comes from the wise perspective of your Inner Guide.

A guidance card can show a new approach, offer a note of caution, or simply encourage. Only you can assess the guidance in each case. If you feel positive, the guidance is encouraging. If you feel negative, the guidance is a note of caution. In either case, your Inner Guide is standing by, ready to support you.

You can assume guidance comes with your best interests at heart. It doesn't tell you what to do or think. It's offered with loving wisdom as something for you to ponder. You're always free to respond in whatever way you think best, without judgment from your Inner Guide.

Reversed: The guidance card suggests your Inner Guide wants you to understand there is a low level of something involving the main subject. You are being asked to recognize that the main subject is not experiencing much of some factor.

Flex-spread location: right of the main subject, centered below any factors

- -

INACTIVE

Keywords: downplayed • idle • inoperative • low-key • on hold • on the shelf • on the sidelines • out of service • unused

Description: A card in inactive shows something about the main subject that is idle or out of service for the moment. This factor is normally present, but on the shelf. Perhaps the idle quality could be restarted, but for now, it's not being used.

An inactive quality is often in the background. It exists, but there's not much energy in it for the moment. You can feel glad or concerned about an inactive factor depending on conditions.

Reversed: A reversed card in this position shows a low level of some factor is inactive for the main subject.

Examples: (inactive factor in *italics*)

I am *not using* my usual **hyper-analytical approach** (Knight of Swords).

My friend is putting her sense of **responsibility** (Justice) *on hold* by taking a vacation.

The government is *deactivating* some **regulations** (Emperor).

My supervisor is **no longer** *downplaying* her **pessimism** (reversed Knight of Pentacles).

The **conventions** (reversed Ten of Pentacles) that are **not often necessary** in this program are being *put back in place*.

Opposite Position: active

Flex-spread location: right of the main subject

- -

INSIDE

Keywords: below the surface • inconspicuous • inner • inner face • interior • internal • out of view • unapparent • hidden • within

Description: Sometimes outward appearances belie inner reality. A card in inside shows something going on below the surface of the main subject. It offers a glimpse into that interior. The inside position looks past the obvious to the deeper factor within. For a moment the veil is lifted.

For people, inside often shows thoughts, feelings, or intentions. For an area of life or situation, inside exposes the inner dynamics. Sometimes, inside and outside are the same. In this case, a card in inside will be consistent with other cards in a reading.

Reversed: There is a low level of some factor within the main subject.

Examples: (inside factor in *italics*)

I feel a new surge of **confidence** (Ace of Wands) *within* myself.

My children feel very **excited** (Four of Wands) on *the inside*.

There's a lot of **resourcefulness** (Queen of Pentacles) *within* the group.

My friend may be **less unfeeling** (reversed Knight of Swords) *inside* than she seems on the surface.

The **low level of discipline** (reversed Nine of Pentacles) in the company was *hidden*.

Opposite Position: outside

Flex-spread location: right of the main subject

· ·

KNOWN

Keywords: acquainted with • aware of • comprehended • conscious of • familiar • informed of • out in the open • perceived • public • realized • recognized • understood

Description: To know is to be aware of. Before something can be known, it must first be revealed. A card in known can show some factor brought to light for or about the main subject. It's no longer a secret.

Knowing can also mean accepting as true. A card in known can show something that's "common knowledge" to or about the main subject. It's recognized as fact. Knowing can also imply understanding. You can be exposed to something and yet not know it. You must first comprehend its essence, perhaps at many levels, before you know it deeply.

Reversed: The main subject knows there is a low level of some factor. It is recognized and understood that something concerning the main subject is not fully developed.

Examples: (known factor in *italics*)

A **hidden dishonor** (Seven of Swords) within the group is *exposed*.

I *know* a **direction change** (Seven of Pentacles) is planned.

A lawyer who is *recognized* to be **ethical** (King of Swords) is being hired to handle the case.

Everyone *understands* that the <u>startup company</u> has **little knowledge** (reversed Six of Pentacles) of the field.

My wife is *aware* that she has **low energy** (reversed Queen of Wands) <u>health</u>-wise.

Opposite Position: unknown

Flex-spread location: right of the main subject

. . . .

NEW

Keywords: different • fresh • just out • novel • unfamiliar • unique • unusual• un-tested • untried • unused

Description: New is different. A card in new shows a factor that's novel or unfamiliar for the main subject. The new can appear quietly and go unnoticed. Or, it can arrive suddenly and full-blown. Without warning, all the rules are different. No matter what, a new factor creates change.

The new can also be something that is untested or untried by the main subject. You don't know whether or not this novel approach will bring desired change until you try. It may not, but often old ways need to be set aside to allow for new developments.

Reversed: A low level of some factor is new for the main subject.

Examples: (new factor in *italics*)

A *new* opportunity for **prosperity** (Page of Pentacles) has suddenly presented itself to <u>me</u>.

Arthur's *untested new* <u>invention</u> strikes me as an **apparent folly** (Fool).

A recent *new hire* offers me a **creative opportunity** (Page of Wands) in <u>my career</u>.

This **first loss** (reversed Five of Cups) is a *new development* for <u>the team</u>.

<u>My boss</u> has been **less judgmental** (reversed Judgement). This is *new*.

Opposite Position: old

Flex-spread location: right of the main subject

. . . .

OLD

Keywords: customary • traditional • usual • classic • time-honored • behind the times • dated • obsolete • old-fashioned • old hat • out of date • passé • stale • timeworn • tired

Description: The old is something that's been around for a long time. A card in old can show a factor that's endured and persisted. The old can be time-honored—valued because of its age and worth.

Sometimes the old is something that's outlived its usefulness. It's stale and tired. You can honor and appreciate what's old, but other times, you need to make room for the new.

Reversed: The main subject experiences a low level of something as old, traditional, or perhaps passé.

Examples: (old factor in *italics*)

>I think of myself as a **martyr** (Ten of Swords); it's *an old habit* of mine.

>My *old, forever* <u>friend</u> is always **reliable and steadfast** (King of Pentacles).

>The **apathy** (Four of Cups) in <u>the group</u> is getting *old*.

>It's *traditional* for the participants at this <u>event</u> to be **less than forthright** (reversed Queen of Swords).

><u>The boss</u> is *tired* of the fact that his **wishes are rarely met** (reversed Nine of Pentacles).

Opposite Position: new

Flex-spread location: right of the main subject

· ·

OUTSIDE

Keywords: apparent • conspicuous • displayed • exterior • external • obvious • on view • ostensible • outer • outward face • presented • shown • surface • without

Description: A card in outside shows some quality that is the outer face of the main subject—its external appearance. This includes the physical, but goes beyond it as well. The factor may represent what is conspicuous or clearly presented by the main subject. Outside can also indicate how the main subject is coming across to others.

Sometimes outside shows a style of interacting with the outer world. Other times, outside describes what seems to be true on the surface, even though it doesn't match what's inside. Compare a card in outside with other cards to see if they're consistent. If not, then appearances may not be the whole story.

Reversed: The main subject is outwardly displaying a low level of some factor. From the outside, the main subject appears not to have much of some quality.

Examples: (outside factor in *italics*)

><u>I</u> am the picture of confident **authority** (King of Swords) on the *outside*.

>An <u>incident</u> appears to be a **call for justice** (Ace of Swords) on the *surface*.

><u>My minister</u> has been *outwardly* **searching** (Hermit) for a deeper faith.

>A stern judge *appears* to have **little compassion** (reversed Strength) during <u>a court case</u>.

>To *everyone else*, <u>I</u> seem to **rarely disagree** (reversed Five of Wands) in my <u>marriage</u>.

Opposite Position: Inside

Flex-spread location: right of the main subject

. . . .

RESULTING FROM

Keywords: arising out of • coming to pass • deriving from • ensuing • following • happening after • springing out of • stemming from

Description: Resulting from shows some factor that may come to pass due to the circumstances in or around the main subject in the present. A card in this position indicates one probable outcome—what may transpire if the present conditions for the main subject remain unchanged.

An outcome position is one of the most popular in the tarot. People always want to know what will happen in the future, but the future is never a certainty. The resulting from position only suggests a possibility that may materialize. You can view this as a pleasing development or a warning depending on circumstances.

Reversed: A low level of some factor could result due to current conditions for the main subject. A result may be a lessening of some quality.

Examples: (resulting from factor in *italics*)

> **Discord and disagreement** (Five of Swords) may *result from* an incident in <u>the situation</u>.
>
> An **opportunity for love** (Page of Cups) may *come to pass* based on what is happening with <u>me</u> now.
>
> <u>The public figure</u> may *eventually receive* **absolution** (Judgement) because of his apology.
>
> A **loss of community** (reversed Three of Cups) may *follow* my <u>choice to move</u>.
>
> A **shortage of money** (reversed Ten of Pentacles) may *ensue* because of current conditions in <u>the marketplace</u>.

Opposite Position: contributing to

Flex-spread usage: right of main subject

. . . .

STABILIZING

Keywords: balancing • calming • establishing • firming • fixing in place • grounding • ordering • securing • settling • smoothing • solidifying • steadying

Description: A stabilizing force steadies and calms. It discourages swings from one extreme to the other. Conditions become secure and predictable. A card in stabilizing shows a factor that's balancing for the main subject.

When change is needed, a stabilizing force can mean stagnation. It can fix an unwelcome situation in place or reinforce a dull routine. A stabilizing energy can be welcome or not depending on circumstances.

Reversed: A low level of some factor is stabilizing for the main subject.

Examples: (stabilizing factor in *italics*)

> Being in **nature** (Empress) makes <u>me</u> feel *grounded*.

> <u>My son</u> feels more *secure* since he **moved on** (Eight of Cups) from a bad relationship.

> **Avoiding** (Two of Swords) a difficult decision makes <u>me</u> feel *calm* even though I'll have to face it eventually.

> <u>The family</u> is feeling *stable* since all the **sudden changes have diminished** (reversed Tower).

> <u>The office</u> has *settled down* since the **overbearing manager** (reversed Knight of Swords) was **dismissed**.

Opposite Position: disrupting

Flex-spread location: right of the main subject

. . . .

STRONG

Keywords: abundant • big • dominant • extensive • extra • influential • large • major • powerful • vital

Description: There are two dimensions to strong—size and power. A card in strong shows a factor that's abundant or powerful for the main subject. A strong quality can also be dominant. It has extra power and scope for the moment.

A strong quality is not necessarily mighty in and of itself. It may simply be strongly present. Often we believe what's strong is preferable, but that's not always true. A strong quality can be welcomed or not, but it's not easily dismissed.

Reversed: A low level of something is strongly true for the main subject. Sometimes a low level of something strengthens the main subject.

Examples: (strong factor in *italics*)

> <u>I</u> am experiencing a *strong* need for **sensual pleasure** (Nine of Cups).

> A **stalemate** (Two of Swords) is the *dominant* feature of <u>the problem</u>.

> A **resourceful person** (Queen of Pentacles) is *especially vital* in <u>this crisis</u>.

> There is *quite* a **low level of competence** (reversed Three of Pentacles) in the <u>engineering department</u>.

> <u>Marcia</u> feels *strengthened* by the **low level of hard control** (reversed Chariot).

Opposite Position: weak

Flex-spread location: right of the main subject

TEMPORARY

Keywords: brief • ephemeral • flash-in-the-pan • fleeting • impermanent • interim •
momentary • passing • provisional • short-lived • transient • transitory

Description: Temporary means short-term or provisional. A card in temporary shows a factor that's not expected to last for the main subject. Sometimes, a stopgap measure is in place, but only until a permanent solution can be found.

Sometimes you can hope something will last, but find out it's only temporary. You know conditions are going to change. Sometimes you're glad a situation is short-term; other times you wish it would endure.

Reversed: There is temporarily a low level of some factor for the main subject. A certain quality is less, but only for a time.

Examples: (temporary factor in *italics*)

I am having to be more **self-reliant** (Nine of Pentacles) because my assistant is gone *temporarily*.

The members of the cast are **conforming to the rules** (Hierophant), but that *won't last*.

Today I may have a *fleeting* **opportunity for intimacy** (Ace of Cups) with my partner.

The candidate *briefly* **lost his cockiness** (reversed Knight of Wands) after his humbling defeat.

The task was **not much fun** (reversed Two of Pentacles) for the short time I was doing it by myself.

Opposite Position: enduring

Flex-spread location: right of main subject

UNKNOWN

Keywords: blind to • hidden • in the dark • mysterious • secret • unacquainted with •
unaware of • unconscious of • unfamiliar • unrealized • unrecognized • unsuspected

Description: The unknown is secret and mysterious. It lies hidden or unexposed. The unknown can be something of which the main subject is not yet aware. The main subject can also be in the dark or blind to some feature of himself or the situation.

An unknown quality can also be something rarely, if ever, experienced. It's so unfamiliar as to be unknown. Sometimes the unknown is simply strange and baffling.

Reversed: The main subject is unaware of the fact that there is a low level of something.

Examples: (unknown factor in *italics*)

I *don't suspect* how **lonely** (Three Swords) I really am.

My spouse is *blind to* the fact that I am **innocent** (Six of Cups).

The protest group is completely *unfamiliar* with what **victory** (Chariot) feels like.

Paul has *no idea* that he is **not much of a charmer** (reversed Knight of Wands).

I am *unaware* that there is **very little planning** (reversed Three of Pentacles) for the big event.

Opposite Position: known

Flex-spread location: right of the main subject

· ·

WEAK

Keywords: debilitating • incapacitating • ineffectual • in short supply • limited • low • meager • minor • powerless • reduced • scant • small • subordinate

Description: Weakness has a negative connotation. We tend to admire strength, but a card in the weak position doesn't necessarily show something inferior. It simply points out a factor that's reduced for the main subject. It's less available.

Sometimes, weak shows something with little power or endurance. It is in a reduced state. Something can also be weakening or incapacitating the main subject. Weakness can be valued or not depending on circumstances.

Reversed: A low level of something is weakly true for the main subject. The fact that some factor is low debilitates the main subject in some way.

Examples: (weak factor in *italics*)

I tend to be reserved; I am *weak* in the area of **boldness** (Two of Wands).

A choice offers *scant* **opportunities for me to use my mind** (Page of Swords).

My partner has *few* **illusions** (Moon) about the success of the mission.

My health is *deteriorating* because I have **so little time to rest** (reversed Four of Swords).

Lisa feels **less healthy** (reversed Temperance), but the ailment is *not serious*.

Opposite Position: strong

Flex-spread location: right of the main subject

Part Five

REFERENCE

Simplified Reading Procedure

This is a simplified procedure for readings using small spreads, such as the daily reading.

Shuffle the deck once or twice.

Hold the deck facedown in one hand and cover it with your other hand.

Pause a moment to become calm and centered.

Ask your Inner Guide to give you the guidance you need.

Place the deck facedown in front of you.

Cut the deck to the left and restack it.

Turn over the first card and place it in front of you.

Continue placing cards if your spread contains more than one position.

Make a note of your reading, if you want.

Return card(s) to the deck, and shuffle once or twice.

Full Reading Procedure

This is a full procedure for doing a tarot reading for yourself. It's based on the procedure described in Chapter Two, page 15.

Step 1—Choose and label the main subject of your reading

Step 2—Assemble all desired materials in the reading space

Step 3—Set the mood

Step 4—Opening Statement

Step 5—Shuffle the cards

Step 6—Cut the cards

Step 7—Lay out the cards

Step 8—Respond to the cards

Step 9—Analyze the reading

Step 10—Create the story

Step 11—Create the summary statement

Step 12—Finish up

Step 13—Use what you have learned

Interpretation Procedure for a Single Card

Here is a procedure to help you uncover the meaning of a single card in a reading (see page 22).

Step 1—What is the card's energy?

Step 2—What is the context for this card's energy?

Step 3—How strong does this card's energy feel to me?

Step 4—Does this card form a pair with another card?

Step 5—Is the card in a group, and, if so, how does this impact its interpretation?

Step 6—What is the energy phase of the card, if reversed?

Step 7—Does my feeling about the card's energy from step 3 match its orientation?

Step 8—Is this a repeating energy?

Step 9—If the card is in a group (step 5), does its orientation affect the card's meaning within the group?

Step 10—What do I want to do about this energy?

Procedure for Writing a Question

You can choose to write a question as the subject of a reading.

First, review your situation thoroughly. Think about all the people involved, directly or indirectly. Let your mind wander freely. You want to look at your problem without judging or censoring any part. Keep the following guidelines in mind:

Accept Responsibility

Example: What do I need to know to find the best living arrangements for my father?

Keep Your Options Open

Example: How might I encourage my mother-in-law to consider her health?

Find the Best Level of Detail

Example: How can I improve the flow of work within our office?

Focus on Yourself

Example: What role do I play in Arthur's drinking problem?

Stay Neutral

Example: How can I foster a spirit of cooperation concerning chores?

Be Positive

Example: Can you help me understand how to push on to victory in a tournament?

Useful ways to begin a question:

Can you give me insight into . . .

What do I need to understand about . . .

What is the meaning of . . .

What is the lesson or purpose of . . .

What are the circumstances underlying . . .

How can I improve my chances of. . .

How might I . . .

Questions to avoid:

Those to be answered "Yes" or "No"

Those beginning with "Should . . ."

Those beginning with "When will . . .

Shuffling Methods

Card Player's Method

The Card Player's Method is often used to shuffle playing cards. Hold about half the cards facedown in each hand and intermingle them as they drop to the surface of the table. This technique mixes the cards thoroughly, but it can be awkward with tarot cards because they are bigger than normal. This method can also be hard on your cards; they tend to form a bend in the middle. The Card Player's Method is effective, but somewhat mechanical in spirit.

Insertion Method

Hold about half the deck in each hand, and insert one half in a scattered fashion down through the other half. You can hold the cards on their long or short side. This method is fast and efficient with a lot of hand-to-card contact. Be careful with the edges as they can fray.

Cowie Push/Put Method

I discovered this style in a book by Norma Cowie.[10] Her technique thoroughly mixes the cards with maximum hand contact and little or no damage. Hold the deck facedown in your dominant hand. Push some cards from the top with your thumb into your other hand. Then, push again, but this time to the bottom of the new pile. Continue alternating a push to the top, then one to the bottom until all the cards have been transferred. At this point, put the entire deck back into your dominant hand and start over. This method can be difficult at first. You may push too many at a time or drop some, but your technique will improve with practice.

Scrambling Method

The Scrambling Method is about as basic as you can get. Spread all the cards face down on the floor or table, and start scrambling. You do need room to shuffle in this way. The technique creates a good mix with few ill effects on the cards, but it does create reversed cards — a disadvantage if you are not using them. This shuffle also has a rather ill-composed feel which some find objectionable.

To Avoid Reversed Cards

Start with your cards all facing the same direction. Every time you divide the deck before shuffling, make sure the two piles stay facing the same way.

To Get Reversed Cards

Every time you divide the deck before shuffling, rotate one of the piles 180 degrees.

Areas of Life

Career	Investments	Marriage or Partnership
Job	Money	Relationship
Vocation	Friendships	Romance
Community	Health	Sexuality
Neighborhood	Body	Spirituality or Religion
Creative Expression	Physical Condition	Sports
Talent	Diet	Volunteer Work
Family Life	Exercise	
Finances	Hobby or Pastime	

Suit Qualities

Each of the four suits has its own special quality or energy. The lists on pages 334–335 will help give you a feel for these energies. Each list has words that show different facets of a suit's character.

There is a positive and negative list for each suit. This split is not ideal because it implies good and bad. We tend to judge qualities based on their impact on us. Our language reflects these judgments. The tarot is more neutral. The cards show energies as they are in their essence, not as we might judge them.

How we view a quality also depends on our circumstances and personality. Is being aggressive positive or negative? It all depends.

Wands-Positive	Wands-Negative	Cups—Positive	Cups-Negative
adventurous	aggressive	aesthetic	broody
aggressive	brash	affectionate	delicate
ardent	cocky	agreeable	doleful
attractive	daredevilish	amiable	escapist
audacious	devil-may-care	benevolent	fanciful
avid	foolhardy	calm	fragile
bold	hasty	caring	frail
brave	headstrong	compassionate	gushy
buoyant	heedless	concerned	huffy
charismatic	hotheaded	considerate	hypersensitive
charming	hot-tempered	diplomatic	hysterical
cheerful	impatient	dreamy	impressionable
confident	impetuous	emotional	indolent
courageous	impulsive	empathetic	introverted
creative	imprudent	forbearing	lazy
daring	incautious	gentle	maudlin
eager	irresponsible	good-hearted	melancholic
ebullient	nervy	gracious	mopish
energetic	overconfident	healing	moody
enthusiastic	overzealous	humane	morose
exuberant	precipitous	imaginative	narcissistic
extroverted	presumptuous	inner	overemotional
fiery	rash	intimate	overrefined
forceful	reckless	introspective	petulant
heroic	restless	intuitive	passive
inspiring	rootless	joyful	sulky
intrepid	self-absorbed	kind	sullen
inventive	superficial	loving	temperamental
magnetic	thoughtless	mellow	thin-skinned
optimistic	unprepared	merciful	touchy
original		mild	vapory
outgoing		nice	waspish
passionate		pacific	wishy-washy
risk-taking		patient	
self-assured		peaceful	
self-confident		perceptive	
undaunted		psychic	
valiant		quiet	
wholehearted		refined	
		responsive	
		romantic	
		sensitive	
		soft	
		spiritual	
		subjective	
		sweet	
		sympathetic	
		telepathic	
		tender	
		tenderhearted	
		tolerant	
		understanding	
		wise	

Swords-Positive	Swords-Negative	Pentacles-Positive	Pentacles-Negative
analytical	abstruse	able	bullheaded
articulate	aloof	adept	colorless
astute	arrogant	adroit	compulsive
authoritative	autocratic	assiduous	conventional
clearheaded	biting	bighearted	drab
clever	blunt	capable	gloomy
dignified	cold	careful	grim
direct	condescending	cautious	grinding
discerning	controlling	competent	hardheaded
dispassionate	cool	concrete	humorless
equitable	critical	conscientious	inflexible
ethical	cutting	constant	intractable
evenhanded	detached	dogged	intransigent
forthright	distant	efficient	materialistic
frank	dogmatic	enterprising	mulish
honest	domineering	dependable	obdurate
honorable	high-handed	determined	obsessive
impartial	imperious	down-to-earth	obstinate
incisive	insensitive	factual	ordinary
intellectual	intolerant	firm	overcautious
just	judgmental	generous	overorganized
keen-minded	opinionated	handy	pedestrian
knowledgeable	overbearing	hardworking	perfectionistic
learned	overintellectualizing	industrious	pertinacious
literate	patronizing	loyal	pessimistic
logical	remote	meticulous	pigheaded
lucid	standoffish	nurturing	prim
magisterial	thoughtless	orderly	prosaic
mental	unaffectionate	organized	rigid
moral	unfeeling	painstaking	staid
objective	unresponsive	persevering	stiff
observant	unsparing	practical	stiff-necked
outspoken		productive	stodgy
penetrating		proficient	stubborn
perspicacious		prudent	timid
quick-witted		realistic	unadventurous
rational		reliable	unbending
reasonable		resolute	uncompromising
smart		resourceful	unexciting
trenchant		responsible	unimaginative
truthful		sensible	unquestioning
unbiased		skillful	unromantic
unprejudiced		solid	unspontaneous
well-informed		stable	unyielding
witty		stalwart	
		steadfast	
		steady	
		sturdy	
		supporting	
		tenacious	
		thorough	
		trusting	
		trustworthy	
		unwavering	

Suit Pair Meanings

Wands/Cups

Fire/Water
Outer/Inner
Aggressive/Passive
Extrovert/Introvert
Passionate/Tender
Eros/Agape
Intense/Mild
Energetic/Restful
Militant/Peace-Loving
Individual/Group
Competitive/Cooperative
Actions/Feelings
Overt/Covert
Direct/Indirect

Wands/Swords

Fire/Air
Hot/Cool
Passionate/Reserved
Engaged/Detached
Charisma/Authority
Partisan/Unbiased
Inspiration/Analysis
Artist/Critic

Wands/Pentacles

Fire/Earth
Showy/Sedate
New/Old
Risk/Security
Impetuous/Deliberate
Inspiration/Perspiration
Adventurous/Cautious
Liberal/Conservative
Original/Traditional
Big Picture/Detail
Cursory/Thorough
Fast/Slow
Optimistic/Pessimistic

Cups/Swords

Water/Air
Feelings/Thoughts
Right Brain/Left Brain
Love/Truth
Emotion/Logic
Intuition/Reason
Heart/Head
Connection/Separation
Mercy/Justice
Subjective/Objective
Intimacy/Distance
McCoy/Spock

Cups/Pentacles

Water/Earth
Spirit/Matter
Religion/Science
Dreamy/Down-to-Earth
Fantasy/Reality
Delicate/Tough
Flexible/Firm
Soft/Hard
Romantic/Practical
Sentimental/
    Matter-of-Fact
Play/Work

Swords/Pentacles

Air/Earth
Theory/Practice
Abstract/Concrete
Mental/Physical
Book Learning/
    Common Sense
Thinking/Doing
Ideas/Implementation
Perfection/Compromise
What is Right/
    What Works
Ideals/Realities

Court Card Rank Pair Meanings

King/King

Adult/Adult, Two equals
Two mature, well-developed,
    but different aspects of self
Masculine/Masculine
King qualities doubled
Concern with external events

Queen/Queen

Adult/Adult, Two equals
Two mature, well-developed,
    but different aspects of self
Feminine/Feminine
Queen qualties doubled
Concern with inner states

King/Queen

Man/Woman
Masculine/Feminine
Outer/Inner
Aggressive/Passive
Extrovert/Introvert
Direct/Indirect
Intense/Mild
Individual/Relationship
Actions/Feelings
Doing/Being
Logical/Intuitive
Competitive/Cooperative
Strong/Gentle
Offense/Defense

King or Queen/Knight

Adult/Teen or Young Adult
Moderate/Immoderate
Conservative/Liberal
Old/Young
Traditional/New
Establishment/Challenger
Slow/Fast
Cautious/Adventurous
Security/Risk
Stable/Unstable

King or Queen/Page

Adult/Child
Serious/Lighthearted
Responsible/Carefree
Restrained/Unrestrained
Dignified/Uninhibited
Grown-up/Childish
Planned/Spontaneous
Jaded/Innocent
Sedate/Showy
Ant/Grasshopper

Knight/Knight

Adult or Teen/Adult or Teen
Two extreme sides of self
Two in extreme positions
Knight qualities doubled

Knight/Page

Adult or Teen/Child
Older Child/Younger Child
Drastic/Mild
Obsessive/Easygoing
Grim/Merry
Pessimistic/Optimistic
Complicated/Simple
Questioning/Accepting

Page/Page

Child/Child
Two childlike people
Page qualities doubled
Strong urge to action

Appendix A

FOOL'S JOURNEY

The Fool's Journey is a metaphor for the journey through life. Each major arcana card stands for a stage on that journey—an experience that a person must incorporate to realize his wholeness. These 22 descriptions are based on the keywords for each major arcana card. A card's number is in parentheses.

The Fool

We begin with the Fool (0), a card of beginnings. The Fool stands for each of us as we begin our journey of life. He is a fool because only a simple soul has the innocent faith to undertake such a journey with all its potential hazards and pain.

At the start of his trip, the Fool is newborn—fresh, open, and spontaneous. The figure on Card 0 has his arms flung wide, and his head held high. He is ready to embrace whatever comes his way, but he is also oblivious to the cliff edge he is about to cross. The Fool is unaware of the hardships he will face as he ventures out to learn the lessons of the world.

The Fool stands somewhat outside the rest of the major arcana. Zero is an unusual number. It rests in the exact middle of the number system—poised between the positive and negative. At birth, the Fool is set in the middle of his own individual universe. He is strangely empty (as is zero), but imbued with a desire to go forth and learn. This undertaking would seem to be folly, but is it?

The Magician and the High Priestess

On setting out, the Fool immediately encounters the Magician (1) and the High Priestess (2)—the great balancing forces that make up the perceived world. It is a feature of the material universe that as soon as we name some aspect of experience, we automatically evoke its opposite.

The Magician is the positive side. He represents the active, masculine power of creative impulse. He is also conscious awareness. The Magician is the force that allows us to impact the world through a concentration of individual will and power. The High Priestess is the so-called negative side. She is the mysterious unconscious. She provides the fertile ground in which creative events occur. The High Priestess is our unrealized potential waiting for an active principle to bring it to expression.

The words positive and negative do not imply "good" and "bad." These are human distinctions that do not apply in the tarot. The Magician and the High Priestess are absolutely equal in value and importance. Each is necessary for balance. We may view the negative as our Shadow, but without shadows, we cannot see the light, and without a ground of potential, we cannot create.

The Empress

As he grows, the Fool becomes more and more aware of his surroundings. As with most babies, he first recognizes his mother—the warm, loving woman who nourishes and cares for him. He also comes to know Mother Earth, who nurtures him in a larger sense.

The Empress (3) represents the world of nature and sensation. A baby delights in exploring everything he touches, tastes, and smells. He cannot get enough of the sights and sounds that enchant his senses. It is natural to delight in the abundant goodness of Mother Earth who surrounds us with her support.

The Emperor

The next person the Fool encounters is the father in the figure of the Emperor (4). He is the representative of structure and authority. When a baby leaves his mother's arms, he learns that there are patterns to his world. Objects respond in predictable ways that can be explored. The child experiences a new kind of pleasure that comes from discovering order.

The Fool also encounters rules. He learns his will is not always paramount, and there are certain behaviors necessary for his well-being. There are people in authority who will enforce such guidelines. These restrictions can be frustrating, but through the patient direction of the Father, the Fool begins to understand their purpose.

The Hierophant

Eventually, the Fool ventures out of his home into the wider world. He is exposed to the beliefs and traditions of his culture and begins his formal education. The Hierophant (5) represents the organized belief systems that begin to surround and inform the growing child.

A hierophant is someone who interprets arcane knowledge and mysteries. On Card 5 we see a religious figure blessing two acolytes. Perhaps he is inducting them into church membership. Although this image is religious, it is really a symbol for initiations of all kinds.

The child is trained in the practices of his society and becomes part of a particular culture and worldview. He learns to identify with a group and discovers a sense of belonging. He enjoys learning the customs of his society and showing how well he can conform to them.

The Lovers

Eventually, the Fool faces two new challenges. He experiences the powerful urge for sexual union with another person. Before, he was mainly self-centered. Now he feels the balancing tendency, pictured in the Lovers (6), to reach out and become half of a loving partnership. He yearns for relationship.

THE BIG BOOK OF TAROT

The Fool also needs to decide upon his own beliefs. It is well enough to conform while he learns and grows, but at some point, he must determine his own values if he is to be true to himself. He must start to question received opinion.

The Chariot

By the time the Fool becomes an adult, he has a strong identity and a certain mastery over himself. Through discipline and willpower, he has developed an inner control which allows him to triumph over his environment.

The Chariot (7) represents the vigorous ego that is the Fool's crowning achievement so far. On Card 7 we see a proud, commanding figure riding victoriously through his world. He is in visible control of himself and all he surveys. For the moment, the Fool's assertive success is all he might wish, and he feels a certain self-satisfaction. His is the assured confidence of youth.

Strength

Over time, life presents the Fool with new challenges, some that cause suffering and disillusionment. He has many occasions to draw on the quality of strength (8). He is pressed to develop his courage and resolve and find the heart to keep going despite setbacks.

The Fool also discovers the quiet attributes of patience and tolerance. He realizes the willful command of the Chariot must be tempered by kindliness and the softer power of a loving approach. At times, intense passions surface, just when the Fool thought he had everything, including himself, under control.

The Hermit

Sooner or later, the Fool is led to ask himself the age-old question "Why?" He becomes absorbed with the search for answers, not from an idle curiosity, but out of a deeply felt need to find out why people live, if only to suffer and die. The Hermit (9) represents the need to find deeper truth.

The Fool begins to look inward, trying to understand his feelings and motivations. The sensual world holds less attraction for him, and he seeks moments of solitude away from the frantic activity of society. In time he may seek a teacher or guide who can give him advice and direction.

Wheel of Fortune

After much soul-searching, the Fool begins to see how everything connects. He has a vision of the world's wondrous design; its intricate patterns and cycles. The Wheel of Fortune (10) is a symbol of the mysterious universe whose parts work together in harmony. When the Fool glimpses the beauty and order of the world, if only briefly, he finds some of the answers he is seeking.

Sometimes his experiences seem to be the work of fate. A chance encounter or miraculous occurrence begins the process of change. The Fool may recognize his destiny in the sequence of events that led him to this turning point. Having been solitary, he feels ready for movement and action again. His perspective is wider, and he sees himself within the grander scheme of a universal plan. His sense of purpose is restored.

Justice

The Fool must now decide what this vision means to him personally. He looks back over his life to trace the cause and effect relationships that brought him to this point. He takes responsibility for his past actions so he can make amends and ensure a more honest course for the future. The demands of justice (11) must be served so he can wipe the slate clean.

This is a time of decision for the Fool. He is making important choices. Will he remain true to his insights, or slip back into an easier, more unaware existence that closes off further growth?

The Hanged Man

Undaunted, the Fool pushes on. He is determined to realize his vision, but he finds life is not so easily tamed. Sooner or later, he encounters his personal cross—an experience that seems too difficult to endure. This overwhelming challenge humbles him until he has no choice but to give up and let go.

At first, the Fool feels defeated and lost. He believes he has sacrificed everything, but from the depths he learns an amazing truth. He finds that when he relinquishes his struggle for control, everything begins to work as it should. By becoming open and vulnerable, the Fool discovers the miraculous support of his Inner Self. He learns to surrender to his experiences, rather than fighting them. He feels a surprising joy and begins to flow with life.

The Fool feels suspended in a timeless moment, free of urgency and pressure. In truth, his world has been turned upside-down. The Fool is the Hanged Man (12), apparently martyred, but actually serene and at peace.

Death

The Fool now begins to eliminate old habits and tired approaches. He cuts out nonessentials because he appreciates the basics of life. He goes through endings as he puts the outgrown aspects of his life behind him. This process may seem like dying because it is the death of his familiar self to allow for the growth of a new one. At times this inexorable change seems to be crushing the Fool, but eventually he rises up to discover that Death (13) is not a permanent state. It is simply a transition to a new, more fulfilling way of life.

Temperance

Since embracing the Hermit, the Fool has swung wildly back and forth on an emotional pendulum. Now, he realizes the balancing stability of temperance (14). He discovers true poise and equilibrium. By experiencing the extremes, he has come to appreciate moderation. The Fool has combined all aspects of himself into a centered whole that glows with health and well-being. How graceful and soft is the angel on Card 14 compared to the powerful but rigid ruler on the Chariot (Card 7)?[11] The Fool has come a long way in realizing the harmonious life.

The Devil

The Fool has his health, peace of mind, and a graceful composure. What more could he need? On everyday terms, not much, but the Fool is courageous and continues to pursue the deepest levels of his being. He soon comes face to face with the Devil (15).

The Devil is not an evil, sinister figure residing outside of us. He is the knot of ignorance and hopelessness lodged within each of us at some level. The seductive attractions of the material world bind us so compellingly that we often do not even realize our slavery to them.

We live in a limited range of experience, unaware of the glorious world that is our true heritage. The couple on Card 15 are chained, but acquiescent. They could so easily free themselves, but they do not even apprehend their bondage.[12] They look like the Lovers, but are unaware that their love is circumscribed within a narrow range. The price of this ignorance is an inner core of despair.

The Tower

How can the Fool free himself from the Devil? Can he ever root out his influence? The Fool may only find release through the sudden change represented by the Tower (16). The Tower is the ego fortress each of us has built around his beautiful inner core. Gray, cold, and rock-hard, this fortress seems to protect, but is really a prison.

Sometimes only a monumental crisis can generate enough power to smash the wall of the Tower. On Card 16 we see an enlightening bolt striking this building. It has ejected the occupants who seem to be tumbling to their deaths. The crown indicates they were once proud rulers; now they are humbled by a force stronger than they.

The Fool may need such a severe shake-up if he is to free himself, but the resulting revelation makes the painful experience worthwhile. The dark despair is blasted away in an instant, and the light of truth is free to shine down.

The Star

The Fool is suffused with a serene calm. The beautiful images on the Star (17) attest to this tranquility. The woman pictured on Card 17 is naked, her soul no longer hidden behind any disguise. Radiant stars shine in a cloudless sky serving as a beacon of hope and inspiration.

The Fool is blessed with a trust that completely replaces the negative energies of the Devil. His faith in himself and the future is restored. He is filled with joy and his one wish is to share it generously with the rest of the world. His heart is open and his love pours out freely. This peace after the storm is a magical moment for the Fool.

The Moon

What effect could spoil this perfect calm? Is there another challenge for the Fool? In fact, it is his bliss that makes him vulnerable to the illusions of the Moon (18). The Fool's joy is a feeling state. His positive emotions are not subject to mental clarity. In his dreamy condition, the Fool is susceptible to fantasy, distortion, and a false picture of the truth.

The Moon stimulates the creative imagination. It opens the way for bizarre and beautiful thoughts to bubble up from the unconscious, but deep-seated fears and anxieties can also arise. These experiences may cause the Fool to feel lost and bewildered.

The Sun

It is the lucid clarity of the Sun (19) that directs the Fool's imagination. The Sun's illumination shines in all the hidden places. It dispels the clouds of confusion and fear. It enlightens, so the Fool both feels and understands the goodness of the world.

Now, he enjoys a vibrant energy and enthusiasm. The Star's openness has solidified into an expansive assurance. The Fool is the naked babe pictured on Card 19, riding out joyously to face a new day. No challenge is too daunting. The Fool feels a radiant vitality, involved in grand undertakings as he draws to himself everything he needs. He is able to realize his greatness.

Judgement

The Fool has been reborn. His false ego-self has been shed, allowing his radiant, true self to manifest. He has discovered that joy, not fear, is at life's center.

The Fool feels absolved. He forgives himself and others, knowing that his real self is pure and good. He may regret past mistakes, but he knows they were due to his ignorance of his nature. He feels cleansed and refreshed, ready to start anew.

It is time for the Fool to make a deeper judgment (20) about his life. His own personal day of reckoning has arrived. Since he now sees himself truly he can make the necessary decisions about the future. He can choose wisely which values to cherish, and which to discard.

The angel on Card 20 is the Fool's Higher Self calling him to rise up and fulfill his promise. He discovers his true vocation—his reason for entering this life. Doubts and hesitations vanish, and he is ready to follow his dream.

The World

The Fool reenters the World (21), but this time with a more complete understanding. He has integrated all the disparate parts of himself and achieved wholeness. He has reached a new level of happiness and fulfillment.

The Fool experiences life as full and meaningful. The future is filled with infinite promise. In line with his personal calling, he becomes actively involved in the world. He renders service by sharing his unique gifts and talents and finds that he prospers at whatever he attempts. Because he acts from inner certainty, the whole world conspires to see that his efforts are rewarded. His accomplishments are many.

• • •

So, the Fool's Journey was not so foolish after all. Through perseverance and honesty, he reestablished the spontaneous courage that first impelled him on his search for Self, but now he is fully aware of his place in the world. This cycle is over, but the Fool will never stop growing. Soon he will be ready to begin a new journey that will lead him to ever greater levels of understanding.

READING FOR OTHERS

Once, years ago, I went to a coworker's office to say goodbye on my last day of work. I happened to mention the tarot, and he immediately whisked me into his room for a reading. It turned out to be a beautiful session—meaningful for both of us. In that half hour, I got to know this man better than during all the time I'd worked with him.

Once you start studying the tarot, sooner or later, someone's going to ask you for a reading. People are curious—about the process and about themselves. You may jump at the opportunity or hesitate, wondering if you can handle this new direction.

I encourage you to try reading for someone else if an opportunity presents itself and you feel ready. In our rushed society, there are so few occasions to sit with someone and share. Take this one when you can, but keep one important point in mind. You don't need to present yourself as more adept then you are, or adopt some artificial stance. Be yourself, and encourage the other person to explore this intriguing adventure with you.

Here are some thoughts I'd like to share about reading for someone else.

Seekers

In tarot literature, a person asking for a reading is often called the "querent," someone making a query. I prefer the term "seeker." For our purposes, then, a seeker is simply someone who asks you for a reading.

You may encounter two kinds of seekers: those you know (friends, relations, or coworkers) and those you don't know. For seekers you know, you can't help being aware of your "real" relationship. Don't jeopardize that relationship in any way, but do try to set it aside for now. Stay in the present moment by focusing on the cards and the immediate experience. Treat the reading as an event out of time for both of you.

Seekers can be eager or hesitant, open or closed, quiet or talkative, laughing or somber. Don't let any of these differences concern you. They're simply expressions of personality. If someone seems nervous, be calm and reassuring.

The Seeker's Goal

In readings, we come face-to-face with the mysterious. People remember readings with great feeling—especially their first. They can often recall details years later. My mother visited a storefront reader in downtown San Francisco when she was just eighteen. She talked about that reading off and on her whole life. It was a whim of the moment, but it was special to her because it opened a door into the unknown.

Seekers may request readings for many reasons, but they only ask when they are ready to look below the surface of their lives—at least a little. Even the most casual seekers are drawn for this purpose, although they may not acknowledge it. Those who are totally uninterested will never cross your path. So, readings should always be done only at the seeker's request. Never force or even encourage a reading. The desire for insight needs to come from the seeker.

Inner Guides

A tarot reading actually involves four "entities"—you, the seeker, and both your Inner Guides.

Your Inner Guide is by your side throughout the reading. It sends you intuitive messages that you pass on to the seeker, who absorbs those understandings with the help of his or her Inner Guide. Together, the four of you create an event that is meaningful on many levels.

Choosing a Layout

For most seekers, a good, all-purpose main subject is "my life." Occasionally, someone will be concerned about something in particular and ask you to focus on that topic. This is more common when you read for someone often. In this case, pick a main subject and type that you feel suits the seeker's concern. It's better for you to choose because the seeker will not be expecting this request. Asking can disrupt the flow of the process. However, do check with the seeker to make sure your choice is acceptable.

Choose a layout based on a quick assessment of the moment. Here are some points to consider:

What is the reading environment?

Keep the reading "lighter" when the environment is public or casual. Deeply personal readings are best kept for private moments.

How much time do you have?

Use small layouts if time is an issue so you can finish without feeling rushed.

What is the seeker's stated goal, if any?

Always accommodate a seeker's spoken requests for the reading, if possible.

What do I know about the seeker?

Bear in mind what you know of the seeker, but don't let preconceived ideas get in the way. Things are not always as they seem!

Do I have any pre-reading "flashes"?

Be aware of intuitive flashes before a reading. These can arrive as you're sitting down, or even days before! Accommodate these in your layout, if you can.

How much energy do I have?

Assess your own energy level. Don't take on a complicated or heavy reading when you're feeling drained. Also, keep the layout simple if you plan to do many readings in a row for different people.

Be prepared with a few all-purpose layouts you know well. You can use one as is or adapt it to suit the moment. A good layout offers a variety of opportunities for open-ended insights in different areas.

If you have time, you can do a small preliminary reading about a few area-of-life subjects. If the seeker shows special interest in one of these, you can use that area of life as the main subject of a follow-up reading.

The Process

You can follow the reading procedure described in Chapter Two, but delete time-consuming steps such as taking notes and writing a summary statement. These break up the flow.

I recommend having a separate deck devoted to readings you do for others. The seeker should shuffle and cut the cards, if possible. Hand him the cards, and tell him to shuffle until he feels ready to stop. Then, direct him through the cut, and have him hand the cards back to you. Maintain the orientation he established after the cut.

You should lay out the cards. I try to sit next to the seeker so we can look at the cards together. This arrangement fosters sharing. If you must sit opposite, try to place the cards so you can both view them easily.

Your Role

As you might guess, when you do a reading for someone else, all the cards in the reading are a message for that person from his or her perspective. Your role as the reader is to help the seeker make discoveries through the cards. You don't have to be a tarot expert to achieve this goal! It's the desire to be of service that counts.

The secret is to keep the focus on the seeker and away from yourself. This is easier said than done. Your pesky ego will get in the way by offering such "useful" thoughts as:

"You don't know what you're doing."

"Who do you think you are? You're just a beginner."

"These interpretations are really lame."

"He's not pleased with your efforts."

"Other readers are better than you."

"This is really going well. I'm pretty impressive."

"I'm special because I can do this."

Your ego can come up with many such "helpful" comments. If one crosses your mind, simply smile to yourself, let it go, and return to the seeker. With experience, you'll forget yourself more and more, and, ironically, become more confident and relaxed.

Create an environment in which the seeker feels free to contribute. Some won't want to, but others will become engaged and vocal. Let the seeker know what you're doing as appropriate, but it's best not to get too wordy. Be truthful, but positive. Never say something is absolutely going to happen, as this can't be known. Leave the seeker with a hopeful orientation toward the future.

Turn to your Inner Guide frequently. It will help you know what to do if you trust and stay open. Have faith in its wise counsel. Know the reading will work out just as it should.

BECOMING AWARE OF YOUR EGO

As you go about your daily affairs, practice becoming aware of your ego's comments. These are thoughts you have about yourself that are critical or self-inflating. When one of these thoughts comes to mind, acknowledge it, and then gently set it aside. Don't engage the thought, just move quietly past it. If you like, you can turn your thoughts instead to your wise and loving Inner Guide. This practice will serve you well when you read for others.

IMAGINARY READING

Choose a familiar spread to work with. Now, pretend to do a reading for an imaginary seeker. Imagine the seeker sitting right next to you. This is most effective if you really get into the role. Feel and act as if the reading were actually happening. Then, when you do read for someone, the process will feel familiar. Of course, a real reading is going to be unpredictable, but you'll be ready!

THREE SAMPLE READINGS— CELTIC CROSS

J ill's tale is a series of three readings I did for a friend over the course of a year. In this series about one woman's experience, you can see how new elements interact with those that endure. These readings illustrate how the tarot can reflect developments over time. Every reading is a snapshot of a given moment. As events unfold, the snapshots change, but there is a common thread that connects them. I recommend laying out the cards selected so you can experience these readings too.

Jill's First Reading

Jill (not her real name) had been adopted at eleven months. She wanted to learn all she could about her first year. For several months, she had been trying to gain information about her birth mother and, to a lesser extent, her birth father.

Jill tried to go through the agency that handled her adoption, but found that most of the information was closed to her. At the time of the reading, she had decided to pursue legal options to gain access. The cards she drew for her first reading are shown on page 348.

When these cards were laid down, both of us were immediately drawn to the Three of Swords—the root cause of the situation. This card perfectly symbolizes the heartbreak and loneliness Jill must have felt as a baby being abruptly separated from her birth parents and foster family. Note the three swords—Jill and her two parents—piercing their communal heart.

The betrayal meaning is also important. At some level, Jill feels betrayed by many people: her adoptive parents who deny her search, the agency who thwarts it, and her birth parents whom Jill may unconsciously resent for leaving her.

The many court cards suggest a need for balance. First, there is the central Cups/Pentacles pair (Cards 1 and 2). They symbolize the conflict between Jill's wish to fantasize about the future (Cups) and her need to be realistic (Pentacles). This theme will turn out to be a primary focus for Jill in the months to come.

The Page of Pentacles shows Jill's need to focus on practical matters in order to win her legal case and learn about her origins. The Knight of Cups shows her countertendency to dream

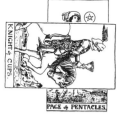

Jill's First Reading

unrealistically about what finding her birth mother will be like. He suggests that Jill lacks moderation in her emotions. As a Knight, he shows that her hopes are overly romantic.

This idea is reinforced by the Queen of Cups as Card 4. The word "mother" popped into my mind in relation to this card. It occurred to me that the Queen of Cups had a special meaning in this case. She is the dream mother Jill hopes to find; one who is completely loving and tenderhearted. This desire from the past is propelling Jill into her current situation.

Another important pair is the King of Swords as Card 7 and the Knight of Pentacles as Card 8. The King of Swords suggests that Jill sees herself as the agent of honesty and justice in this situation. She feels it is her right to learn the truth about her first year of life. Also, in the week before the reading, Jill had prepared a position paper for the court. She used the talents of the King of Swords—his keen analytical ability, intellect, and writing skills.

The Knight of Pentacles suggests that other people may be seeing Jill as too serious and driven. Since they do not appreciate her intensity, they judge her as too obsessed to compromise. Whether or not this view is justified, it is valuable information. If Jill alienates the agency and the legal system, she reduces her chances for success. The Knight of Pentacles hints that Jill should temper any appearance of inflexibility with a moderated, reasonable approach.

The Five of Cups as Card 9 is the key to the whole situation. It represents loss, beginning with the original loss of her birth parents. Now, Jill must be willing to let go of her dream mother so a true relationship can form with her actual birth mother, whoever she may be. Jill is also afraid she may lose her court case.

The Eight of Swords suggests that some confusing moments lie ahead. There will be times when Jill feels powerless as she tries to balance her conflicting feelings. Also, outside forces may temporarily restrict her search.

On the other hand, the Six of Wands as Card 5 and the Magician as Card 10 could not be more positive. The Six of Wands shows the strength of Jill's conscious belief in her ability to overcome her legal obstacles and emerge triumphant. She knows she can achieve the victory predicted by the Magician. As the only major arcana card in the reading, the Magician shows the extra dimension of power waiting for Jill when she realizes her goal. If she can consolidate her inner strengths and accept her losses consciously, she will meet with great success.

Jill's Second Reading

Six months later, I did a reading for myself about Jill and her situation (see page 350). The events which had transpired were so dramatic that I felt drawn to see what the tarot would say about them.

A few months after her first reading, Jill met with a judge who was so convinced by the validity of her search that she ruled the adoption files should be opened. Through hard work, Jill located her birth parents within three weeks. Her father was reluctant to speak with her at first, but her mother welcomed her warmly after a surprise meeting in a distant city.

I truly felt Jill had realized the positive outcome projected for her in the first reading. She trusted her abilities and accomplished all her goals in a very short time; however, this drama was about to take an unexpected turn.

Jill and her birth mother quickly formed a close relationship. While Jill was staying with her mother, her birth father reestablished contact. Her birth parents spoke to each other for the first time in over thirty years, and soon they renewed their original romantic relationship! It was at this time that I decided to do a reading. I wanted to understand the highly charged energy that surrounded this situation.

The main-subject question I wrote: "What is the nature and cause of the intertwining life dramas of Jill, her birth mother, and her birth father?" The reading was for me—offering me insights about Jill's situation that I could appreciate as her friend. Here are the cards I chose:

We again see a Page as Card 1. Jill's situation is still an opportunity to act, but this time she is facing a challenge. Jill could be truthful with herself and approach this situation with fortitude and clarity of thought (Swords).

The Four of Swords as Card 2 tells her how to support herself through this period. She could examine her actions and motivations scrupulously. She could also nurture a still, quiet center in herself so that she can ride this emotional roller coaster.

In Cards 3 and 5 we see the links between this reading and the first. In Card 5, we again see the "dream mother"—the Queen of Cups. It seems that perhaps Jill has not let this ideal go, but has instead placed it firmly in her conscious mind. She is thinking and feeling about her birth mother most of the time.

In that first reading, the Five of Cups showed that transmuting emotional loss is a key lesson for Jill in this drama. Now, this card has moved to Card 3. The regret Jill feels about her birth may have become lodged firmly in her unconscious. At a deep level, she may be mourning the loss of her loved ones and the dream of what might have been. This reenactment of her birth triangle may also be triggering a fear that she will lose her parents again.

QUEEN of CUPS.

PAGE of SWORDS.

THE MOON.

THE LOVERS.

Jill's Second Reading

The Three of Pentacles as Card 4 could suggest that the teamwork Jill has enjoyed with her birth parents may become a thing of the past. The position of the figures on this card is revealing. Two are together while the other stands alone. The solitary figure is half turned away as if she can't decide if she is part of the twosome or not. In studying this card, I noticed for the first time the tipped cup in the right hand of the lone figure. How clearly it echoes the overturned cups in the Five of Cups and the losses they represent!

The Four of Wands as Card 6 is cause for celebration. Whatever else Jill's situation may bring, it seems that perhaps the near future will be exciting.

Cards 7 and 8 carry extra weight because they are major arcana cards. They spell out an important conflict between Jill and her environment as I see it. Jill's point of view is the Lovers. She wants to forge the bonds of love and relationship that were denied her originally. She is also coming to terms with the fact that her parents are becoming lovers literally.

Unfortunately, Jill's environment may be one of fear and illusion. The Moon symbolizes the uncertainties that arise when events are not what they seem and people do not mean what they say. In this case, there is no willful deceit, just lack of clarity. No one means any harm, but everyone is unsure of their real needs.

It appears that I am perceiving Jill as heading toward some rejection as pictured in the Five of Pentacles (Card 10). The lack of unity showing up throughout this reading suggests that Jill could find herself left out in the cold and shunned as the odd person out.

Perhaps Jill's strength lies with the truth. The Page of Swords (Card 1) suggests a central need for clarity and honesty. In the meantime, Jill might want to prepare for challenges. From my perspective, the Nine of Wands as Card 9 suggests she might need to be defensive and prepare to draw on her hidden reserves. There may be celebration in the near future, but there will also be hard times as Jill seeks to find her way with truth in her new relationships.

THE BIG BOOK OF TAROT

Jill's Third Reading

The third reading (page 352) for Jill was held in her presence five months after the second reading. During that period, Jill's birth father had visited her mother, and the budding romance between the two blossomed. Soon after, Jill and her mother traveled to the distant state where her father lived. There were positive aspects to the trip, but the visit took a troubling turn toward the end. Jill experienced the rejection anticipated in the second reading I did for myself. Her father's door was literally slammed in her face one night. She was turned out onto the street when the tensions between them reached a climax.

Jill's mother never returned from that trip. She left her husband and all her belongings to move in with Jill's father. From that point on, Jill's interaction with the two was often tense. There were several dramatic, even frightening, occurrences that were very upsetting to Jill. At the time of the reading, she wanted very much to find out where this situation was heading. The question she wrote was: "How will my relationship with my birth mother and birth father develop in the future?"

We can see that the energies of Jill's situation are still in evidence in the cards she drew. There are four repeat cards. The Eight of Swords has moved from Card 6 (reading 1) to Card 3. The restriction that was in the future is now the basis of the situation. The emotional events of the past year have been so turbulent that Jill feels powerless at a fundamental level.

The Nine of Wands has moved from Card 9 (reading 2) to Card 5. This card was an indication that Jill might need to take care of herself and prepare for the worst. Well, she has certainly started to think along those lines. Having been burned, she knows she has to be strong and defensive emotionally.

The Four of Wands has moved from Card 6 (reading 2) to Card 4. Any celebration over the reunion is fading. The excitement of the good times has moved through Jill's life and is now way behind her.

Cards 7 and 8 show that Jill's expectations still do not match her parents' point of view. Jill longs for a secure, orderly family life (Ten of Pentacles). She wants a solution that will endure—nothing more than the chance to experience the ordinary routines of a normal family.

Her parents, however, are locked into an obsessive relationship symbolized by the Devil. What Jill viewed as the Lovers in reading 2 is really the bondage of two souls who do not seem to have enough self-understanding to create a love that includes their daughter.

Jill needs a resolution, and there are two cards that suggest it is coming. First is the Eight of Wands as Card 1. This card shows that a conclusion is likely. Jill will be able to complete unfinished business if she takes quick, decisive action.

Death shows that a major ending is approaching in the near future. Perhaps the three will suffer a parting of the ways. Maybe Jill will make a transition into a new kind of relationship with her parents.

The Empress as the outcome or resolution is a positive sign because it shows that the ideal of the Mother is the understanding awaiting Jill in this situation. The Empress is the archetype of mothering—the ability to love, cherish, and nurture despite all temptations away from that response. Jill felt this card also meant a refocusing on her own role as a mother.

How is Jill to proceed if she wants to bring about this positive resolution? The key lies in the two Pentacles court cards. The Page as Card 9 is the fourth repeat card; it appeared first as Card 1 (reading 1). It reinforces the idea that Jill's lesson is about trust and the ability to act on your dreams.

 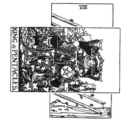 

Jill found her birth parents despite many formidable obstacles, but she discovered that the reality was not the same as her fantasy. She learned to trust herself and not rely on the support of others to see her through. The King of Pentacles as Card 2 tells Jill not to seek salvation through other people. She must develop within herself the mature (kingly) Pentacles qualities of steadiness *and* dependability.

The Page is encouraging her to claim her power and find a solution that works. She must release her dream of an ideal family once and for all so she can relate

Jill's Third Reading

to her actual parents with all their faults and limitations.

Although this reading is about love and the ties that bind people from birth, there is not a single Cups card. These cards of love and emotion are totally absent. The lessons of love are not always easy. For Jill, they have taken the form of challenges that have drawn out her inner reserves and made her a stronger and wiser person.

BIBLIOGRAPHY

Abraham, Sylvia. *How to Read the Tarot: The Key Word System*. St Paul, MN: Llewellyn, 1994.

——— . *How to Use Tarot Spreads: Answers to Every Question*. St. Paul, MN: Llewellyn, 1997.

Almond, Jocelyn, and Keith Seddon. *Understanding Tarot: A Practical Guide to Tarot Card Reading*. London: Aquarian, 1991.

Amaral, Geraldine, and Nancy Brady Cunningham. *Tarot Celebrations: Honoring the Inner Voice*. York, ME: Samuel Weiser, 1997.

Amberstone, Ruth Ann, and Wald Amberstone. *Tarot Tips*. St. Paul: Llewellyn, 2003.

Anonymous. *Meditations on the Tarot: A Journey into Christian Hermeticism*. Rockport, MA: Element, 1985.

Aviza, Edward A. *Thinking Tarot*. New York: Fireside, 1997.

Banzhaf, Hajo. *Tarot and the Journey of the Hero*. Boston, MA: Samuel Weiser, 2000.

——— . *The Tarot Handbook*. Stamford, CT: U. S. Games, 1993.

Banzhaf, Hajo, and Elisa Hemmerlein. *Tarot as Your Companion: A Practical Guide to the Rider-Waite and Crowley Thoth Tarot Decks*. Stamford, CT: U. S. Games, 1999.

Berres, Janet. *Textbook of the Tarot*. Morton Grove, IL: International Tarot Society, 1990.

Braden, Nina Lee. *Tarot for Self-Discovery*. St. Paul: Llewellyn, 2002.

Burger, Evelin, and Johannes Fiebig. *Complete Book of Tarot Spreads*. New York: Sterling, 1995.

Clarson, Laura E. *Tarot Unveiled: The Method to Its Magic*. Stamford, CT: U. S. Games, 2002.

Connolly, Eileen. *Tarot: A New Handbook for the Apprentice*. North Hollywood, CA: Newcastle, 1979.

——— . *Tarot: A New Handbook for the Journeyman*. North Hollywood, CA: Newcastle, 1987.

Cortellesi, Linda. *The User-Friendly Tarot Guidebook*. Worthington, OH: Chalice Moon Publications, 1996.

Cowie, Norma. *Tarot for Successful Living*. White Rock, Canada: NC Publishing, 1979.

D'Agostino, Joseph D. *Tarot: The Royal Path to Wisdom*. York, ME: Samuel Weiser, 1976.

Decker, Ronald, and Michael Dummett. *A History of the Occult Tarot: 1870–1970*. London: Duckworth, 2002.

Denning, Melita, and Osborne Phillips. *The Magick of the Tarot*. St. Paul, MN: Llewellyn, 1983.

Doane, Doris Chase, and King Keyes. *How to Read Tarot Cards*. New York: Barnes & Noble, 1967.

Echols, Signe E., Robert Mueller, and Sandra A. Thomson. *Spiritual Tarot: Seventy-Eight Paths to Personal Development*. New York: Avon, 1996.

Fairfield, Gail. *Choice-Centered Relating and the Tarot*. Boston, MA: Samuel Weiser, 2000.

——— . *Choice Centered Tarot*. North Hollywood, CA: Newcastle, 1984.

Galenorn, Yasmine. *Tarot Journeys: Adventures in Self-Transformation*. St. Paul, MN: Llewellyn, 1999.

Garen, Nancy. *Creating Your Own Tarot Cards*. New York: Fireside, 1991.

——— . *Tarot Made Easy*. New York: Fireside, 1989.

Gerulskis-Estes, Susan. *The Book of Tarot*. Dobbs Ferry, NY: Morgan & Morgan, 1981.

Giles, Cynthia. *The Tarot: History, Mystery, and Lore*. New York: Fireside, 1992.

Gillentine, Julie. *Tarot & Dream Interpretation*. St. Paul, MN: Llewellyn, 2003.

Graves, F. D. *The Windows of Tarot*. Dobbs Ferry, NY: Morgan & Morgan, 1973.

Gray, Eden. *A Complete Guide to the Tarot*. New York: Bantam, 1970.

———. *Mastering the Tarot: Basic Lessons in an Ancient, Mystic Art*. New York: New American Library, 1971.

———. *The Tarot Revealed*. New York: New American Library, 1960.

Greer, Mary K. *The Complete Book of Tarot Reversals*. St. Paul, MN: Llewellyn, 2002.

———. *Tarot for Yourself: A Workbook for Personal Transformation*. North Hollywood, CA: Newcastle, 1984.

Greer, Mary K., and Rachel Pollack, eds. *New Thoughts on Tarot*. North Hollywood, CA: Newcastle, 1989.

Greer, Mary K., and Tom Little. *Understanding the Tarot Court*. St. Paul, MN: Llewellyn, 2004.

Gregory, James. *How to Perform a Psychic Reading: A Beginner's Guide to Reading Tarot Cards*. Colorado Springs, CO: Zymore Press, 1999.

Haga, Enoch. *TARO Solution: A Complete Guide to Interpreting the Tarot*. Livermore, CA: Enoch Haga Publisher, 1994.

Hamaker-Zondag, Karen. *Tarot as a Way of Life: A Jungian Approach to the Tarot*. York, ME: Samuel Weiser, 1997.

Hazel, Elizabeth. *Tarot Decoded: Understanding and Using Dignities and Correspondences*. Boston, MA: Weiser Books, 2004.

Hollander, P. Scott. *Tarot for Beginners*. St. Paul, MN: Llewellyn, 1995.

Irwin, Lee. *Gnostic Tarot: Mandalas for Spiritual Transformation*. York, ME: Samuel Weiser, 1998.

Jette, Christine. *Professional Tarot: The Business of Reading, Consulting & Teaching*. St. Paul, MN: Llewellyn, 2003.

———. *Tarot for All Seasons*. St. Paul, MN: Llewellyn, 2001.

———. *Tarot for the Healing Heart: Using Inner Wisdom to Heal Body and Mind*. St. Paul, MN: Llewellyn, 2001.

———. *Tarot Shadow Work: Using the Dark Symbols to Heal*. St. Paul, MN: Llewellyn, 2001.

Junjulas, Craig. *Psychic Tarot*. Stamford, CT: U. S. Games, 1985.

K, Amber, and Azrael Arynn K. *Heart of Tarot: An Intuitive Approach*. St. Paul, MN: Llewellyn, 2002.

Kaplan, Stuart R. *The Encyclopedia of Tarot: Volumes 1–3*. Stamford, CT: U. S. Games, 1978, 1986, 1990.

———. *Tarot Cards for Fun and Fortune Telling*. Stamford, CT: U. S. Games, 1970.

Kaser, R. T. *Tarot in Ten Minutes*. New York: Avon, 1992.

Kelly, Dorothy. *Tarot Card Combinations*. Boston, MA: Weiser Books, 2003.

Knight, Gareth. *The Magical World of the Tarot: Fourfold Mirror of the Universe*. York, ME: Samuel Weiser, 1991.

Konraad, Sandor. *Classic Tarot Spreads*. Atglen, PA: Whitford Press, 1985.

Louis, Anthony. *Tarot Plain and Simple*. St. Paul, MN: Llewellyn, 1997.

MacGregor, Trish, and Phyllis Vega. *Power Tarot*. New York: Fireside, 1998.

Masino, Marcia. *Easy Tarot Guide*. San Diego, CA: ACS Publications, 1987.

McElroy, Mark. *Putting the Tarot to Work*. St. Paul, MN: Llewellyn, 2004.

Michelsen, Teresa. *Designing Your Own Tarot Spreads*. St. Paul, MN: Llewellyn, 2003.

Moura, Ann. *Tarot for the Green Witch*. St. Paul, MN: Llewellyn, 2003.

Nichols, Sallie. *Jung and Tarot: An Archetypal Journey*. York, ME: Samuel Weiser, 1980.

Oken, Alan. *Pocket Guide to the Tarot*. Berkeley, CA: Crossing Press, 1996.

Peach, Emily. *The Tarot Workbook: Understanding and Using Tarot Symbolism*. New York: Sterling, 1990.

Pielmeier, Heidemarie, and Marcus Schirner. *Illustrated Tarot Spreads: 78 New Layouts for Personal Discovery*. New York: Sterling, 1999.

Pollack, Rachel. *Complete Illustrated Guide to Tarot: How to Unlock the Secrets of the Tarot*. New York: Gramercy Books, 1999.

——— . *The Forest of Souls: A Walk through the Tarot*. St. Paul, MN: Llewellyn, 2002.

——— . *Seventy-Eight Degrees of Wisdom: A Book of Tarot, Part 1: The Major Arcana*. London: Aquarian, 1980.

——— . *Seventy-Eight Degrees of Wisdom: A Book of Tarot, Part 2: The Minor Arcana and Readings*. London: Aquarian, 1980.

Porter, Tracy. *Tarot Companion: An Essential Reference Guide*. St. Paul, MN: Llewellyn, 2000.

Prosapio, Richard, with Elizabeth Prosapio. *Intuitive Tarot: Discovering the Power of Your Intuition*. Stamford, CT: U. S. Games, 1996.

Renee, Janina. *Tarot for a New Generation*. St. Paul, MN: Llewellyn, 2002.

——— . *Tarot Spells*. St. Paul, MN: Llewellyn, 1990 and 2000.

——— . *Tarot: Your Everyday Guide*. St. Paul, MN: Llewellyn, 2000.

Ricklef, James. *Tarot Tells the Tale: Explore Three-Card Readings through Familiar Stories*. St. Paul, MN: Llewellyn, 2003.

Riley, Jana. *Tarot: Dictionary and Compendium*. York, ME: Samuel Weiser, 1995.

Rosengarten, Arthur. *Tarot and Psychology: Spectrums of Possibility*. St. Paul, MN: Paragon House, 2000.

Sharman-Burke, Juliet. *The Complete Book of Tarot: A Step-by-Step Guide to Reading the Cards*. New York: St. Martin's, 1985.

——— . *Understanding the Tarot: A Personal Teaching Guide*. New York: St. Martin's, 1998.

Shavick, Nancy. *The Tarot Reader*. New York: Berkley, 1991.

Simon, Sylvie. *The Tarot: Art, Mysticism, Divination*. Rochester, VT: Inner Traditions, 1986.

Sterling, Stephen Walter. *Tarot Awareness: Exploring the Spiritual Path*. St. Paul, MN: Llewellyn, 2000.

Townley, Kevin. *The Cube of Space; Container of Creation*. Boulder, CO: Archive Press, 1993.

Vega, Phyllis. *Romancing the Tarot*. New York: Fireside, 2001.

Waite, Arthur Edward. *Pictorial Key to the Tarot*. York, ME: Samuel Weiser, 1993.

Wang, Robert. *Qabalistic Tarot*. York, ME: Samuel Weiser, 1983.

Wanless, James. *New Age Tarot: A Workbook and Glossary of Symbols*. Carmel, CA: Merrill-West Publishing, 1986.

Woudhuysen, Jan. *Tarot Therapy: A New Approach to Self Exploration*. Los Angeles: Jeremy P. Tarcher, 1979.

NOTES

i. Michael Dummett, *The Visconti-Sforza Tarot Cards* (New York: George Braziller, Inc, 1986), p. 13.

ii. Cynthia Giles, *The Tarot: History, Mystery and Lore* (New York: Simon & Schuster, 1992), chapter 2 and 3.

iii. J.A. and Magda Gonzalez, Native American Tarot Deck; Michael Tierra and Candis Cantin, The Herbal Tarot; Koji Furata and Stuart R. Kaplan, The Ukiyoe Tarot, all published by U.S. Games (Stamford, CT); and Juliet Sharmon-Burke and Liz Greene, *The Mythic Tarot*, a book and deck set published by Simon & Schuster.

iv. Hermann Rorschach, *The Rorschach® Test* (Switzerland, Hans Huber, 1927).

1. Myers, B., *The Myers-Briggs Type Indicator* (Palo Alto, CA: Consulting Psychologists Press, 1962).

2. Italo Calvino, *The Castle of Crossed Destinies* (New York: Harcourt Brace Jovanovich, 1969).

3. Pollack, Rachel, *Seventy-Eight Degrees of Wisdom, Part 1* (London: Aquarian Press, 1980), p. 30.

4. For example, *Tarot of Marseilles* (Clumhout, Belgium: Carta Mundi, 1996). Distributed by U.S. Games.

5. Phrase from Judith Viorst, *Alexander and the Terrible, Horrible, No Good, Very Bad Day* (New York: Atheneum, 1972).

6. Dante Alighieri, *The Purgatorio*, John Ciardi, trans. (New York: New American Library, 1957), p. 123.

7. Paul Reps, compilator, *Zen Flesh, Zen Bones: A Collection of Zen and Pre-Zen Writings* (Tokyo: Tuttle, 1957), pp. 7–8.

8. Bunyan, John, *The Pilgrim's Progress*. Excerpt from the Norton Anthology of English Literature: vol. l, 3rd ed. (New York: W W Norton, 1974), p. 1780.

9. Konraad, Sandor, *Classic Tarot Spreads* (Atglen, PA: Whitford Press, 1985), pp. 96-97

10. Cowie, Norma, *Tarot for Successful Living* (White Rock, British Columbia: NC Publishing, 1979), pp. 23–25. Used by kind permission.

11. Pollack, Rachel, *Seventy-Eight Degrees of Wisdom, Part 1* (London: Aquarian Press, 1980), p. 65.

12. Pollack, Rachel, *Seventy-Eight Degrees of Wisdom, Part 1* (London: Aquarian Press, 1980), p. 102.

ACKNOWLEDGMENTS

As always, I wish to thank my husband Steve whose love, support and technical prowess have seen me through another project. I also wish to express my love for David, Jonathan, Alona and new arrival Jake. You enrich my life in so many ways.

I'd like to thank the staff at Red Wheel/Weiser for their support over the years and for helping to bring this book to life. In particular, I'm grateful to Peter Turner who first envisioned this composite of my earlier books. It's given me the chance to review and update my thoughts about the tarot for a new audience.

I also wish to thank Kathyrn Sky-Peck for her excellent design work and Christine LeBlond, my editor. Your insightful comments and encouraging emails smoothed the way and added so much to this book.

Finally, I'd like to thank you the reader for being willing to explore the mysteries of life with open wonder. May this book encourage you on this path!

To Our Readers